lonely planet

SPANISH

Travel Phrasebook & Dictionary

Credits

Production Editor Aileen Cudmore

Language Writers Marta López, Cristina Hernández Montero

Thanks

Sofie Andersen, Marc Backwell, Fergal Condon, Gwen Cotter, Sally Davies, Kellie Langdon, Saralinda Turner, Clifton Wilkinson

Published by Lonely Planet Global Limited
CRN 554153

Digital Depot, Roe Lane off Thomas Street, Dublin
D08 TCV4, Ireland (EU authorised representative)

10th Edition – Sep 2026
ISBN 978 1 80653 130 1

Printed in China 10 9 8 7 6 5 4 3 2 1

Contact lonelyplanet.com/contact

HOW TO USE THIS BOOK

Look out for the following icons throughout the book:

'Shortcut' Phrase
Easy-to-remember alternative to the full phrase

Q&A Pair
'Question-and-answer' pair – we suggest a response to the question asked

Look for
Phrases you may see on signs, menus etc

Listen for
Phrases you may hear from officials, locals etc

LANGUAGE TIP

An insight into Spanish

CULTURE TIP

An insight into the local culture

How to read the phrases:

- Coloured words and phrases throughout the book are phonetic guides to help you pronounce Spanish.
- Lists of phrases with tinted background are options you can choose to complete the phrase above them.

These abbreviations will help you choose the right words and phrases in this book:

f	feminine	m	masculine	sg	singular
inf	informal	pl	plural		
lit	literal	pol	polite		

CONTENTS

INTRO

Spanish

ESPAÑOL (ES·PA·*NYOL*)

Who speaks Spanish?

Why Bother

You'll be seduced by this melodic language and have fun trying to roll your *rr*'s like the locals – not to mention ordering scrumptious tapas or engaging in all the shouting at the *fútbol*.

Distinctive Sounds

The strong and rolled r, harsh and guttural kh and, in European Spanish, 'lisping' th.

Spanish in the World

Over the last 500 years, Spanish in Latin America has evolved differently to

500 MILLION speak Spanish as their first language

100 MILLION speak Spanish as their second language

the Spanish of Europe. Among other differences, you'll easily recognise Latin Americans by the lack of lisp in their speech – ie *cerveza* (beer) is ther·*ve*·tha in most of Spain but ser·*ve*·sa across the Atlantic.

Spanish in Spain

Spanish, or Castilian (*castellano* ka·ste·*lya*·no) is primarily the language of Castille (covering the largest territory in Spain). However, Catalan, Galician and Basque are also official languages, and locals in these regions are very proud of their own language.

False Friends

Warning: many Spanish words look like English words but have a different meaning altogether, eg *suburbio* soo·*boor*·byo is a slum district, not a suburb (which is *barrio* *ba*·ryo in Spanish).

Language Family

Romance (developed from Vulgar Latin spoken by Roman soldiers and merchants during the conquest of the Iberian peninsula from the 3rd to the 1st century BCE). Close relatives include Portuguese, Italian, French and Romanian.

Must-Know Grammar

Spanish has a formal and informal word for 'you' (*usted* oo·*sted* and *tú* too respectively for 'you' singular). The verbs also have a different ending for each person, like the English 'I do' vs 'he/she does'.

Donations to English

Thanks to Columbus landing in the New World in 1492, a large corpus of words from indigenous American languages has entered English via Spanish. You may recognise *canyon, guerrilla, ranch,* and *tornado.*

5 Phrases TO LEARN BEFORE YOU GO

01 What time does it open/close?

¿A qué hora abren/cierran? a ke *o*·ra *ab*·ren/*thye*·ran

The Spanish tend to observe long lunch hours, so opening times may surprise you.

02 Are these complimentary?

¿Son gratis? son *gra*·tees

Tapas (bar snacks) are available pretty much around the clock at Spanish bars. You'll find they're free in some places.

03 When is admission free?

¿Cuándo es la entrada gratuita?

kwan·do es la en·*tra*·da gra·*twee*·ta

Many museums and galleries in Spain have admission-free times, so check before buying tickets.

04 Where can we go (salsa) dancing?

¿Dónde podemos ir a bailar (salsa)?

don·de po·*de*·mos eer a bai·*lar* (*sal*·sa)

Flamenco may be the authentic viewing experience in Spain, but to actively enjoy the music you'll want to do some dancing.

05 How do you say this in (Catalan/Galician/Basque)?

¿Cómo se dice esto en (catalán/gallego/euskera)?

ko·mo se *dee*·the *es*·to en (ka·ta·*lan*/ga·*lye*·go/e·oos·*ke*·ra)

Spain has four official languages, and people in these regions will appreciate it if you try to use their local language.

10 Phrases TO SOUND LIKE A LOCAL

What's up?	¿Qué pasa?	ke *pa*·sa
Great!	¡Genial!	khe·*nyal*
How cool!	¡Qué guay!	ke gwai
That's fantastic!	¡Estupendo!	es·too·*pen*·do
Really?	¿En serio?	en *se*·ryo
You don't say!	¡No me digas!	no me *dee*·gas
Sure.	Claro.	*kla*·ro
OK.	Vale.	*va*·le
Of course!	¡Por supuesto!	por soo·*pwes*·to
Whatever.	Lo que sea.	lo ke *se*·a

SPANISH

Pronunciation

Spanish pronunciation isn't difficult, as most sounds are similar to those found in English. The relationship between Spanish sounds and their spelling is straightforward and consistent. There are some easy rules to follow and once you learn them you shouldn't have problems being understood. As in most languages, Spanish pronunciation can vary according to region – this book focuses on Castilian Spanish.

VOWEL SOUNDS

SYMBOL	ENGLISH EQUIVALENT	SPANISH EXAMPLE	TRANSLITERATION
a	cat	agua	a·gwa
ai	aisle	bailar	bai·*lar*
e	red	número	*noo*·me·ro
ee	bee	día	*dee*·a
ey	hey	seís	seys
o	hot	ojo	o·kho
oo	book	gusto	*goo*·sto
ow	cow	autobús	ow·to·*boos*
oy	boy	hoy	oy

CONSONANT SOUNDS

SYMBOL	ENGLISH EQUIVALENT	SPANISH EXAMPLE	TRANSLITERATION
b	big	barco	*bar*·ko
ch	chili	chica	*chee*·ka
d	din	dinero	dee·*ne*·ro
f	fun	fiesta	*fye*·sta
g	go	gato	*ga*·to
k	kick	cabeza, queso	ka·*be*·tha, *ke*·so
kh	as in the *ch* in the Scottish *loch*	jardín, gente	khar·*deen*, *khen*·te
l	loud	lago	*la*·go
ly	million	llamada	lya·*ma*·da
m	man	mañana	ma·*nya*·na
n	no	nuevo	*nwe*·vo
ny	canyon	señora	se·*nyo*·ra
p	pig	padre	*pa*·dre
r	run (but stronger and rolled)	ritmo, burro, mariposa	*reet*·mo, *boo*·ro, ma·ree·*po*·sa
s	so	semana	se·*ma*·na
t	tin	tienda	*tyen*·da
th	thin	Barcelona, manzana	bar·the·*lo*·na, man·*tha*·na
v	soft 'b', between 'v' and 'b'	vaca	*va*·ka
w	win	guardia	*gwar*·dya
y	yes	viaje, ya	*vya*·khe, ya

READING & WRITING

There are some key things to remember about consonants in written Spanish:

- The letter *c* is pronounced with a lisp, eg *cerveza* ther·ve·tha, except when it comes before *a*, *o* and *u* or a consonant. Then, it's pronounced hard like the *k* in 'king'.
- When ending a word, the letter *d* is also pronounced soft, like a th, or is pronounced as a very slight, gentle d.
- The letter *j* stands for a harsh and guttural sound, and we use the kh symbol in our pronunciation guides.
- Try to roll your double *r*'s.
- The letter *q* is pronounced hard, like a k.
- The letter *v* sounds more like a b, said with the lips pressed together.
- There are a few letter combinations which you may find slightly unusual: *ch*, *ll* and *ñ*. The *ch* (che) and *ll* (e·lye) are no longer considered separate letters in the Spanish alphabet, so in dictionaries and the like, you'll find words starting with *ch* amongst the *c* listings, and those starting with *ll*, amongst the *l* listings. The letter *ñ* (e·nye) is considered a separate letter in the Spanish alphabet.

SPANISH ALPHABET

A a a	**B b** be	**C c** the
D d de	**E e** e	**F f** e·fe
G g khe	**H h** a·che	**I i** ee
J j *kho*·ta	**K k** ka	**L l** e·le
M m e·me	**N n** e·ne	**Ñ ñ** e·nye
O o o	**P p** pe	**Q q** koo
R r e·re	**S s** e·se	**T t** te
U u oo	**V v** *oo*·ve	**W w** *oo*·ve *do*·ble
X x e·kees	**Y y** ee·*grye*·ga	**Z z** *the*·ta

WORD STRESS

There is word stress in Spanish, which means you emphasise one syllable in a word over another. Rule of thumb: when a written word ends in *n*, *s* or a vowel, the stress falls on the second-last syllable, eg *lejos* *le*·khos (far), *casa* *ka*·sa (house). Otherwise, the final syllable is stressed, eg *hablar* a·*blar* (talk). If you see an accent mark over a syllable, it cancels out these rules and you just stress that syllable instead, eg *número* *noo*·me·ro (number).

LANGUAGE TIP: FALSE FRIENDS

Beware of false friends – those words that sound like familiar English, but could land you in a bit of trouble if you use them unwittingly in Spanish. Here are some mistakes that it's a little too easy to make:

el suburbio	el soo·*boor*·byo slum district, not 'suburb' which is *el barrio*, el *ba*·ryo
Estoy constipado/a. m/f	es·*toy* kons·tee·*pa*·do/a I have a cold, not 'I'm constipated', which is *estoy estreñido/a* m/f es·*toy* es·tre·*nyee*·do/a
Estoy embarazada.	es·*toy* em·ba·ra·*tha*·da I'm pregnant, not 'I'm embarassed', which is *estoy avergonzado/a* m/f es·*toy* a·ver·gon·*tha*·do/a
la injuria	la een·*khoo*·ree·a insult, not 'injury', which is *la herida*, la e·*ree*·da
los parientes	los pa·ree·*yen*·tes relatives, not 'parents', which is *los padres*, los *pa*·dres
sensible	sen·*see*·ble sensitive, not 'sensible', which is *prudente*, proo·*den*·te

SPANISH Grammar

This chapter is designed to explain the main grammatical structures you need in order to make your own sentences. Look under each heading for information on functions which these grammatical categories express in a sentence. For example, demonstratives are used for giving instructions, so you'll need them to tell the taxi driver where your hotel is, etc. A glossary of grammatical terms is included at the end of this chapter to help you.

ADJECTIVES & ADVERBS

Describing People/Things • Doing Things

When using an adjective to describe a noun, you need to use a different ending depending on whether the noun is masculine or feminine, and singular or plural. See also **gender** (p19) and **plurals** (p23). Most adjectives use the following four endings:

ADJECTIVES

	singular		plural	
m	fantástico	fan·*tas*·tee·ko	fantásticos	fan·*tas*·tee·kos
f	fantástica	fan·*tas*·tee·ka	fantásticas	fan·*tas*·tee·kas

a fantastic hotel	un hotel fantástico (lit: a-m-sg hotel fantastic-m-sg) oon o·*tel* fan·*tas*·tee·ko

a fantastic meal	una comida fantástica (lit: a-f-sg meal fantastic-f-sg) *oo*·na ko·*mee*·da fan·*tas*·tee·ka
some fantastic books	unos libros fantásticos (lit: some-m-pl books fantastic-m-pl) *oo*·nos *lee*·bros fan·*tas*·tee·kos
some fantastic tapas	unas tapas fantásticas (lit: some-f-pl tapas fantastic-f-pl) *oo*·nas *ta*·pas fan·*tas*·tee·kas

Adjectives generally come after the noun in Spanish. However, adjectives expressing quantity (such as 'much', 'a lot', 'little', 'few', 'many') always precede the noun. See also **demonstratives** (p18) and **possessives** (p23).

a comfortable hotel	un hotel cómodo (lit: a-m-sg hotel comfortable-m-sg) oon o·*tel* *ko*·mo·do
many tourists	muchos turistas (lit: many-m-pl tourists) *moo*·chos too·*rees*·tas

Most adverbs in Spanish are derived from adjectives by adding the ending *-mente* ·*men*·te to the singular feminine form of the adjective (ie the form ending in *-a*), just like you add the ending '-ly' to the adjective in English. In Spanish, adverbs are generally placed after the verb they refer to.

a slow train	un tren lento (lit: a-m-sg train slow-m-sg) oon tren *len*·to
to speak slowly	hablar lentamente (lit: to-speak slowly) ab·*lar* len·ta·*men*·te

ARTICLES

Naming People/Things

There are four words for the definite article (ie equivalents of 'the' in English) in Spanish, used depending on the gender and the number of the noun. See also **gender** (p19) and **plurals** (p23). The masculine singular form of the definite article is joined to some prepositions when it's placed after them, so *a el* (to the-m-sg) becomes *al* al and *de el* (of the-m-sg) becomes *del* del. See also **prepositions** (p25).

DEFINITE ARTICLES

m sg	**the car**	el coche	el *ko*·che
m pl	**the cars**	los coches	los *ko*·ches
f sg	**the shop**	la tienda	la *tyen*·da
f pl	**the shops**	las tiendas	las *tyen*·das

Similarly, Spanish has four words for the indefinite article (ie 'a/an' in English), depending on the gender and number of the noun.

INDEFINITE ARTICLES

m sg	**an egg**	un huevo	oon *we*·vo
m pl	**some eggs**	unos huevos	*oo*·nos *we*·vos
f sg	**a house**	una casa	*oo*·na *ka*·sa
f pl	**some houses**	unas casas	*oo*·nas *ka*·sas

BE

Describing People/Things • Making Statements

Spanish has two words for the English verb 'be': *ser* ser and *estar* es·*tar*, which are used depending on the context.

USE OF *SER* (TO BE)

permanent characteristics of persons/things	Liz es muy guapa. leez es mooy *gwa*·pa	Liz is very pretty.
occupations or nationality	Ana es de España. a·na es de e·*spa*·nya	Ana is from Spain.
time or location of events	Son las tres. son las tres	It's 3 o'clock.
possession	¿De quién es este bolso? de kyen es *es*·te *bol*·so	Whose bag is this?

USE OF *ESTAR* (TO BE)

temporary characteristics of persons/things	La sopa está fría. la so·pa es·*ta* *free*·a	The soup is cold.
time or location of persons/things	Estamos en Madrid. es·*ta*·mos en ma·*dreeth*	We're in Madrid.
mood of a person	Estoy contento/a. m/f es·*toy* kon·*ten*·to/a	I'm happy.

SER (TO BE) – PRESENT TENSE

I	**am**	yo	soy	yo	soy
you sg inf	**are**	tú	eres	too	e·res
you sg pol	**are**	usted	es	oo·*sted*	es
he	**is**	él	es	el	es
she	**is**	ella	es	e·lya	es
we	**are**	nosotros m nosotras f	somos	no·so·tros no·so·tras	so·mos
you pl inf	**are**	vosotros m vosotras f	sois	vo·so·tros vo·so·tras	soys
you pl pol	**are**	ustedes	son	oo·*ste*·des	son
they	**are**	ellos m ellas f	son	e·lyos e·lyas	son

***ESTAR* (TO BE) – PRESENT TENSE**

I	**am**	yo	estoy	yo	es·*toy*
you sg inf	**are**	tú	estás	too	es·*tas*
you sg pol	**are**	usted	está	oo·*sted*	es·*ta*
he	**is**	él	está	el	es·*ta*
she	**is**	ella	está	e·lya	es·*ta*
we	**are**	nosotros m nosotras f	estamos	no·so·tros no·so·tras	es·*ta*·mos
you pl inf	**are**	vosotros m vosotras f	estáis	vo·so·tros vo·so·tras	es·*tais*
you pl pol	**are**	ustedes	están	oo·*ste*·des	es·*tan*
they	**are**	ellos m ellas f	están	e·lyos e·lyas	es·*tan*

DEMONSTRATIVES

Giving Instructions • Indicating Location • Pointing Things Out

To point something out, the easiest phrases to use are *es* es (it is), *esto es* *es*·to es (this is) or *eso es* *e*·so es (that is).

It's a guide to Seville.

Es una guía de Sevilla.
(lit: is a-f-sg guide of Seville)
es *oo*·na *gee*·a de se·*vee*·lya

The Spanish words for 'this' and 'that' vary, depending on whether something is close (ie 'this'), away from you (ie 'that'), or even further away in time or space (ie 'that over there'). Each of these words changes form depending on the gender and number of the noun it refers to. See also **gender** and **plurals** (p23).

DEMONSTRATIVES

	m sg		m pl	
this (close)	este	e·ste	estos	e·stos
that (away)	ese	e·se	esos	e·sos
that (further away)	aquel	a·*kel*	aquellos	a·*ke*·lyos
	f sg		**f pl**	
this (close)	esta	e·sta	estas	e·stas
that (away)	esa	e·sa	esas	e·sas
that (further away)	aquella	a·*ke*·lya	aquellas	a·*ke*·lyas

GENDER

Naming People/Things

In Spanish, all nouns (words which denote a thing, person or idea) have either masculine or feminine gender. You can recognise the noun's gender by the article, demonstrative, possessive or any other adjective accompanying the noun, as they all change form to agree with the noun's gender. See also **adjectives & adverbs** (p14), **articles** (p16), **demonstratives** and **possessives** (p23). The gender of words is also indicated in the dictionary, but here are some general rules:

- A word is masculine/feminine if it refers to a man/woman.
- Words ending in *-o* or *-or* are generally masculine.
- Words ending in *-a*, *-d*, *-z* or *-ión* are usually feminine.

The masculine and feminine forms of words are indicated with m and f throughout this book where relevant. See also the box **masculine & feminine** (p138).

HAVE

Possessing

Possession can be indicated in various ways in Spanish. See also **possessives** (p23). One way is by using the verb *tener* te·*ner* (have). For negative forms with 'have', see **negatives**.

***TENER* (TO HAVE)**

I	**have**	yo	tengo	yo	*ten*·go
you sg inf	**have**	tú	tienes	too	*tye*·nes
you sg pol	**have**	usted	tiene	oo·*sted*	*tye*·ne
he	**has**	él	tiene	el	*tye*·ne
she	**has**	ella	tiene	e·lya	*tye*·ne
we	**have**	nosotros m nosotras f	tenemos	no·*so*·tros no·*so*·tras	te·*ne*·mos
you pl inf	**have**	vosotros m vosotras f	tenéis	vo·*so*·tros vo·*so*·tras	te·*neys*
you pl pol	**have**	ustedes	tienen	oo·*ste*·des	*tye*·nen
they	**have**	ellos m ellas f	tienen	e·lyos e·lyas	*tye*·nen

The word *hay* ai – which is the impersonal form of the verb *haber* ha·*ber* (have) – is used to mean 'there is/are' and in questions for 'is/are there ...?':

Is there hot water?	¿Hay agua caliente? (lit: is-there water hot-f-sg) ai a·gwa ka·*lyen*·te

NEGATIVES

Negating

To make a negative statement in Spanish, just add the word *no* no (not) before the main verb of the sentence:

I'm not going to try that.	No voy a probarlo. (lit: not I-go to to-try-it) no voy a pro·*bar*·lo

Contrary to English, Spanish uses double negatives:

I have nothing to declare.	No tengo nada que declarar. (lit: not I-have nothing that to-declare) no *ten*·go *na*·da ke dek·la·*rar*

PERSONAL PRONOUNS

Making Statements • Naming People/Things

Personal pronouns ('I', 'you' etc) change form in Spanish depending on whether they're the subject or the object of a sentence. It's the same in English, which has 'I' and 'me' as subject and object pronouns (eg 'I see her' and 'She sees me'). Note, however, that the subject pronoun is usually omitted in Spanish as the subject is understood from the corresponding verb form. See also **verbs** (p27).

I'm a student.	Soy estudiante. (lit: I-am student-m&f-sg) soy es·too·*dyan*·te

SUBJECT PRONOUNS

I	yo	yo	**we**	nosotros m nosotras f	no·so·tros no·so·tras
you sg inf	tú	too	**you** pl inf	vosotros m vosotras f	vo·so·tros vo·so·tras
you sg pol	usted	oo·*sted*	**you** pl pol	ustedes	oo·*ste*·des
he **she**	él ella	el e·lya	**they**	ellos m ellas f	e·lyos e·lyas

As the tables show, Spanish has two 'you' forms. With people familiar to you or younger than you, it's usual to use the informal form of 'you', *tú* too, rather than the polite form, *usted* oo·*sted*. Phrases in this book use the form that is appropriate to the situation. Where both forms are used, they are indicated by pol and inf. See also the box **addressing people** (p95).

OBJECT PRONOUNS

me	me	me	**us**	nos	nos
you sg inf	te	te	**you** pl inf	os	os
you sg pol	lo/le m la/le f	lo/le la/le	**you** pl pol	los/les m las/les f	los/les las/les
him **it**	lo/le	lo/le	**them**	los/les m las/les f	los/les las/les
her **it**	la/le	la/le			

In this table, the forms separated by a slash are direct/indirect object pronouns.

The direct and indirect object pronouns differ only for the third person ('he', 'she', 'it', 'they') and the polite 'you' forms.

I don't know her.	No la conozco. (lit: not her I-know) no la ko·*noth*·ko
I'm talking to her.	Le hablo. (lit: to-her I-talk) le *a*·blo

The object pronouns generally come before the verb. The indirect object pronoun comes before the direct object pronoun.

I'll show it to you.	Te lo mostraré. (lit: to-you-sg-inf it-m-sg I-will-show) te lo mos·tra·*re*

PLURALS

Naming People/Things

To form plurals in Spanish, add *-s* if the noun ends in a vowel and *-es* if it ends in a consonant. In this book singular and plural forms are shown with sg and pl respectively where needed.

SINGULAR			PLURAL		
bed	cama	*ka*·ma	**beds**	camas	*ka*·mas
woman	mujer	moo·*kher*	**women**	mujeres	moo·*khe*·res

POSSESSIVES

Possessing

A common way of indicating possession is by using possessive adjectives before the noun they refer to. Like other adjectives, they agree with the noun in number, and in case of 'our' and 'your' they also agree in gender. See also **gender** (p19) and **plurals**.

our daughter	nuestra hija (lit: our-f-sg daughter) *nwes*·tra *ee*·kha

POSSESSIVE ADJECTIVES

my	mi/mis	mee/ mees	**our**	nuestro/ nuestros m nuestra/ nuestras f	*nwes*·tro/ *nwes*·tros *nwes*·tra/ *nwes*·tras
your sg inf	tu/tus	too/toos	**your** pl inf	vuestro/ vuestros m vuestra/ vuestras f	*vwes*·tro/ *vwes*·tros *vwes*·tra/ *vwes*·tras
your sg pol	su/sus	soo/soos	**your** pl pol	su/sus	soo/soos
his her its	su/sus	soo/soos	**their**	su/sus	soo/soos

Note that in the table above, the Spanish possessive adjective forms separated by a slash are used with a singular and plural noun respectively.

my child	mi hijo (lit: my-m-sg child) mee *ee*·kho
my children	mis hijos (lit: my-m-pl children) mees *ee*·khos

Another way to indicate possession is by using possessive pronouns (see the table opposite), which also agree in gender and number with the noun.

The book is mine.	El libro es mío. (lit: the-m-sg book is mine-m-sg) el *lee*·bro es *mee*·o

POSSESSIVE PRONOUNS

mine	mío/ míos m mía/ mías f	*mee*·o/ *mee*·os *mee*·a/ *mee*·as	**ours**	nuestro/ nuestros m nuestra/ nuestras f	*nwes*·tro/ *nwes*·tros *nwes*·tra/ *nwes*·tras
yours sg inf	tuyo/ tuyos m tuya/ tuyas f	*too*·yo/ *too*·yos *too*·ya/ *too*·yas	**yours** pl inf	vuestro/ vuestros m vuestra/ vuestras f	*vwes*·tro/ *vwes*·tros *vwes*·tra/ *vwes*·tras
yours sg pol **his hers its**	suyo/ suyos m suya/ suyas f	*soo*·yo/ *soo*·yos *soo*·ya/ *soo*·yas	**yours** pl pol **theirs**	suyo/ suyos m suya/ suyas f	*soo*·yo/ *soo*·yos *soo*·ya/ *soo*·yas

The four alternatives in this table are used with m sg, m pl, f sg and f pl nouns.

Ownership can also be expressed in Spanish using the construction '*de* de (of) + noun', just like in English. See also **have** (p20).

my friend's bag	el bolso de mi amigo (lit: the-m-sg bag of my friend-m-sg) el *bol*·so de mee a·*mee*·go

PREPOSITIONS

Giving Instructions • Indicating Location • Pointing Things Out

Like English, Spanish uses prepositions to explain where things are in time or space. Some common prepositions are listed in the table that follows. For more prepositions, see the **dictionary** (p205).

When certain prepositions are followed by a definite article, they are contracted into a single word. See also **articles** (p16).

PREPOSITIONS

after	después de	des·*pwes* de	**from**	de	de
at (time)	a	a	**in (place)**	en	en
before	antes de	*an*·tes de	**to**	a	a

QUESTIONS

Asking Questions • Negating

The easiest way of forming 'yes/no' questions in Spanish is to add the phrase *verdad* ver·*dad* (literally 'truth') to the end of a statement, similar to 'isn't it?' in English. You can also turn a statement into a question by putting the verb before the subject of the sentence, just like in English.

This is the right stop, isn't it?	¿Ésta es la parada, verdad? (lit: this-f-sg is the-f-sg stop truth) *es*·ta es la pa·*ra*·da ver·*dad*
Is this the right stop?	¿Es ésta la parada? (lit: is this-f-sg the-f-sg stop) es *es*·ta la pa·*ra*·da

As in English, there are also question words for more specific questions. These words go at the start of the sentence.

QUESTION WORDS

how	cómo	*ko*·mo	**where**	dónde	*don*·de
what	qué	ke	**who**	quién sg quiénes pl	kyen *kye*·nes
when	cuándo	*kwan*·do	**why**	por qué	por ke

VERBS

Doing Things

There are three verb categories in Spanish, depending on whether the infinitive ends in *-ar*, *-er* or *-ir*, eg *hablar* ab·*lar* (talk), *comer* ko·*mer* (eat), *vivir* vee·*veer* (live). Tenses are formed by adding various endings for each person to the verb stem (after removing *-ar*, *-er* or *-ir* from the infinitive) or to the infinitive, and for most verbs these endings follow regular patterns. The verb endings for the present, past and future tenses are presented in the tables on the following pages. For negative forms of verbs, see **negatives** (p21).

PRESENT TENSE

		hablar	**comer**	**vivir**
I	yo	hablo	como	vivo
you sg inf	tú	hablas	comes	vives
you sg pol	usted	habla	come	vive
he/she	él/ella	habla	come	vive
we	nosotros m nosotras f	hablamos	comemos	vivimos
you pl inf	vosotros m vosotras f	habláis	coméis	vivís
you pl pol	ustedes	hablan	comen	viven
they	ellos m ellas f	hablan	comen	viven

See also **be** (p16) and **have** (p20).

PAST TENSE

		hablar	comer	vivir
I	yo	hablé	comí	viví
you sg inf	tú	hablaste	comiste	viviste
you sg pol	usted	habló	comió	vivió
he/she	él/ella	habló	comió	vivió
we	nosotros m nosotras f	hablamos	comimos	vivimos
you pl inf	vosotros m vosotras f	hablasteis	comisteis	vivisteis
you pl pol	ustedes	hablaron	comieron	vivieron
they	ellos m ellas f	hablaron	comieron	vivieron

In case of the future tense, the endings follow the same pattern for all three verb categories, and they are simply added to the infinitive (dictionary form of the verb), not the verb stem:

FUTURE TENSE

		hablar	comer	vivir
I	yo	hablaré	comeré	viviré
you sg inf	tú	hablarás	comerás	vivirás
you sg pol	usted	hablará	comerá	vivirá
he/she	él/ella	hablará	comerá	vivirá
we	nosotros m nosotras f	hablaremos	comeremos	viviremos
you pl inf	vosotros m vosotras f	hablaréis	comeréis	viviréis
you pl pol	ustedes	hablarán	comerán	vivirán
they	ellos m ellas f	hablarán	comerán	vivirán

WORD ORDER

Making Statements

Spanish has a basic word order of subject–verb–object, just like English. However, the subject pronoun is usually omitted in Spanish because the subject is understood from the corresponding verb form. See also **verbs** (p27). Both of the following examples are correct, but the second one is more common:

I study business.	Yo estudio comercio. (lit: I I-study business) yo es·*too*·dyo ko·*mer*·thyo
	Estudio comercio. (lit: I-study business) es·*too*·dyo ko·*mer*·thyo

See also **negatives** (p21) and **questions** (p26).

CULTURE TIP: PROVERBS IN SPAIN

Proverbs are big in Spain. The Marqués de Santillana compiled a national collection in the second half of the 15th century, and one of the characters in *Don Quixote*, Sancho Panza, speaks almost entirely in proverbs. The novel's author, Cervantes, described these popular sayings as 'short sentences based on long experience'.

Ser como el perro del hortelano, que ni come las berzas, ni las deja comer al amo.	ser *ko*·mo el *pe*·ro del or·te·*la*·no ke nee *ko*·me las *ber*·thas nee las *de*·kha ko·*mer* al *a*·mo (to be like the market gardener's dog, who doesn't eat the cabbages and won't let his master eat them either)

GRAMMAR GLOSSARY

adjective	a word that describes something – 'he was the **greatest** player of his time'
adverb	a word that explains how an action is done – 'he turned around **quickly**'
article	the words 'a', 'an' and 'the'
demonstrative	a word that means 'this' or 'that'
direct object	the thing or person in the sentence that has the action directed to it – 'and the ball missed **him**'
gender	classification of *nouns* into classes (like masculine and feminine), requiring other words (eg *adjectives*) to belong to the same class
indirect object	the person or thing in the sentence that is the recipient of the action – 'the public yelled to **him**'
infinitive	dictionary form of a verb – 'to **play** more'
noun	a thing, person or idea – 'the **match** was exciting'
number	whether a word is singular or plural – 'and he scored more **points**'
personal pronoun	a word that means 'I', 'you' etc
possessive adjective	a word that means 'my', 'your' etc
possessive pronoun	a word that means 'mine', 'yours' etc
preposition	a word like 'for' or 'before' in English
subject	the thing or person in the sentence that does the action – '**his opponent** fell to the ground'
tense	form of a *verb* that tells you whether the action is in the present, past or future – eg 'run' (present), 'ran' (past), 'will run' (future)
verb	a doing word – 'when the ball **hit** the net again'
verb stem	part of a *verb* that doesn't change – eg '**move**' in '**mov**ing' and '**mov**ed'

BASICS

Understanding

KEY PHRASES

Do you speak English?	¿Habla inglés? pol	*ab*·la een·*gles*
I (don't) understand.	(No) Entiendo.	(no) en·*tyen*·do
What does ... mean?	¿Qué significa ...?	ke seeg·nee·*fee*·ka ...

There are two words for 'Spanish': *español* es·pa·*nyol* and *castellano* kas·te·*lya*·no. Both are used in different contexts.

Q **Do you speak (English)?**	¿Habla (inglés)? *ab*·la (een·*gles*)
Q **Does anyone speak (English)?**	¿Hay alguien que hable (inglés)? ai al·*gyen* ke *ab*·le een·*gles*
A **I (don't) speak Spanish.**	(No) Hablo español. (no) *ab*·lo es·pa·*nyol*
A **I speak a little (Spanish).**	Hablo un poco de (español). *ab*·lo oon *po*·ko de (es·pa·*nyol*)
I'd like to practise Spanish.	Me gustaría practicar español. me goos·ta·*ree*·a prak·tee·*kar* es·pa·*nyol*
I need an interpreter who speaks (English).	Necesito un intérprete que hable (inglés). ne·the·*see*·to oon in·*ter*·pre·te ke *ab*·le (een·*gles*)

LISTEN FOR

¿Cómo?	*ko*·mo	Pardon?
No.	no	No.
Sí.	see	Yes.

Would you like me to teach you some English?	¿Quieres que te enseñe algo de inglés? inf *kye*·res ke te en·se·nye *al*·go de een·*gles*
Q **Do you understand me?**	¿Me entiende/entiendes? pol/inf me en·*tyen*·de/en·*tyen*·des
A **I (don't) understand.**	(No) Entiendo. (no) en·*tyen*·do
How do you pronounce this word?	¿Cómo se pronuncia esta palabra? *ko*·mo se pro·*noon*·thya *es*·ta pa·*lab*·ra
How do you write 'ciudad'?	¿Cómo se escribe 'ciudad'? *ko*·mo se es·*kree*·be thyu·*dad*
What does ... mean?	¿Qué significa ...? ke seeg·nee·*fee*·ka ...
Could you repeat that?	¿Puede repetirlo? *pwe*·de re·pe·*teer*·lo
Could you please write it down?	¿Puede escribirlo, por favor? *pwe*·de es·kree·*beer*·lo por fa·*vor*
Could you please speak more slowly?	¿Puede hablar más despacio, por favor? *pwe*·de ab·*lar* mas des·*pa*·thyo por fa·*vor*

Slowly, please!	Más despacio, por favor.	mas des·*pa*·thyo por fa·*vor*

Numbers & Amounts

KEY PHRASES

How much?	¿Cuánto?	*kwan*·to
a little	un poquito	oon po·*kee*·to
some	algunos/as m/f	al·*goo*·nos/as

CARDINAL NUMBERS

0	cero	*the*·ro
1	uno	*oo*·no
2	dos	dos
3	tres	tres
4	cuatro	*kwa*·tro
5	cinco	*theen*·ko
6	seis	seys
7	siete	*sye*·te
8	ocho	*o*·cho
9	nueve	*nwe*·ve
10	diez	dyeth
11	once	*on*·the
12	doce	*do*·the
13	trece	*tre*·the
14	catorce	ka·*tor*·the
15	quince	*keen*·the
16	dieciséis	dye·thee·*seys*
17	diecisiete	dye·thee·*sye*·te
20	veinte	*veyn*·te

21	veintiuno	veyn·tee·*oo*·no
30	treinta	*treyn*·ta
40	cuarenta	kwa·*ren*·ta
50	cincuenta	theen·*kwen*·ta
60	sesenta	se·*sen*·ta
70	setenta	se·*ten*·ta
80	ochenta	o·*chen*·ta
90	noventa	no·*ven*·ta
100	cien	thyen
101	ciento uno	*thyen*·to *oo*·no
500	quinientos	kee·*nyen*·tos
1000	mil	mil
1,000,000	un millón	oon mee·*lyon*

ORDINAL NUMBERS

1st	primero/a m/f	pree·*me*·ro/a
2nd	segundo/a m/f	se·*goon*·do/a
3rd	tercero/a m/f	ter·*the*·ro/a

AMOUNTS

How much?	¿Cuánto?	*kwan*·to
a little	un poquito	oon po·*kee*·to
many	muchos/as m/f	*moo*·chos/as
some	algunos/as m/f	al·*goo*·nos/as
more/less	más/menos	mas/*me*·nos
a quarter/half	un cuarto/medio	oon *kwar*·to/*me*·dyo
a third	un tercio	oon *ter*·thyo
all/none	todo/nada	*to*·do/*na*·da

For other amounts, see **self-catering** (p184).

Time & Dates

KEY PHRASES

What time is it?	¿Qué hora es?	ke *o*·ra es
At what time ...?	¿A qué hora ...?	a ke *o*·ra ...
What date?	¿Qué día?	ke *dee*·a

TELLING THE TIME

Q **What time is it?**	¿Qué hora es? ke *o*·ra es
A **It's one o'clock.**	Es la una. es la *oo*·na
A **It's (10) o'clock.**	Son las (diez). son las (dyeth)
Quarter past one.	Es la una y cuarto. es la *oo*·na ee *kwar*·to
Twenty past one.	Es la una y veinte. es la *oo*·na ee *veyn*·te
Half past one.	Es la una y media. es la *oo*·na ee *me*·dya
Twenty to one.	Es la una menos veinte. es la *oo*·na *me*·nos *veyn*·te
Quarter to one.	Es la una menos cuarto. es la *oo*·na *me*·nos *kwar*·to
It's early.	Es temprano. es tem·*pra*·no
It's late.	Es tarde. es *tar*·de

At what time?	¿A qué hora? a ke *o*·ra
At ...	A las ... a las ...
am	de la mañana de la ma·*nya*·na
pm	de la tarde de la *tar*·de

THE CALENDAR

Monday	lunes m	*loo*·nes
Tuesday	martes m	*mar*·tes
Wednesday	miércoles m	*myer*·ko·les
Thursday	jueves m	*khwe*·ves
Friday	viernes m	*vyer*·nes
Saturday	sábado m	*sa*·ba·do
Sunday	domingo m	do·*meen*·go

January	enero m	e·*ne*·ro
February	febrero m	fe·*bre*·ro
March	marzo m	*mar*·tho
April	abril m	a·*breel*
May	mayo m	*ma*·yo
June	junio m	*khoo*·nyo
July	julio m	*khoo*·lyo
August	agosto m	a·*gos*·to
September	septiembre m	sep·*tyem*·bre
October	octubre m	ok·*too*·bre
November	noviembre m	no·*vyem*·bre
December	diciembre m	dee·*thyem*·bre

summer	verano m	ve·*ra*·no
autumn	otoño m	o·*to*·nyo
winter	invierno m	een·*vyer*·no
spring	primavera f	pree·ma·*ve*·ra

What date?	¿Qué día? ke *dee*·a
Q **What date is it today?**	¿Qué día es hoy? ke *dee*·a es oy
A **It's (18 October).**	Es (el dieciocho de octubre). es (el dye·thee·*o*·cho de ok·*too*·bre)

PRESENT

now	ahora	a·*o*·ra
right now	ahora mismo	a·*o*·ra *mees*·mo
this afternoon	esta tarde	*es*·ta *tar*·de
this month	este mes	*es*·te mes
this morning	esta mañana	*es*·ta ma·*nya*·na
this week	esta semana	*es*·ta se·*ma*·na
this year	este año	*es*·te *a*·nyo
today	hoy	oy
tonight	esta noche	*es*·ta *no*·che

PAST

(three) days ago	hace (tres) días	*a*·the (tres) *dee*·as
half an hour ago	hace media hora	*a*·the *me*·dya *o*·ra
a while ago	hace un rato	*a*·the un *ra*·to
(five) years ago	hace (cinco) años	*a*·the (*theen*·ko) *a*·nyos

day before yesterday	anteayer	an·te·a·*yer*
last month	el mes pasado	el mes pa·*sa*·do
last night	anoche	a·*no*·che
last week	la semana pasada	la se·*ma*·na pa·*sa*·da
last year	el año pasado	el *a*·nyo pa·*sa*·do
since (May)	desde (mayo)	*des*·de (*ma*·yo)
yesterday	ayer	a·*yer*
yesterday afternoon	ayer por la tarde	a·*yer* por la *tar*·de
yesterday evening	ayer por la noche	a·*yer* por la *no*·che
yesterday morning	ayer por la mañana	a·*yer* por la ma·*nya*·na

FUTURE

in (six) days	dentro de (seis) días	*den*·tro de (seys) *dee*·as
in an hour	dentro de una hora	*den*·tro de *oo*·na *o*·ra
in (five) minutes	dentro de (cinco) minutos	*den*·tro de (*theen*·ko) mee·*noo*·tos
in a month	dentro de un mes	*den*·tro de oon mes
next month	el mes que viene	el mes ke *vye*·ne
next week	la semana que viene	la se·*ma*·na ke *vye*·ne
next year	el año que viene	el *a*·nyo ke *vye*·ne
tomorrow	mañana	ma·*nya*·na
tomorrow morning	mañana por la mañana	ma·*nya*·na por la ma·*nya*·na

tomorrow afternoon	mañana por la tarde	ma·*nya*·na por la *tar*·de
tomorrow evening	mañana por la noche	ma·*nya*·na por la *no*·che
day after tomorrow	pasado mañana	pa·*sa*·do ma·*nya*·na
until (June)	hasta (junio)	as·ta (*khoo*·nyo)

DURING THE DAY

afternoon	tarde f	*tar*·de
day	día m	*dee*·a
evening	noche f	*no*·che
midday	mediodía m	me·dyo·*dee*·a
midnight	medianoche f	me·dya·*no*·che
early morning (midnight to 5am)	madrugada f	ma·droo·*ga*·da
morning	mañana f	ma·*nya*·na
night	noche f	*no*·che
sunrise	amanecer m	a·ma·ne·*ther*
sunset	puesta f del sol	*pwes*·ta del sol

PRACTICAL

Transport

KEY PHRASES

What time's the next bus?	¿A qué hora es el próximo autobús?	a ke o·ra es el *prok*·see·mo ow·to·*boos*
One ... ticket, please.	Un ... billete, por favor.	oon ... bee·*lye*·te, por fa·*vor*
Can you tell me when we get to (Valladolid)?	¿Puede avisarme cuando lleguemos a (Valladolid)?	*pwe*·de a·vee·*sar*·me *kwan*·do lye·*ge*·mos a (va·lya·do·*leeth*)
Please take me to this address.	Por favor, lléveme a esta dirección.	por fa·*vor* *lye*·ve·me a es·ta dee·rek·*thyon*
I'd like to hire a car.	Quería alquilar un coche.	ke·*ree*·a al·kee·*lar* oon *ko*·che

GETTING AROUND

At what time does the ... leave/arrive? ¿A qué hora sale/llega el ...? a ke o·ra *sa*·le/*lye*·ga el ...

boat	barco	*bar*·ko
bus (city)	autobús	ow·to·*boos*
bus (intercity)	autocar	ow·to·*kar*
plane	avión	a·*vyon*
train	tren	tren
tram	tranvía	tran·*vee*·a

What time's the first (bus)?	¿A qué hora es el primer (autobús)? a ke *o*·ra es el pree·*mer* (ow·to·*boos*)
What time's the last (train)?	¿A qué hora es el último (tren)? a ke *o*·ra es el *ool*·tee·mo (tren)
What time's the next (boat)?	¿A qué hora es el próximo (barco)? a ke *o*·ra es el *prok*·see·mo (*bar*·ko)
How long will it be delayed?	¿Cuánto tiempo se retrasará? *kwan*·to *tyem*·po se re·tra·sa·*ra*
Is this seat free?	¿Está libre este asiento? es·*ta lee*·bre es·te a·*syen*·to

Is it free? ¿Está libre? es·*ta lee*·bre

That's my seat.	Ése es mi asiento. *e*·se es mee a·*syen*·to
I'd like to get off at (Aranjuez).	Me gustaría bajarme en (Aranjuez). me goos·ta·*ree*·a ba·*khar*·me en (a·ran·*khweth*)
I want to get off here!	¡Quiero bajarme aquí! *kye*·ro ba·*khar*·me a·*kee*
I'd prefer to walk there.	Prefiero ir a pie. pre·*fye*·ro eer a pye
Can we get there by public transport?	¿Se puede ir en transporte público? se *pwe*·de eer en trans·*por*·te *poo*·blee·ko

BUYING TICKETS

Do I need to book?	¿Tengo que reservar? *ten*·go ke re·ser·*var*
How much is it?	¿Cuánto cuesta? *kwan*·to *kwes*·ta
Where can I buy a ticket?	¿Dónde puedo comprar un billete? *don*·de *pwe*·do kom·*prar* oon bee·*lye*·te
Is it a direct route?	¿Es un viaje directo? es oon *vya*·khe dee·*rek*·to
Is there a toilet?	¿Hay servicios? ai ser·*vee*·thyos
How long does the trip take?	¿Cuánto se tarda? *kwan*·to se *tar*·da
Can I go on the waiting list?	¿Puede ponerme en la lista de espera? *pwe*·de po·*ner*·me en la *lees*·ta de es·*pe*·ra
I'd like an aisle seat.	Quería un asiento de pasillo. ke·*ree*·a oon a·*syen*·to de pa·*see*·lyo
I'd like a window seat.	Quería un asiento junto a la ventana. ke·*ree*·a oon a·*syen*·to *khoon*·to a la ven·*ta*·na
I'd like a (non) smoking seat.	Quería un asiento de (no) fumadores. ke·*ree*·a oon a·*syen*·to de (no) foo·ma·*do*·res

Buying a Ticket

WHAT TIME IS THE NEXT ...?
¿A qué hora sale el próximo ...?
a ke *o*·ra *sa*·le el *prok*·see·mo ...

BOAT
barco
bar·ko

BUS
autobús
ow·to·*boos*

TRAIN
tren
tren

ONE ... TICKET, PLEASE.
Un billete ..., por favor.
oon bee·*lye*·te ... por fa·*vor*

ONE-WAY
sencillo
sen·*thee*·lyo

RETURN
de ida y vuelta
de *ee*·da ee *vwel*·ta

I'D LIKE A/AN ... SEAT.
Quería un asiento ...
ke·*ree*·a oon a·*syen*·to ...

AISLE
de pasillo
de pa·*see*·lyo

WINDOW
junto a la ventana
khoon·to a la ven·*ta*·na

WHICH PLATFORM DOES IT DEPART FROM?
¿De cuál andén sale?
de kwal an·*den* *sa*·le

I'd like to ... my ticket.	Me gustaría ... mi billete. *me goos·ta·ree·a ... mee bee·lye·te*

cancel	cancelar	kan·the·*lar*
change	cambiar	kam·*byar*
collect	recoger	re·ko·*kher*
confirm	confirmar	kon·feer·*mar*

(Two) ... tickets, please.	(Dos) billetes ..., por favor. (dos) bee·*lye*·tes ... por fa·*vor*

1st-class	de primera clase	de pree·*me*·ra *kla*·se
2nd-class	de segunda clase	de se·*goon*·da *kla*·se
child's	infantil	een·fan·*teel*
return	de ida y vuelta	de ee·da ee *vwel*·ta
student's	de estudiante	de es·too·*dyan*·te

A one-way ticket to (Barcelona).	Un billete sencillo a (Barcelona). oon bee·*lye*·te sen·*thee*·lyo a (bar·the·*lo*·na)

LUGGAGE

My luggage has been damaged/lost.	Mi equipaje ha sido dañado/perdido. mee e·kee·*pa*·khe a *see*·do da·*nya*·do/ per·*dee*·do

LISTEN FOR

Esta parada es ...	es·*ta* pa·*ra*·da es ... This stop is ...
La próxima parada es ...	la *prok*·see·ma pa·*ra*·da es ... The next stop is ...
Está completo.	es·*ta* kom·*ple*·to It's full.
El ... está retrasado/ cancelado.	el ... es·*ta* re·tra·*sa*·do/ kan·the·*la*·do The ... is delayed/ cancelled.

My luggage has been stolen.	Mi equipaje ha sido robado. mee e·kee·*pa*·khe a *see*·do ro·*ba*·do
I'd like a luggage locker.	Quería un casillero de consigna. ke·*ree*·a oon ka·see·*lye*·ro de kon·*seeg*·na

BUS

Which bus goes to (Madrid)?	¿Qué autobús va a (Madrid)? ke ow·to·*boos* va a (ma·*dreeth*)
Where's the bus stop?	¿Dónde está la parada del autobús? *don*·de es·*ta* la pa·*ra*·da del ow·to·*boos*
What's the next stop?	¿Cuál es la próxima parada? kwal es la *prok*·see·ma pa·*ra*·da

Please tell me when we get to (Valladolid).	¿Puede avisarme cuando lleguemos a (Valladolid)? *pwe*·de a·vee·*sar*·me *kwan*·do lye·*ge*·mos a (va·lya·do·*leeth*)
Bus number ...	El autobús número ... el ow·to·*boos noo*·me·ro ...

For bus numbers, see **numbers & amounts** (p34).

TRAIN

What station is this?	¿Cuál es esta estación? kwal es *es*·ta es·ta·*thyon*
What's the next station?	¿Cuál es la próxima estación? kwal es la *prok*·see·ma es·ta·*thyon*
Does this train stop at (Valencia)?	¿Para el tren en (Valencia)? *pa*·ra el tren en (va·*len*·thya)
Do I need to change trains?	¿Tengo que cambiar de tren? *ten*·go ke kam·*byar* de tren
Which carriage is for (Bilbao)?	¿Cuál es el coche para (Bilbao)? kwal es el *ko*·che *pa*·ra (beel·*bow*)

BOAT

Are there life jackets?	¿Hay chalecos salvavidas? ai cha·*le*·kos sal·va·*vee*·das
What's the sea like today?	¿Cómo está el mar hoy? *ko*·mo es·*ta* el mar oy
I feel seasick.	Estoy mareado/a. m/f es·*toy* ma·re·a·do/a

TAXI

I'd like a taxi at (9am).	Quería un taxi a (las nueve de la mañana). ke·*ree*·a oon *tak*·see a (las *nwe*·ve de la ma·*nya*·na)
I'd like a taxi tomorrow.	Quería un taxi mañana. ke·*ree*·a oon *tak*·see ma·*nya*·na
Where's the taxi stand?	¿Dónde está la parada de taxis? *don*·de es·*ta* la pa·*ra*·da de *tak*·sees
Is this taxi free?	¿Está libre este taxi? es·*ta* *lee*·bre es·te *tak*·see

Is it free? ¿Está libre? es·*ta* *lee*·bre

Where's the bus stop?

don·de es·*ta* la pa·*ra*·da del ow·to·*boos*

¿Dónde está la parada del autobús?

How much is the flag fall/ hiring charge?	¿Cuánto es la bajada de bandera? *kwan*·to es la ba·*kha*·da de ban·*de*·ra
Please put the meter on.	Por favor, ponga el taxímetro. por fa·*vor pon*·ga el tak·*see*·me·tro
How much is it to (the Prado)?	¿Cuánto cuesta ir (al Prado)? *kwan*·to *kwes*·ta eer (al *pra*·do)
Please take me to (this address).	Por favor, lléveme a (esta dirección). por fa·*vor lye*·ve·me a (*es*·ta dee·rek·*thyon*)
To ...	A ...
	a ...
How much is the final fare?	¿Cuánto es en total? *kwan*·to es en to·*tal*
Please slow down.	Por favor vaya más despacio. por fa·*vor va*·ya mas des·*pa*·thyo
Please wait here.	Por favor espere aquí. por fa·*vor* es·*pe*·re a·*kee*
Stop here!	¡Pare aquí! *pa*·re a·*kee*

For other useful phrases, see **directions** (p57).

CAR & MOTORBIKE

Where can I hire a ...?	¿Dónde se puede alquilar ...? *don*·de se *pwe*·de al·*kee*·lar ...
Does that include insurance/mileage?	¿Incluye el seguro/ kilometraje? een·*kloo*·ye el se·*goo*·ro/ kee·lo·me·*tra*·khe
I'd like to hire a/an ...	Quería alquilar ... ke·*ree*·a al·*kee*·lar ...

4WD	un todoterreno	oon to·do·te·*re*·no
automatic car	un coche automático	oon *ko*·che ow·to·*ma*·tee·ko
manual car	un coche manual	oon *ko*·che man·*wal*
motorbike	una moto	*oo*·na *mo*·to

How much for hourly/ daily hire?	¿Cuánto cuesta el alquiler por hora/día? *kwan*·to *kwes*·ta el al·*kee*·ler por *o*·ra/*dee*·a
How much for weekly hire?	¿Cuánto cuesta el alquiler por semana? *kwan*·to *kwes*·ta el al·*kee*·ler por se·*ma*·na
Is this the road to (Seville)?	¿Se va a (Sevilla) por esta carretera? se va a (se·*vee*·lya) por *es*·ta ka·re·*te*·ra
Where's a petrol station?	¿Dónde hay una gasolinera? *don*·de ai *oo*·na ga·so·lee·*ne*·ra

LOOK FOR

Acceso	ak·*the*·so	Entrance
Aparcamiento	a·par·ka·*myen*·to	Parking
Ceda el Paso	*the*·da el *pa*·so	Give Way
Desvío	des·*vee*·o	Detour
Dirección Única	dee·rek·*thyon* *oo*·nee·ka	One Way
Frene	*fre*·ne	Slow Down
Peaje	pe·a·khe	Toll
Peligro	pe·*lee*·gro	Danger
Prohibido Aparcar	pro·ee·*bee*·do a·par·*kar*	No Parking
Prohibido el Paso	pro·ee·*bee*·do el *pa*·so	No Entry
Stop	es·*top*	Stop
Vía de Acceso	*vee*·a de ak·*the*·so	Exit Motorway

What's the (city) speed limit?	¿Cuál es el límite de velocidad (en la ciudad)? kwal es el *lee*·mee·te de ve·lo·thee·*dad* (en la thyu·*dad*)
Please fill it up.	Por favor, lléneme el depósito. por fa·*vor* *lye*·ne·me el de·*po*·see·to
I'd like (20) litres of ...	Quiero (veinte) litros de ... *kye*·ro (*veyn*·te) *lee*·tros de ...
Please check the oil/water.	Por favor, revise el nivel del aceite/agua. por fa·*vor* re·*vee*·se el nee·*vel* del a·*they*·te/*a*·gwa

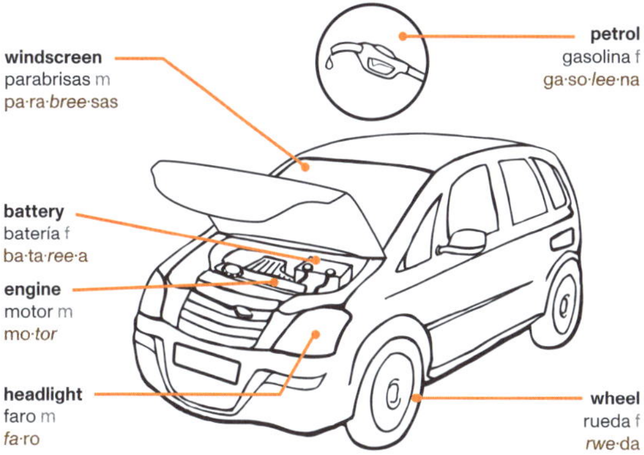

Please check the tyre pressure.	Por favor, revise la presión de los neumáticos. por fa·*vor* re·*vee*·se la pre·*syon* de los ne·oo·*ma*·tee·kos
(How long) Can I park here?	¿(Por cuánto tiempo) Puedo aparcar aquí? (por *kwan*·to *tyem*·po) *pwe*·do a·par·*kar* a·*kee*
I need a mechanic.	Necesito un/una mecánico/a m/f ne·the·see·to oon/*oo*·na me·*ka*·nee·ko/a
The car has broken down (at Salamanca).	El coche se ha averiado (en Salamanca). el *ko*·che se a a·ve·*rya*·do (en sa·la·*man*·ka)
I had an accident.	He tenido un accidente. e te·*nee*·do oon ak·thee·*den*·te

BICYCLE

Can we get there by bike?	¿Se puede ir en bici? se *pwe*·de eer en *bee*·thee
Where can I hire a bicycle?	¿Dónde se puede alquilar una bicicleta? *don*·de se *pwe*·de al·kee·*lar* *oo*·na bee·thee·*kle*·ta
Where can I buy a (secondhand) bike?	¿Dónde se puede comprar una bicicleta (de segunda mano)? *don*·de se *pwe*·de kom·*prar* *oo*·na bee·thee·*kle*·ta (de se·*goon*·da *ma*·no)
How much is it per day?	¿Cuánto cuesta por día? *kwan*·to *kwes*·ta por *dee*·a
How much is it per hour?	¿Cuánto cuesta por hora? *kwan*·to *kwes*·ta por *o*·ra
I have a puncture.	Se me ha pinchado una rueda. se me a peen·*cha*·do *oo*·na *rwe*·da
I'd like to have my bicycle repaired.	Me gustaría arreglar mi bicicleta. me goo·sta·*ree*·a a·reg·*lar* mee bee·thee·*kle*·ta
Are there cycling paths?	¿Hay carril bici? ai ka·*reel bee*·thee
Is there bicycle parking?	¿Hay aparcamiento de bicicletas? ai a·par·ka·*myen*·to de bee·thee·*kle*·tas
Can I take my bike on the train?	¿Puedo llevar mi bicicleta en el tren? *pwe*·do lye·*var* mee bee·thee·*kle*·ta en el tren

Border Crossing

KEY PHRASES

I'm here for ... days.	Estoy aquí por ... días.	es·*toy* a·*kee* por ... *dee*·as
I'm staying at ...	Me estoy alojando en ...	me es·*toy* a·lo·*khan*·do en ...
I have nothing to declare.	No tengo nada que declarar.	no *ten*·go *na*·da ke de·kla·*rar*

PASSPORT CONTROL

I'm here on business.	Estoy aquí de negocios. es·*toy* a·*kee* de ne·*go*·thyos
I'm here on holiday.	Estoy aquí de vacaciones. es·*toy* a·*kee* de va·ka·*thyo*·nes
I'm here in transit.	Estoy aquí en tránsito. es·*toy* a·*kee* en *tran*·see·to
I'm here for ... days.	Estoy aquí por ... días. es·*toy* a·*kee* por ... *dee*·as
I'm here for ... weeks.	Estoy aquí por ... semanas. es·*toy* a·*kee* por ... se·*ma*·nas
I'm here for ... months.	Estoy aquí por ... meses. es·*toy* a·*kee* por ... *me*·ses
I'm going to (Salamanca).	Voy a (Salamanca). voy a (sa·la·*man*·ka)
I'm staying at ...	Me estoy alojando en ... me es·*toy* a·lo·*khan*·do en ...

LISTEN FOR

Su pasaporte, por favor.	soo pa·sa·*por*·te por fa·*vor* Your passport, please.
Su visado, por favor.	soo vee·*sa*·do por fa·*vor* Your visa, please.
¿Está viajando en un grupo?	es·*ta* vya·*khan*·do en oon *groo*·po Are you travelling in a group?
¿Está viajando con familia?	es·*ta* vya·*khan*·do kon fa·*mee*·lya Are you travelling with family?
¿Está viajando solo/a? m/f	es·*ta* vya·*khan*·do *so*·lo/a Are you travelling on your own?

CUSTOMS

I have nothing to declare.	No tengo nada que declarar. no *ten*·go *na*·da ke de·kla·*rar*
I have something to declare.	Quería declarar algo. ke·*ree*·a de·kla·*rar al*·go
That's (not) mine.	Eso (no) es mío. *e*·so (no) es *mee*·o
I didn't know I had to declare it.	No sabía que tenía que declararlo. no sa·*bee*·a ke te·*nee*·a ke de·kla·*rar*·lo

For phrases on payments and receipts, see **money & banking** (p91).

Directions

KEY PHRASES

Where's ...?	¿Dónde está ...?	*don*·de es·*ta* ...
What's the address?	¿Cuál es la dirección?	kwal es la dee·rek·*thyon*
How far is it?	¿A cuánta distancia está?	a *kwan*·ta dees·*tan*·thya es·*ta*

Excuse me.	Perdón. per·*don*
Could you help me, please?	¿Perdón, puede ayudarme, por favor? per·*don pwe*·de a·yoo·*dar*·me por fa·*vor*
Where's ...?	¿Dónde está ...? *don*·de es·*ta* ...
I'm looking for ...	Busco ... *boos*·ko ...
Which way is ...?	¿Por dónde se va a ...? por *don*·de se va a ...
How can I get there?	¿Cómo se puede ir? *ko*·mo se *pwe*·de eer
How far is it?	¿A cuánta distancia está? a *kwan*·ta dees·*tan*·thya es·*ta*
What's the address?	¿Cuál es la dirección? kwal es la dee·rek·*thyon*

Can you show me (on the map)?	¿Me lo puede indicar (en el mapa)? me lo *pwe*·de een·dee·*kar* (en el *ma*·pa)
It's ...	Está ... es·*ta* ...

behind ...	detrás de ...	de·*tras* de ...
far away	lejos	*le*·khos
here	aquí	a·*kee*
in front of ...	enfrente de ...	en·*fren*·te de ...
left	por la izquierda	por la eeth·*kyer*·da
near	cerca	*ther*·ka
next to ...	al lado de ...	al *la*·do de ...
opposite ...	frente a ...	*fren*·te a ...
right	por la derecha	por la de·*re*·cha
straight ahead	todo recto	*to*·do *rek*·to
there	ahí	a·ee

Turn at the corner.	Doble en la esquina. *do*·ble en la es·*kee*·na
Turn at the traffic lights.	Doble en el semáforo. *do*·ble en el se·*ma*·fo·ro
Turn left/right.	Doble a la izquierda/ derecha. *do*·ble a la eeth·*kyer*·da/ de·*re*·cha
(two) kilometres	(dos) kilómetros (dos) kee·*lo*·me·tros
(three) metres	(tres) metros (tres) *me*·tros
(six) minutes	(seis) minutos (seys) mee·*noo*·tos

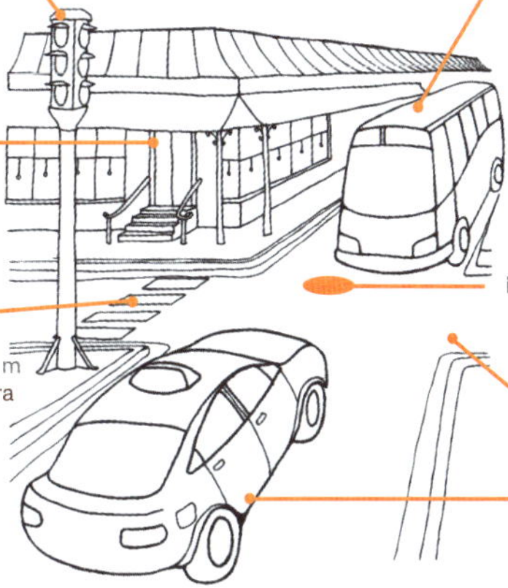

by bus	por autobús por ow·to·*boos*
by taxi	por taxi por *tak*·see
by train	por tren por tren
on foot	a pie a pye
avenue	avenida f a·ve·*nee*·da
lane	callejón m ka·lye·*khon*
street	calle f *ka*·lye

For locations and compass directions, see the **dictionary** (p205).

Accommodation

KEY PHRASES

Where is there a hotel?	¿Dónde hay un hotel?	*don*·de ai oon o·*tel*
Do you have a double room?	¿Tiene una habitación doble?	*tye*·ne *oo*·na a·bee·ta·*thyon* *do*·ble
How much is it per night?	¿Cuánto cuesta por noche?	*kwan*·to *kwes*·ta por *no*·che
Is breakfast included?	¿El desayuno está incluido?	el de·sa·*yoo*·no es·*ta* een·kloo·*ee*·do
What time is checkout?	¿A qué hora hay que dejar libre la habitación?	a ke *o*·ra ai ke de·*khar* *lee*·bre la a·bee·ta·*thyon*

FINDING ACCOMMODATION

Where's a ...?	¿Dónde hay ...? *don*·de ai ...	
bed & breakfast	una pensión con desayuno	*oo*·na pen·*syon* kon de·sa·*yoo*·no
camping ground	terreno de cámping	te·*re*·no de *kam*·peeng
guesthouse	una pensión	*oo*·na pen·*syon*
hotel	un hotel	oon o·*tel*
youth hostel	un albergue juvenil	oon al·*ber*·ge khoo·ve·*neel*

Can you recommend somewhere (cheap)?	¿Puede recomendar algún sitio (barato)? *pwe*·de re·ko·men·*dar* al·*goon* see·tyo (ba·*ra*·to)
Can you recommend somewhere (nearby)?	¿Puede recomendar algún sitio (cercano)? *pwe*·de re·ko·men·*dar* al·*goon* see·tyo (ther·*ka*·no)
Can you recommend somewhere (luxurious)?	¿Puede recomendar algún sitio (de lujo)? *pwe*·de re·ko·men·*dar* al·*goon* see·tyo (de *loo*·kho)
What's the address?	¿Cuál es la dirección? kwal es la dee·rek·*thyon*

For more on how to get there, see **directions** (p57).

BOOKING AHEAD & CHECKING IN

I'd like to book a room, please.	Quería reservar una habitación. ke·*ree*·a re·ser·*var* *oo*·na a·bee·ta·*thyon*

Are there rooms?	¿Hay habitaciones?	ai a·bee·ta·*thyo*·nes

I have a reservation.	He hecho una reserva. e *e*·cho *oo*·na re·*ser*·va
My name's ...	Me llamo ... me *lya*·mo ...
For (three) nights/weeks.	Por (tres) noches/semanas. por (tres) *no*·ches/se·*ma*·nas
From (July 2) to (July 6).	Desde (el dos de julio) hasta (el seis de julio). *des*·de (el dos de *khoo*·lyo) *as*·ta (el seys de *khoo*·lyo)

LISTEN FOR

Lo siento, está completo.	lo *syen*·to es·*ta* kom·*ple*·to I'm sorry, we're full.
¿Por cuántas noches?	por *kwan*·tas *no*·ches For how many nights?
Su pasaporte, por favor.	soo pa·sa·*por*·te por fa·*vor* Your passport, please.

Do I need to pay upfront?	¿Necesito pagar por adelantado? ne·the·*see*·to *pa*·gar por a·de·lan·*ta*·do
Do you offer (long-stay) discounts?	¿Ofrecen descuentos (por larga estancia)? of·*re*·then des·*kwen*·tos (por *lar*·ga es·*tan*·thya)
Is breakfast included?	¿El desayuno está incluido? el de·sa·*yoo*·no es·*ta* een·kloo·*ee*·do
Is there parking?	¿Hay aparcamiento? ai a·par·ka·*myen*·to
Is there wi-fi here?	¿Hay wi-fi aquí? ai *wee*·fee a·*kee*
How much is it per person?	¿Cuánto cuesta por persona? *kwan*·to *kwes*·ta por per·*so*·na
How much is it per night/week?	¿Cuánto cuesta por noche/semana? *kwan*·to *kwes*·ta por *no*·che/se·*ma*·na

Finding a Room

DO YOU HAVE A ... ROOM?
¿Tiene una habitación ...?
tye·ne *oo*·na a·bee·ta·*thyon* ...

DOUBLE
doble
do·ble

SINGLE
individual
een·dee·vee·*dwal*

HOW MUCH IS IT PER ...?
¿Cuánto cuesta por ...?
kwan·to *kwes*·ta por ...

NIGHT
noche
no·che

PERSON
persona
per·*so*·na

IS BREAKFAST INCLUDED?
¿El desayuno está incluido?
el de·sa·*yoo*·no es·*ta* een·kloo·*ee*·do

CAN I SEE THE ROOM?
¿Puedo verla?
pwe·do *ver*·la

I'LL TAKE IT.
La alquilo.
la al·*kee*·lo

I WON'T TAKE IT.
No la alquilo.
no la al·*kee*·lo

Can I pay by credit card?	¿Puedo pagar con tarjeta de crédito? *pwe*·do pa·*gar* con tar·*khe*·ta de *kre*·dee·to

For other methods of payment, see **money & banking** (p91).

Do you have a double room?	¿Tiene una habitación doble? *tye*·ne *oo*·na a·bee·ta·*thyon* *do*·ble
Do you have a single room?	¿Tiene una habitación individual? *tye*·ne *oo*·na a·bee·ta·*thyon* een·dee·vee·*dwal*
Do you have a twin room?	¿Tiene una habitación con dos camas? *tye*·ne *oo*·na a·bee·ta·*thyon* con dos *ka*·mas
Do you have a room with/ without (a) ...?	¿Tiene una habitación con/sin ...? *tye*·ne *oo*·na a·bee·ta·*thyon* kon/seen ...
Can I see it?	¿Puedo verla? *pwe*·do *ver*·la
It's fine, I'll take it.	Vale, la alquilo. *va*·le la al·*kee*·lo

REQUESTS & QUERIES

When/Where's breakfast served?	¿Cuándo/Dónde se sirve el desayuno? *kwan*·do/*don*·de se *seer*·ve el de·sa·*yoo*·no
Please wake me at (seven).	Por favor, despiérteme a (las siete). por fa·*vor* des·*pyer*·te·me a (las *sye*·te)

Can I have another ...?	¿Puede darme otro/a ...? m/f *pwe*·de *dar*·me *o*·tro/a ...
Can I use the ...?	¿Puedo usar ...? *pwe*·do oo·*sar* ...

internet	el internet	el *een*·ter·net
kitchen	la cocina	la ko·*thee*·na
laundry	el lavadero	el la·va·*de*·ro
telephone	el teléfono	el te·*le*·fo·no

Is there a/an ...?	¿Hay ...? ai ...

lift (elevator)	ascensor	as·then·*sor*
message board	tablón de anuncios	ta·*blon* de a·*noon*·thyos
safe	una caja fuerte	*oo*·na *ka*·kha *fwer*·te
swimming pool	piscina	pees·*thee*·na

Do you arrange tours here?	¿Aquí organizan recorridos? a·*kee* or·ga·*nee*·than re·ko·*ree*·dos
Do you change money here?	¿Aquí cambian dinero? a·*kee* *kam*·byan dee·*ne*·ro
Is there a message for me?	¿Tiene un mensaje para mí? *tye*·ne oon men·*sa*·khe *pa*·ra mee
I've locked myself out of my room.	Cerré la puerta y se me olvidaron las llaves dentro. the·*re* la *pwer*·ta y se me ol·vee·*da*·ron las *lya*·ves *den*·tro

The (bathroom) door is locked.	La puerta (del baño) está cerrada. la *pwer*·ta (del *ba*·nyo) es·*ta* the·*ra*·da
There's no need to change my sheets.	No hace falta cambiar las sábanas. no *a*·the *fal*·ta kam·*byar* las *sa*·ba·nas

COMPLAINTS

It's too ...	Es demasiado ... es de·ma·*sya*·do ...

cold	fría f	*free*·a
dark	oscura f	os·*koo*·ra
light/bright	clara f	*kla*·ra
noisy	ruidosa f	rwee·*do*·sa
small	pequeña f	pe·*ke*·nya

The ... doesn't work.	No funciona ... no foon·*thyo*·na ...

air-conditioning	el aire acondicionado	el *ai*·re a·kon·dee·thyo·*na*·do
fan	el ventilador	el ven·tee·la·*dor*
heater	la estufa	la es·*too*·fa
toilet	el retrete	el re·*tre*·te
window	la ventana	la ven·*ta*·na

This ... isn't clean.	Este/Esta ... no está limpio/a. m/f *es*·te/*es*·ta ... no es·*ta* *leem*·pyo/a
There's no hot water.	No hay agua caliente. no ai *a*·gwa ka·*lyen*·te

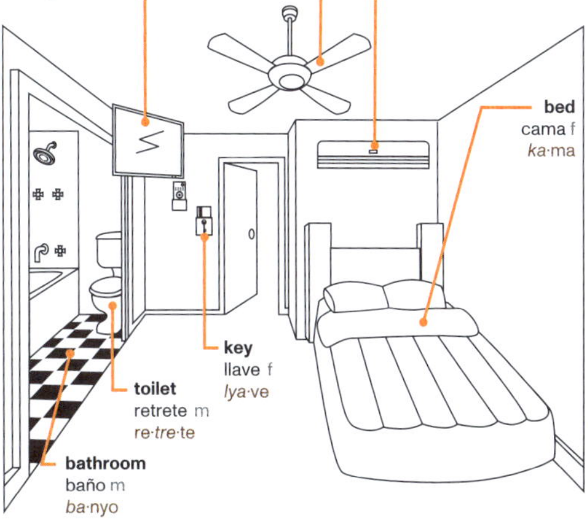

ANSWERING THE DOOR

Who is it?	¿Quién es? kyen es
Just a moment.	Un momento. oon mo·*men*·to
Come in.	Adelante. a·de·*lan*·te
Can you come back later, please?	¿Puede volver más tarde, por favor? *pwe*·de vol·*ver* mas *tar*·de por fa·*vor*

CHECKING OUT

What time is checkout?
¿A qué hora hay que dejar libre la habitación?
a ke *o*·ra ai ke de·*khar* *lee*·bre la a·bee·ta·*thyon*

How much extra to stay until (6 o'clock)?
¿Cuánto más cuesta quedarse hasta (las seis)?
kwan·to mas *kwes*·ta ke·*dar*·se *as*·ta (las seys)

Can I have a late check out?
¿Puedo dejar la habitación más tarde?
pwe·do de·*khar* la a·bee·ta·*thyon* mas *tar*·de

Can I leave my bags here?
¿Puedo dejar las maletas aquí?
pwe·do de·*khar* las ma·*le*·tas a·*kee*

There's a mistake in the bill.
Hay un error en la cuenta.
ai oon e·*ror* en la *kwen*·ta

I'm leaving now.
Me voy ahora.
me voy a·*o*·ra

Can you call a taxi for me (for 11 o'clock)?
¿Me puede pedir un taxi (para las once)?
me *pwe*·de pe·*deer* oon *tak*·see (*pa*·ra las *on*·the)

Could I have my deposit, please?
¿Me puede dar mi depósito, por favor?
me *pwe*·de dar mee de·*po*·see·to por fa·*vor*

Could I have my passport, please?	¿Me puede dar mi pasaporte, por favor? me *pwe*·de dar mee pa·sa·*por*·te por fa·*vor*
Could I have my valuables, please?	¿Me puede dar mis objetos de valor, por favor? me *pwe*·de dar mees ob·*khe*·tos de va·*lor* por fa·*vor*
I'll be back on (Tuesday).	Volveré el (martes). vol·ve·*re* el (*mar*·tes)
I'll be back in (three) days.	Volveré en (tres) días. vol·ve·*re* en (tres) *dee*·as

Where is there a hotel?

don·de ai oon o·*tel*

¿Dónde hay un hotel?

I had a great stay, thank you.	He tenido una estancia muy agradable, gracias. e te·*nee*·do *oo*·na es·*tan*·thya mooy a·gra·*da*·ble *gra*·thyas
You've been terrific.	Han sido estupendos. an *see*·do es·too·*pen*·dos
I'll recommend it to my friends.	Se lo recomendaré a mis amigos. se lo re·ko·men·da·*re* a mees a·*mee*·gos

CAMPING

Where's the nearest camp site?	¿Dónde está el cámping más cercano? *don*·de es·*ta* el *kam*·peeng mas ther·*ka*·no
Can I camp here?	¿Se puede acampar aquí? se *pwe*·de a·kam·*par* a·*kee*
Can I park next to my tent?	¿Se puede aparcar al lado de la tienda? se *pwe*·de a·par·*kar* al *la*·do de la *tyen*·da
Do you have ...?	¿Tiene ...? *tye*·ne ...

electricity	electricidad	e·lek·tree·thee·*dad*
shower facilities	duchas	*doo*·chas
a site	un sitio	oon *see*·tyo
tents for hire	tiendas de campaña para alquilar	*tyen*·das de kam·*pa*·nya *pa*·ra al·kee·*lar*

How much is it per ...?	¿Cuánto vale por ...? *kwan*·to *va*·le por ...

caravan	caravana	ka·ra·*va*·na
person	persona	per·*so*·na
tent	tienda	*tyen*·da
vehicle	vehículo	ve·*ee*·koo·lo

Is the water drinkable?	¿Se puede beber el agua? se *pwe*·de *be*·ber el *a*·gwa
I'm looking for the nearest showers.	Estoy buscando las duchas más cercanas. es·*toy* boos·*kan*·do las *doo*·chas mas ther·*ka*·nas
I'm looking for the nearest toilet block.	Estoy buscando los servicios más cercanos. es·*toy* boos·*kan*·do los ser·*vee*·thyos mas ther·*ka*·nos
Could I borrow ...?	¿Me puede prestar ...? me *pwe*·de pres·*tar* ...

For cooking utensils, see **self-catering** (p186) and the **dictionary** (p205).

LOOK FOR

Caballeros	ka·ba·*lye*·ros	Men
Caliente	ka·*lyen*·te	Hot
Dirección Prohibida	dee·rek·*thyon* pro·hee·*bee*·da	No Entry
Frío	*free*·o	Cold
Señoras	se·*nyo*·ras	Women

RENTING

Do you have a/an ... for rent?	¿Tiene ... para alquilar? *tye*·ne ... *pa*·ra al·kee·*lar*

apartment	un piso	oon *pee*·so
cabin	una cabaña	*oo*·na ka·*ba*·nya
house	una casa	*oo*·na *ka*·sa
room	una habitación	*oo*·na a·bee·ta·*thyon*
villa	un chalet	oon cha·*le*

furnished	amueblado/a m/f a·mwe·*bla*·do/a
partly furnished	semi amueblado/a m/f se·mee a·mwe·*bla*·do/a
unfurnished	sin amueblar seen a·mwe·*blar*

STAYING WITH LOCALS

Can I stay at your place?	¿Me puedo quedar en su/tu casa? pol/inf me *pwe*·do ke·*dar* en soo/too *ka*·sa
Thanks for your hospitality.	Gracias por su/tu hospitalidad. pol/inf *gra*·thyas por soo/too os·pee·ta·lee·*dad*
I have my own mattress.	Tengo mi propio colchón. *ten*·go mee *pro*·pyo kol·*chon*
I have my own sleeping bag.	Tengo mi propio saco de dormir. *ten*·go mee *pro*·pyo *sa*·ko de dor·*meer*

Can I bring anything for the meal?	¿Puedo traer algo para la comida? *pwe*·do tra·*er al*·go *pa*·ra la ko·*mee*·da
Can I use your telephone?	¿Puedo usar su/tu teléfono? **pol/inf** *pwe*·do oo·*sar* soo/too te·*le*·fo·no
Can I help?	¿Puedo ayudar? *pwe*·do a·yoo·*dar*
Can I set/clear the table?	¿Puedo poner/quitar la mesa? *pwe*·do po·*ner*/kee·*tar* la *me*·sa
Can I do the dishes?	¿Puedo lavar los platos? *pwe*·do la·*var* los *pla*·tos
Can I take out the rubbish?	¿Puedo sacar la basura? *pwe*·do sa·*kar* la ba·*soo*·ra

For compliments to the chef, see **compliments & complaints** (p174).

Shopping

KEY PHRASES

I'd like to buy ...	Quería comprar ...	ke·*ree*·a kom·*prar* ...
Can I look at it?	¿Puedo verlo?	*pwe*·do *ver*·lo
Can I try it on?	¿Me lo puedo probar?	me lo *pwe*·do pro·*bar*
How much?	¿Cuánto cuesta?	*kwan*·to *kwes*·ta
That's too expensive.	Es muy caro.	es mooy *ka*·ro

LOOKING FOR ...

Where's a (super)market?	¿Dónde está un (super)mercado? *don*·de es·*ta* oon (soo·per·)mer·*ka*·do
Where's a camping store?	¿Dónde está una tienda de camping? *don*·de es·*ta* *oo*·na *tyen*·da de *kam*·peeng
Where can I buy locally produced goods/souvenirs?	¿Dónde puedo comprar recuerdos de la zona? *don*·de *pwe*·do kom·*prar* re·*kwer*·dos de la *tho*·na
Where can I buy ...?	¿Dónde puedo comprar ...? *don*·de *pwe*·do kom·*prar* ...

For more on shops and how to get there, see **directions** (p57) and the **dictionary** (p205).

MAKING A PURCHASE

How much is this?	¿Cuánto cuesta esto? *kwan*·to *kwes*·ta *es*·to
✂ **How much?** ¿Cuánto cuesta?	*kwan*·to *kwes*·ta
I'd like to buy ...	Quería comprar ... ke·*ree*·a kom·*prar* ...
I'm just looking.	Sólo estoy mirando. *so*·lo es·*toy* mee·*ran*·do
Can I look at it?	¿Puedo verlo? *pwe*·do *ver*·lo
Do you have any others?	¿Tiene otros? *tye*·ne *o*·tros
What is this made from?	¿De qué está hecho? de ke es·*ta* *e*·cho
Do you accept credit/ debit cards?	¿Aceptan tarjetas de crédito/débito? a·*thep*·tan tar·*khe*·tas de *kre*·dee·to/*de*·bee·to
Could I have a bag, please?	¿Podría darme una bolsa, por favor? po·*dree*·a *dar*·me *oo*·na *bol*·sa por fa·*vor*
Could I have a receipt, please?	¿Podría darme un recibo, por favor? po·*dree*·a *dar*·me oon re·*thee*·bo por fa·*vor*
✂ **Receipt, please.** El recibo, por favor.	el re·*thee*·bo por fa·*vor*

LISTEN FOR

¿En qué le puedo ayudar?	en ke le *pwe*·do a·yoo·*dar* Can I help you?
No tengo.	no *ten*·go I don't have any.
¿Algo más?	*al*·go mas Anything else?

I don't need a bag, thanks.	No necesito bolsa, gracias. no ne·the·*see*·to *bol*·sa *gra*·thyas
Can you write down the price?	¿Puede escribir el precio? *pwe*·de es·kree·*beer* el *pre*·thyo
Could I have it wrapped?	¿Me lo podría envolver? me lo po·*dree*·a en·vol·*ver*
Does it have a guarantee?	¿Tiene garantía? *tye*·ne ga·ran·*tee*·a
Can I pick it up later?	¿Puedo recogerlo más tarde? *pwe*·do re·ko·*kher*·lo mas *tar*·de
Can I have it sent overseas?	¿Pueden enviarlo por correo a otro país? *pwe*·den en·vee·*ar*·lo por ko·*re*·o a *o*·tro pa·*ees*
It's faulty.	Es defectuoso. es de·fek·*two*·so
I'd like my change, please.	Quería mi cambio, por favor. ke·*ree*·a mee *kam*·byo por fa·*vor*

Making a Purchase

I'D LIKE TO BUY ...
Quería comprar ...
ke·*ree*·a kom·*prar* ...

HOW MUCH IS IT?
¿Cuánto cuesta esto?
kwan·to *kwes*·ta *es*·to

OR

CAN YOU WRITE DOWN THE PRICE?
¿Puede escribir el precio?
pwe·de es·kree·*beer* el *pre*·thyo

DO YOU ACCEPT CREDIT CARDS?
¿Aceptan tarjetas de crédito?
a·*thep*·tan tar·*khe*·tas de *kre*·dee·to

COULD I HAVE A ..., PLEASE?
¿Podría darme ..., por favor?
po·*dree*·a *dar*·me ... por fa·*vor*

RECEIPT
un recibo
oon re·*thee*·bo

BAG
una bolsa
oo·na *bol*·sa

LISTEN FOR

cazador m **de ofertas**	ka·tha·*dor* de o·*fer*·tas	bargain hunter
estafa f	es·*ta*·fa	rip-off
ganga f	*gan*·ga	bargain
rebajas f pl	re·*ba*·khas	specials
ventas f pl	*ven*·tas	sale

I'd like my money back, please.	Quería que me devolviera el dinero, por favor. ke·*ree*·a ke me de·vol·*vye*·ra el dee·*ne*·ro por fa·*vor*
I'd like to return this, please.	Quería devolver esto, por favor. ke·*ree*·a de·vol·*ver es*·to por fa·*vor*

BARGAINING

That's too expensive.	Es muy caro. es mooy *ka*·ro
Do you have something cheaper?	¿Tiene algo más barato? *tye*·ne *al*·go mas ba·*ra*·to
Can you lower the price?	¿Podría bajar un poco el precio? po·*dree*·a ba·*khar* oon *po*·ko el *pre*·thyo
I'll give you ...	Le/Te daré ... pol/inf le/te da·*re* ...

CLOTHES

Can I try it on?	¿Me lo puedo probar? me lo *pwe*·do *pro*·bar
My size is ...	Uso la talla ... *oo*·so la *ta*·lya ...
It doesn't fit.	No me queda bien. no me *ke*·da byen
small	pequeño/a m/f pe·*ke*·nyo/a
medium	mediano/a m/f me·*dya*·no/a
large	grande m&f *gran*·de

For clothing items, see the **dictionary** (p205). For sizes, see **numbers & amounts** (p34).

I'm just looking.
so·lo es·*toy* mee·*ran*·do
Sólo estoy mirando.

REPAIRS

Can I have my (camera) repaired here?	¿Puede reparar mi (cámara) aquí? *pwe*·de re·pa·*rar* mee (*ka*·ma·ra) a·*kee*
When will my (sun) glasses be ready?	¿Cuándo estarán listas mis gafas (de sol)? *kwan*·do es·ta·*ran lees*·tas mees *ga*·fas (de sol)
When will my shoes be ready?	¿Cuándo estarán listos mis zapatos? *kwan*·do es·ta·*ran lees*·tos mees tha·*pa*·tos

BOOKS & READING

Is there a/an (English-language) bookshop?	¿Hay una librería (en inglés)? ai *oo*·na lee·bre·*ree*·a (en een·*gles*)
Is there a/an (English-language) section?	¿Hay una sección (en inglés)? ai *oo*·na sek·*thyon* (en een·*gles*)
I (don't) like ...	(No) Me gusta/gustan ... sg/pl (no) me *goos*·ta/*goos*·tan ...
I'm looking for something by (Javier Marías).	Estoy buscando algo de (Javier Marías). es·*toy* boos·*kan*·do *al*·go de (kha·*vyer* ma·*ree*·as)

For more on books and reading, see **interests** (p124).

CULTURE TIP: HISPANIC LITERATURE

Spanish-language literature has a long history, dating from the 12th century and written across the Spanish-speaking world. The thriving industry includes works from authors such as Ana María Matute, Isabel Allende, Jorge Luis Borges, Miguel de Unamuno, Carmen Martín Gaite, Juan Goytisolo, Miguel Delibes, 1982 Nobel Prize winner Gabriel García Márquez and the 1989 Nobel Prize winner, Camilo José Cela.

MUSIC

I heard a band called ...	Escuché a un grupo que se llama ... es·koo·*che* a oon *groo*·po ke se *lya*·ma ...
What's their best recording?	¿Cuál es su mejor disco? kwal es soo me·*khor dees*·ko
Can I listen to this?	¿Puedo escuchar esto? *pwe*·do es·koo·*char es*·to
I'd like some headphones.	Quería unos auriculares. ke·*ree*·a *oo*·nos ow·ree·koo·*la*·res

VIDEO & PHOTOGRAPHY

Can you print digital photos?
¿Podría imprimir fotos digitales?
po·*dree*·a eem·pree·*meer* *fo*·tos dee·khee·*ta*·les

Can you transfer my photos from camera to a USB?
¿Podría pasar las fotos de mi cámara a un USB?
po·*dree*·a pa·*sar* las *fo*·tos de mee *ka*·ma·ra a oon oo·es·e·*be*

I need a cable to connect my camera to a computer.
Necesito un cable para conectar mi cámara al ordenador.
ne·the·*see*·to oon *ka*·ble *pa*·ra ko·nek·*tar* mee *ka*·ma·ra al or·de·na·*dor*

I need a cable to recharge this battery.
Necesito un cable para recargar esta batería.
ne·the·*see*·to oon *ka*·ble *pa*·ra re·kar·*gar* es·ta ba·te·*ree*·a

CULTURE TIP: THE SPANISH LISP

According to a popular legend, one Spanish king – some say Felipe IV, others Ferdinand I – was unable to pronounce the s sound properly and his court, and eventually all of Spain, mimicked his lisp. Of course, the tale is a myth. Indeed, only the letters *c* and *z* are pronounced th (when they precede an *i* or an *e*), while the letter *s* remains the same as in English – a selectiveness due to the way Spanish evolved from Latin. So when you hear someone say *gracias* *gra*·thyas, they are no more lisping than when you say 'thank you' in English.

Do you have (a) ... for this camera?	¿Tiene ... para esta cámara? *tye*·ne ... *pa*·ra *es*·ta *ka*·ma·ra
Do you have batteries for this camera?	¿Tiene pilas para esta cámara? *tye*·ne *pee*·las *pa*·ra *es*·ta *ka*·ma·ra
Do you have memory cards for this camera?	¿Tiene tarjetas de memoria para esta cámara? *tye*·ne tar·*khe*·tas de me·*mo*·rya *pa*·ra *es*·ta *ka*·ma·ra
I need some passport photos.	Necesito fotos de pasaporte. ne·the·*see*·to *fo*·tos de pa·sa·*por*·te

Communications

KEY PHRASES

I'd like to check my email.	Quería revisar mi correo electrónico.	ke·*ree*·a re·vee·*sar* mee ko·*re*·o e·lek·*tro*·nee·ko
I want to send a parcel.	Quería enviar un paquete.	ke·*ree*·a en·vee·*ar* oon pa·*ke*·te
I'd like a SIM card.	Quería una tarjeta SIM.	ke·*ree*·a *oo*·na tar·*khe*·ta seem

POST OFFICE

I want to send a parcel.	Quería enviar un paquete. ke·*ree*·a en·vee·*ar* oon pa·*ke*·te
I want to send a postcard.	Quería enviar una postal. ke·*ree*·a en·vee·*ar* *oo*·na pos·*tal*
I want to buy an envelope.	Quería comprar un sobre. ke·*ree*·a kom·*prar* oon *so*·bre
I want to buy stamps.	Quería comprar sellos. ke·*ree*·a kom·*prar* *se*·lyos
Please send it by air/ surface mail to ...	Por favor, mándelo por vía aérea/terrestre a ... por fa·*vor* *man*·de·lo por *vee*·a a·e·re·a/te·*res*·tre a ...

LISTEN FOR

buzón m	boo·*thon*	mail box
código m **postal**	*ko*·dee·go pos·*tal*	postcode
correo m **certificado**	ko·*re*·o ther·tee·fee·*ka*·do	registered mail
por vía aérea	por *vee*·a a·e·re·a	airmail
correo m **urgente**	ko·*re*·o oor·*khen*·te	express mail
declaración f **de aduana**	de·kla·ra·*thyon* de a·*dwa*·na	customs declaration
frágil	*fra*·kheel	fragile
internacional	een·ter·na·thyo·*nal*	international
nacional	na·thyo·*nal*	domestic

It contains ...	Contiene ... kon·*tye*·ne ...
Where's the poste restante section?	¿Dónde está la lista de correos? *don*·de es·*ta* la *lees*·ta de ko·*re*·os
Is there any mail for me?	¿Hay alguna carta para mí? ai al·*goo*·na *kar*·ta *pa*·ra mee

PHONE

Q **What's your phone number?**	¿Cuál es su/tu número de teléfono? pol/inf kwal es soo/too *noo*·me·ro de te·*le*·fo·no
A **The number is ...**	El número es ... el *noo*·me·ro es ...

What's the area code for ...?	¿Cuál es el prefijo de la zona de ...? kwal es el pre·*fee*·kho de la *tho*·na de ...
What's the country code for ...?	¿Cuál es el prefijo del país de ...? kwal es el pre·*fee*·kho del pa·*ees* de ...

For telephone numbers, see **numbers & amounts** (p34).

I want to...	Quiero ... *kye*·ro ...

make a call to (Singapore)	hacer una llamada a (Singapur)	a·*ther* *oo*·na lya·*ma*·da a (seen·ga·*poor*)
make a local call	hacer una llamada local	a·*ther* *oo*·na lya·*ma*·da lo·*kal*

It's engaged.	Está comunicando. es·*ta* ko·moo·nee·*kan*·do
The connection's bad.	Es mala conexión. es *ma*·la ko·nek·*syon*
Hello. (calling)	Hola. *o*·la
Hello? (answering)	¿Diga? *dee*·ga

LISTEN FOR

¿De parte de quién?	de *par*·te de kyen	Who's calling?
¿Con quién quiere hablar?	kon kyen *kye*·re a·*blar*	Who do you want to speak to?
Lo siento, pero ahora no está.	lo *syen*·to *pe*·ro a·o·ra no es·*ta*	I'm sorry, he/she is not here.
Lo siento, tiene el numero equivocado.	lo *syen*·to *tye*·ne el *noo*·me·ro e·kee·vo·*ka*·do	Sorry, you have got the wrong number.

Can I speak to ...?	¿Está ...? es·*ta* ...
It's (Julio) ...	Soy (Julio) ... soy (*khoo*·lyo) ...
I've been cut off.	Me han cortado. me an kor·*ta*·do
Can I leave a message?	¿Puedo dejar un mensaje? *pwe*·do de·*khar* oon men·*sa*·khe
Please tell him/her I called.	Sí, por favor, dígale que he llamado. see por fa·*vor dee*·ga·le ke e lya·*ma*·do
I'll call back later.	Ya llamaré más tarde. ya lya·ma·*re* mas *tar*·de

MOBILE/CELL PHONE

I'd like a/an ...	Quería ...	*ke·ree·a ...*
charger for my phone	un cargador para mi teléfono	oon kar·ga·*dor* *pa*·ra mee te·*le*·fo·no
mobile/cell phone	un móvil	oon *mo*·veel
SIM card (for your network)	una tarjeta SIM (para su red)	*oo*·na tar·*khe*·ta seem (*pa*·ra soo red)
What are the rates?	¿Cuál es la tarifa?	kwal es la ta·*ree*·fa

THE INTERNET

Do you have public internet access here?	¿Tiene acceso público a internet?	*tye*·ne ak·*the*·so *poo*·blee·ko a *een*·ter·net
Is there wi-fi here?	¿Hay wi-fi aquí?	ai *wee*·fee a·*kee*

Can I connect my laptop here?	¿Puedo conectar mi portátil aquí? *pwe*·do ko·nek·*tar* mee por·*ta*·teel a·*kee*
Do you have headphones (with a microphone)?	¿Tiene auriculares (con micrófono)? *tye*·ne ow·ree·koo·*la*·res (kon mee·*kro*·fo·no)

LOOK FOR

Here are some Spanish substitutes for common internet-related terms.

charlar	char·*lar*	chat
ciberespacio m	thee·ber·e·*spa*·thyo	cyberspace
navegar por internet	na·ve·*gar* por in·ter·*net*	surf
descargar	des·kar·*gar*	download
en línea	en *lee*·ne·a	online
nombre m **de usuario**	*nom*·bre de oo·*swa*·ryo	username
página f **web inicial**	*pa*·khee·na web ee·nee·*thyal*	homepage
sistema f **de búsqueda**	sees·*te*·ma de *boos*·ke·da	search engine
página f **web**	*pa*·khee·na web	website

I'd like to ...		Quería ... *ke·ree·a ...*
check my email	revisar mi correo electrónico	re·vee·*sar* mee ko·*re*·o e·lek·*tro*·nee·ko
download my photos	descargar mis fotos	des·kar·*gar* mees *fo*·tos
use a printer	usar una impresora	oo·*sar* *oo*·na eem·pre·*so*·ra
use a scanner	usar un escáner	oo·*sar* oon es·*ka*·ner

How much per hour/ page?	¿Cuánto cuesta por hora/ página? *kwan·to kwes·ta por o·ra/ pa·khee·na*
How do I log on?	¿Cómo entro al sistema? *ko·mo en·tro al sees·te·ma*
It's crashed.	Se ha quedado colgado. *se a ke·da·do kol·ga·do*
I've finished.	He terminado. *e ter·mee·na·do*
portable hard drive	disco duro m portátil *dees·ko doo·ro por·ta·teel*
USB flash drive (memory stick)	memoria f USB *me·mo·rya oo·e·se·be*

Money & Banking

KEY PHRASES

How much is it?	¿Cuánto cuesta esto?	*kwan*·to *kwes*·ta es·to
What's the exchange rate?	¿Cuál es el tipo de cambio?	kwal es el *tee*·po de *kam*·byo
Where's the nearest ATM?	¿Dónde está el cajero automático más cercano?	*don*·de es·*ta* el ka·*khe*·ro ow·to·*ma*·tee·ko mas ther·*ka*·no

PAYING THE BILL

Q **How much is it?**	¿Cuánto cuesta esto? *kwan*·to *kwes*·ta *es*·to
A **It's (12) euros.**	Son (doce) euros. son (*do*·the) e·*oo*·ros
A **It's free.**	Es gratis. es *gra*·tees
There's a mistake in the bill.	Hay un error en la cuenta. ai oon e·*ror* en la *kwen*·ta
Do you accept credit/debit cards?	¿Aceptan tarjetas de crédito/débito? a·*thep*·tan tar·*khe*·tas de *kre*·dee·to/*de*·bee·to
I'd like my change, please.	Quería mi cambio, por favor. ke·*ree*·a mee *kam*·byo por fa·*vor*

Could I have a receipt, please?	¿Podría darme un recibo, por favor? po·*dree*·a *dar*·me *oon* re·*thee*·bo por fa·*vor*

See also **bargaining** (p78).

BANKING

Where can I ...?	¿Dónde puedo ...? *don*·de *pwe*·do ...
I'd like to ...	Me gustaría ... me goos·ta·*ree*·a ...

arrange a transfer	hacer una transferencia	ha·*ther oo*·na trans·fe·*ren*·thee·ya
get a cash advance	obtener un adelanto	ob·te·*ner* on a·de·*lan*·to
change money	cambiar dinero	kam·*byar* dee·*ne*·ro
get change for this note	conseguir cambio para este billete	kon·se·*geer kam*·byo *pa*·ra *es*·te bee·*lye*·te
withdraw money	sacar dinero	sa·*kar* dee·*ne*·ro

Where's the nearest ATM?	¿Dónde está el cajero automático más cercano? *don*·de es·*ta* el ka·*khe*·ro ow·to·*ma*·tee·ko mas ther·*ka*·no
Where's the nearest foreign exchange office?	¿Dónde está la oficina de cambio más cercano? *don*·de es·*ta* la o·fee·*thee*·na de *kam*·byo mas ther·*ka*·no

LISTEN FOR

No le quedan fondos.	no le *ke*·dan *fon*·dos You have no money left.
Hay un problema con su cuenta.	ai oon pro·*ble*·ma kon soo *kwen*·ta There's a problem with your account.
¿Puedo ver su identificación, por favor?	*pwe*·do ver soo ee·den·tee·fee·ka·*thyon* por fa·*vor* Can I see your ID, please?
Por favor firme aquí.	por fa·*vor* *feer*·me a·*kee* Please sign here.

What's the exchange rate?	¿Cuál es el tipo de cambio? kwal es el *tee*·po de *kam*·byo
What's the charge for that?	¿Cuánto hay que pagar por eso? *kwan*·to ai ke pa·*gar* por *e*·so
The ATM took my card.	El cajero automático se ha tragado mi tarjeta. el ka·*khe*·ro ow·to·*ma*·tee·ko se a tra·*ga*·do mee tar·*khe*·ta
I've forgotten my PIN.	He olvidado mi PIN. e ol·vee·*da*·do mee peen

Business

KEY PHRASES

I'm attending a conference.	Asisto a un congreso.	a·*sees*·to a oon kon·*gre*·so
I have an appointment with ...	Tengo una cita con ...	*ten*·go *oo*·na *thee*·ta kon ...
Can I have your business card?	¿Puede darme su tarjeta de visita?	*pwe*·de *dar*·me soo tar·*khe*·ta de vee·*see*·ta

People usually chit-chat for a while before they get down to business. For titles and greetings, see **meeting people** (p106).

I'm attending a ... Asisto a ...
a·*sees*·to a ...

conference	un congreso	oon kon·*gre*·so
course	un curso	oon *koor*·so
meeting	una reunión	*oo*·na re·oo·*nyon*
trade fair	una feria de muestras	*oo*·na *fe*·rya de *mwes*·tras

I'm with my colleagues. Estoy con mis colegas. m&f
es·*toy* kon mees ko·*le*·gas

I'm alone. Estoy solo/a. m/f
es·*toy* *so*·lo/a

Where's the business district? ¿Dónde está el centro financiero?
don·de es·*ta* el *then*·tro fee·nan·*thye*·ro

LANGUAGE TIP: ADDRESSING PEOPLE

To show formality or respect, you should use the polite form of address *usted* sg pol oo·*sted* or *ustedes* pl pol oo·*ste*·des in business and with any service providers (be they kiosk attendants or doctors). It's best to take the lead from how people address you, and respond in the same way. For more on polite forms, see **personal pronouns** in the **grammar** chapter, p21.

Where's the conference?	¿Dónde está el congreso? *don*·de es·*ta* el kon·*gre*·so
Where's the meeting?	¿Dónde es la reunión? *don*·de es la re·oo·*nyon*
I have an appointment with ...	Tengo una cita con ... *ten*·go *oo*·na *thee*·ta kon ...
Q **Can I have your business card?**	¿Puede darme su tarjeta de visita? *pwe*·de *dar*·me soo tar·*khe*·ta de vee·*see*·ta
A **Here's my business card.**	Aquí tiene mi tarjeta de visita. a·*kee tye*·ne mee tar·*khe*·ta de vee·*see*·ta
That went very well.	Eso fue muy bien. *e*·so fwe mooy byen
Thank you for your interest/time.	Gracias por su interés/ tiempo. *gra*·thyas por soo een·te·*res*/ *tyem*·po
Shall we go for a drink/ meal?	¿Vamos a tomar/comer algo? *va*·mos a to·*mar*/ko·*mer al*·go
It's on me.	Invito yo. een·*vee*·to yo

Sightseeing

KEY PHRASES

Can we hire a guide?	¿Podemos alquilar un guía?	po·*de*·mos al·kee·*lar* oon *gee*·a
Can I take photographs?	¿Puedo tomar fotos?	*pwe*·do to·*mar* *fo*·tos
What time does the museum open?	¿A qué hora abre el museo?	a ke *o*·ra *ab*·re el moo·*se*·o

REQUESTS & QUERIES

I'd like a/an ... Quería ... ke·*ree*·a ...

audio set	un equipo audio	oon e·*kee*·po *ow*·dyo
catalogue	un catálogo	oon ka·*ta*·lo·go
guidebook in English	una guía turística en inglés	*oo*·na *gee*·a too·*rees*·tee·ka en een·*gles*
(local) map	un mapa (de la zona)	oon *ma*·pa (de la *tho*·na)

I'd like to see ... Me gustaría ver ... me goos·ta·*ree*·a ver ...

Do you have information on local sights?	¿Tiene información sobre los lugares de interés local? *tye*·ne een·for·ma·*thyon* *so*·bre los loo·*ga*·res de een·te·*res* lo·*kal*
Do you have information on historical sights?	¿Tiene información sobre los lugares de interés histórico? *tye*·ne een·for·ma·*thyon* *so*·bre los loo·*ga*·res de een·te·*res* ees·*to*·ree·ko
Do you have information on religious sights?	¿Tiene información sobre los lugares de interés religioso? *tye*·ne een·for·ma·*thyon* *so*·bre los loo·*ga*·res de een·te·*res* re·lee·*khyo*·so
Can we hire a guide?	¿Podemos alquilar un guía? po·*de*·mos al·kee·*lar* oon *gee*·a
Can I take photographs (of you)?	¿(Le/Te) Puedo tomar fotos? pol/inf (le/te) *pwe*·do to·*mar* *fo*·tos
I'll send you the photograph.	Le/Te mandaré la foto. pol/inf le/te man·da·*re* la *fo*·to
Could you take a photograph of me?	¿Me puede hacer una foto? me *pwe*·de a·*ther* *oo*·na *fo*·to
What's that?	¿Qué es eso? ke es *e*·so
How old is it?	¿De qué época es? de ke *e*·po·ka es

GETTING IN

What time does it open/close?	¿A qué hora abre/cierra? a ke *o*·ra *ab*·re/*thye*·ra
What's the admission charge?	¿Cuánto cuesta la entrada? *kwan*·to *kwes*·ta la en·*tra*·da

Is there a discount for ...?	¿Hay descuentos para ...? ai des·*kwen*·tos *pa*·ra ...

children	niños	*nee*·nyos
families	familias	fa·*mee*·lyas
groups	grupos	*groo*·pos
older people	gente mayor	*khen*·te ma·*yor*
students	estudiantes	es·too·*dyan*·tes

GALLERIES & MUSEUMS

What time does the gallery open?	¿A qué hora abre la galería? a ke *o*·ra *a*·bre la ga·le·*ree*·a
What time does the museum open?	¿A qué hora abre el museo? a ke *o*·ra *ab*·re el moo·*se*·o
Q **What's in the collection?**	¿Qué hay en la colección? ke ai en la ko·lek·*thyon*
A **It's a/an ... exhibition.**	Es una exposición de ... es *oo*·na eks·po·see·*thyon* de ...
I like the works of ...	Me gustan las obras de ... me *goos*·tan las *o*·bras de ...
It reminds me of ...	Me recuerda a ... me re·*kwer*·da a ...
... art	arte m ... *ar*·te ...

graphic	gráfico	*gra*·fee·ko
impressionist	impresionista	eem·pre·syo·*nees*·ta
modernist	modernista	mo·der·*nees*·ta
Renaissance	renacentista	re·na·then·*tees*·ta

LOOK FOR

Abierto	a·*byer*·to	Open
Cerrado	the·*ra*·do	Closed
Prohibido	pro·ee·*bee*·do	Prohibited

TOURS

Are there organised walking tours?	¿Organizan recorridos a pie? or·ga·*nee*·than re·ko·*ree*·dos a pye
I'd like to take cooking/ language classes.	Me gustaría ir a clases de cocina/idiomas. me goos·ta·*ree*·a eer a *kla*·ses de ko·*thee*·na/ee·*dyo*·mas
Can you recommend a ...?	¿Puede recomendar algún/alguna ...? m/f *pwe*·de re·ko·men·*dar* al·*goon*/al·*goo*·na ...

Can I take photographs?
pwe·do to·*mar fo*·tos
¿Puedo tomar fotos?

When's the next ...?	¿Cuándo es el/la próximo/a ...? m/f *kwan*·do es el/la *prok*·see·mo/a ...

boat trip	paseo m en barca	pa·*se*·o en *bar*·ka
day trip	excursión f de un día	eks·koor·*syon* de oon *dee*·a
excursion	excursión f	eks·koor·*syon*
tour	recorrido m	re·ko·*ree*·do

Do I need to take (food) with me?	¿Necesito llevar (comida)? ne·the·*see*·to lye·*var* (ko·*mee*·da)
Is (equipment/transport) included?	¿Incluye (equipo/ transporte)? een·*kloo*·ye (e·*kee*·po/ trans·*por*·te)
How long is the tour?	¿Cuánto dura el recorrido? *kwan*·to *doo*·ra el re·ko·*ree*·do
What time should I be back?	¿A qué hora tengo que volver? a ke *o*·ra *ten*·go ke vol·*ver*
Be back here at ...	Vuelva ... *vwel*·va ...
I've lost my group.	He perdido a mi grupo. e per·*dee*·do a mee *groo*·po

Seniors & Travellers with Disabilities

KEY PHRASES

I need assistance.	Necesito asistencia.	ne·the·*see*·to a·sees·*ten*·thya
Is there wheelchair access?	¿Hay acceso para la silla de ruedas?	ai ak·*the*·so *pa*·ra la *see*·lya de *rwe*·das
Are there toilets for people with a disablity?	¿Hay aseos para minusválidos?	ai a·*se*·os *pa*·ra mee·noos·*va*·lee·dos

I have a disability.	Soy discapacitado/a. m/f soy dees·ka·pa·thee·*ta*·do/a
I need assistance.	Necesito asistencia. ne·the·*see*·to a·sees·*ten*·thya
Are guide dogs permitted?	¿Se permite la entrada a los perros lazarillos? se per·*mee*·te la en·*tra*·da a los *pe*·ros la·tha·*ree*·lyos
Is there wheelchair access?	¿Hay acceso para la silla de ruedas? ai ak·*the*·so *pa*·ra la *see*·lya de *rwe*·das
Are there parking spaces for people with a disability?	¿Tiene aparcamiento para discapacitados? *tye*·ne a·par·ka·*myen*·to *pa*·ra dees·ka·pa·thee·*ta*·dos
Are there rails in the bathroom?	¿Hay pasamanos en el baño? ai pa·sa·*ma*·nos en el *ba*·nyo

LOOK FOR

Acceso para Sillas de Ruedas	ak·*the*·so *pa*·ra *see*·lyas de *rwe*·das	Wheelchair Entrance
Ascensor	a·then·*sor*	Elevator/Lift

Are there toilets for people with a disability?	¿Hay aseos para discapacitados? ai a·*se*·os *pa*·ra dees·ka·pa·thee·*ta*·dos
Is there somewhere I can sit down?	¿Hay algun sitio dónde me pueda sentar? ai al·*goon see*·tyo *don*·de me *pwe*·da sen·*tar*
Could you help me cross this street?	¿Me puede ayudar a cruzar la calle? me *pwe*·de a·yoo·*dar* a kroo·*thar* la *ka*·lye
Could you call me a taxi for the disabled?	¿Podría llamar a un taxi para discapacitados? po·*dree*·a lya·*mar* a oon *tak*·see *pa*·ra dees·ka·pa·thee·*ta*·dos
crutches	muletas f pl moo·*le*·tas
guide dog	perro m lazarillo *pe*·ro la·tha·*ree*·lyo
ramp	rampa f *ram*·pa
walking frame	andador m an·da·*dor*
walking stick	bastón m bas·*ton*
wheelchair	silla f de ruedas *see*·lya de *rwe*·das

Travel with Children

KEY PHRASES

Are children allowed?	¿Se admiten niños?	se ad·*mee*·ten *nee*·nyos
Is there a child discount?	¿Hay descuento para niños?	ai des·*kwen*·to *pa*·ra *nee*·nyos
Is there a baby change room?	¿Hay un cambiador para bebés?	ai oon kam·bya·*dor pa*·ra be·*bes*

I need a ... Necesito ...
ne·the·*see*·to ...

baby/child seat	un asiento de seguridad para bebés/niños	oon a·*syen*·to de se·goo·ree·*dad pa*·ra be·*bes*/*nee*·nyos
cot	una cuna	*oo*·na *koo*·na
potty	un orinal de niños	oon o·ree·*nal* de *nee*·nyos
stroller	un cochecito	oon ko·che·*thee*·to

Do you sell baby wipes? ¿Vende toallitas para bebés?
ven·de to·a·*lyee*·tas *pa*·ra be·*bes*

Do you sell nappies/diapers? ¿Vende pañales?
ven·de pa·*nya*·les

Do you sell milk formula?	¿Vende leche de fórmula? *ven*·de *le*·che de *for*·moo·la
Is there a/an ...?	¿Hay ...? ai ...

baby change room	un cambiador para bebés	oon kam·bya·*dor* *pa*·ra be·*bes*
child discount	descuento para niños	des·*kwen*·to *pa*·ra *nee*·nyos
child-minding service	servicio de cuidado de niños	ser·*vee*·thyo de kwee·*da*·do de *nee*·nyos
children's menu	menú infantil	me·*noo* een·fan·*teel*
family discount	descuento familiar	des·*kwen*·to fa·mee·*lyar*
highchair	trona	*tro*·na

Do you mind if I breastfeed here?	¿Le molesta que dé de pecho aquí? le mo·*les*·ta ke de de *pe*·cho a·*kee*
Are children allowed?	¿Se admiten niños? se ad·*mee*·ten *nee*·nyos
Is this suitable for (three)-year-old children?	¿Es apto para niños de (tres) años? es *ap*·to *pa*·ra *nee*·nyos de (tres) *a*·nyos

If your child is sick, see **health** (p158).

SOCIAL

Meeting People

KEY PHRASES

My name is ...	Me llamo ...	me *lya*·mo ...
I'm from ...	Soy de ...	soy de ...
I work in (education).	Trabajo en (enseñanza).	tra·*ba*·kho en (en·se·*nyan*·tha)
I'm ... years old.	Tengo ... años.	*ten*·go ... a·nyos
And you?	¿Y usted/tú? pol/inf	ee oos·*ted*/too

BASICS

Yes.	Sí. see
No.	No. no
Please.	Por favor. por fa·*vor*
Thank you (very much).	(Muchas) Gracias. (*moo*·chas) *gra*·thyas
You're welcome.	De nada. de *na*·da
Excuse me.	Perdón/Discúlpeme. per·*don*/dees·*kool*·pe·me
Sorry.	Lo siento. lo *syen*·to

GREETINGS

In Spain people are often quite casual in their social interactions. It's fine to use the following expressions in both formal and informal situations.

Hello/Hi.	Hola. *o*·la
Good morning.	Buenos días. *bwe*·nos *dee*·as
Good afternoon. (until 8pm)	Buenas tardes. *bwe*·nas *tar*·des
Good evening/night.	Buenas noches. *bwe*·nas *no*·ches
See you later.	Hasta luego. *as*·ta *lwe*·go
Goodbye/Bye.	Adiós. a·*dyos*
Q **How are you?**	¿Qué tal? ke tal
A **Fine, thanks. And you?**	Bien, gracias. ¿Y usted/tú? pol/inf byen *gra*·thyas ee oos·*ted*/too
Q **What's your name?**	¿Cómo se llama usted? pol *ko*·mo se *lya*·ma oos·*ted* ¿Cómo te llamas? inf *ko*·mo te *lya*·mas
A **My name is ...**	Me llamo ... me *lya*·mo ...
I'm pleased to meet you.	Mucho gusto. *moo*·cho *goos*·to

I'd like to introduce you to ...	Quería presentarle a ... pol ke·*ree*·a pre·sen·*tar*·le a ... Quería presentarte a ... inf ke·*ree*·a pre·sen·*tar*·te a ...

This is ...	Esto es...	*es*·to es ...

This is my friend.	Este/a es mi amigo/a. m/f es·te/a es mee a·*mee*·go/a

TITLES & ADDRESSING PEOPLE

Señor and *Señora* tend to be used in everyday speech. *Doña*, although rare, is used as a mark of respect towards older women, while *Don* is sometimes used to address men. An elderly neighbour, for example, might be called *Doña Lola*. For more on polite forms, see **addressing people** (p95), and **personal pronouns** (p21).

Mr	Señor se·*nyor*
Sir	Don don
Miss	Señorita se·nyo·*ree*·ta
Ms/Mrs	Señora se·*nyo*·ra
Madam	Doña *do*·nya

MAKING CONVERSATION

Spain is known for its distinct regional personalities. A great conversation starter in Spain is to ask someone where they come from. Other good topics are sport, politics, history and travel.

Do you live here?	¿Vives aquí? *vee*·ves a·*kee*

LANGUAGE TIP: ADDRESSING FRIENDS

You may hear friends calling each other *tío* m *tee*·o, or *tía* f *tee*·a, but these words are usually used when talking about others. They're a bit crass (a little like using 'sheila' to describe a girl in Australia). Guys use *colega* ko·*le*·ga, and *hombre* *om*·bre, to address their workmates or male friends.

Where are you going?	¿Adónde vas? a·*don*·de vas
What are you doing?	¿Qué haces? ke a·thes
Q **Are you here on holiday?**	¿Estás aquí de vacaciones? es·*tas* a·*kee* de va·ka·*thyo*·nes
A **I'm here for a holiday.**	Estoy aquí de vacaciones. es·*toy* a·*kee* de va·ka·*thyo*·nes
A **I'm here on business.**	Estoy aquí en viaje de negocios. es·*toy* a·*kee* en *vya*·khe de ne·*go*·thyos
A **I'm here to study.**	Estoy aquí estudiando. es·*toy* a·*kee* es·too·*dyan*·do
That's (beautiful), isn't it?	¿Es (precioso), no? es (pre·*thyo*·so) no
Q **How long are you here for?**	¿Cuánto tiempo te vas a quedar? *kwan*·to *tyem*·po te vas a ke·*dar*
A **I'm here for ... weeks/days.**	Estoy aquí por ... semanas/días. es·*toy* a·*kee* por ... se·*ma*·nas/*dee*·as

NATIONALITIES

You'll find that many country names are similar to English, so even if you don't know the Spanish name, it's more than likely you'll be understood. For more countries, see the **dictionary** (p205).

Q **Where are you from?**	¿De dónde es usted? pol de *don*·de es oos·*ted* ¿De dónde eres? inf de *don*·de *e*·res
A **I'm from (the UK).**	Soy del (Reino Unido). soy del (*rey*·no u·*ni*·do)
A **I'm from (the US).**	Soy de (los Estados Unidos). soy de (los e·*sta*·dos u·*ni*·dos)

AGE

Q **How old are you?**	¿Cuántos años tienes? *kwan*·tos *a*·nyos *tye*·nes
A **I'm ... years old.**	Tengo ... años. *ten*·go ... *a*·nyos
Q **How old is your son/daughter?**	¿Cuántos años tiene tu hijo/hija? *kwan*·tos *a*·nyos *tye*·ne too *ee*·kho/*ee*·kha
A **He's/She's ... years old.**	Tiene ... años. *tye*·ne ... *a*·nyos
I'm younger than I look.	Soy más joven de lo que parezco. soy mas *kho*·ven de lo ke pa·*reth*·ko
Too old!	¡Demasiado viejo! de·ma·*sya*·do *vye*·kho

For your age, see **numbers & amounts** (p34).

LISTEN FOR

¡Cojonudo!	ko·kho·*noo*·do	Great!
¿De veras?	de *ve*·ras	Really?
¡Enhorabuena!	e·no·ra·*bwe*·na	Congratulations!
¡Estupendo!	es·too·*pen*·do	That's fantastic!
¡No me digas!	no me *dee*·gas	You don't say!
¡Qué guay!	ke gwai	How cool!
¿Qué hay?	ke ai	What's up?
¡Qué interesante!	ke een·te·re·*san*·te	How interesting!

OCCUPATIONS & STUDY

Q **What do you do?**
¿A qué te dedicas?
a ke te de·*dee*·kas

A **I work in (education/ hospitality).**
Trabajo en (enseñanza/ hostelería).
tra·*ba*·kho en (en·se·*nyan*·tha/ os·te·le·*ree*·a)

A **I'm a/an ...**
Soy ...
soy ...

architect	arquitecto/a m/f	ar·kee·*tek*·to/a
mechanic	mecánico/a m/f	me·*ka*·nee·ko/a
student	estudiante m&f	es·too·*dyan*·te
teacher	profesor/ profesora m/f	pro·fe·*sor*/ pro·fe·*so*·ra

A **I'm self-employed.**
Soy trabajador/ trabajadora autónomo/a. m/f
soy tra·ba·kha·*dor*/ tra·ba·kha·*do*·ra ow·*to*·no·mo/a

(A) **I'm retired.**	Estoy jubilado/a. m/f es·*toy* khoo·bee·*la*·do/a
(A) **I'm unemployed.**	Estoy en el paro. es·*toy* en el *pa*·ro
(Q) **What are you studying?**	¿Qué estudias? ke es·*too*·dyas
(A) **I'm studying (languages).**	Estudio (idiomas). es·*too*·dyo (ee·*dyo*·mas)
I'm studying at ...	Estudio en ... es·*too*·dyo en ...

For more occupations and studies, see the **dictionary** (p205).

FAMILY

(Q) **Do you have (a) ...?**	¿Tiene ...? pol *tye*·ne ... ¿Tienes ...? inf *tye*·nes ...
(A) **I (don't) have (a) ...**	(No) Tengo ... (no) *ten*·go ...

brother	un hermano	oon er·*ma*·no
children	hijos	*ee*·khos
family	una familia	*oo*·na fa·*mee*·lya
partner	una pareja m&f	*oo*·na pa·*re*·kha
sister	una hermana	*oo*·na er·*ma*·na

(Q) **Are you married?**	¿Estás casado/a? m/f es·*tas* ka·*sa*·do/a
(A) **I'm married.**	Estoy casado/a. m/f es·*toy* ka·*sa*·do/a
(A) **I'm single.**	Soy soltero/a. m/f soy sol·*te*·ro/a

Ⓐ **I live with someone.**	Vivo con alguien. *vee*·vo kon *al*·gyen
Ⓐ **I'm separated.**	Estoy separado/a. m/f es·*toy* se·pa·*ra*·do/a

TALKING WITH CHILDREN

Do you go to school or kindergarten?	¿Vas al colegio o a la guardería? vas al ko·*le*·khyo o a la gwar·de·*ree*·a
What grade are you in?	¿En qué curso estás? en ke *koor*·so es·*tas*
Do you like school?	¿Te gusta el colegio? te *goos*·ta el ko·*le*·khyo
Do you like sport?	¿Te gusta el deporte? te *goos*·ta el de·*por*·te
Do you learn (English)?	¿Aprendes (inglés)? a·*pren*·des (een·*gles*)
I come from very far away.	Vengo de muy lejos. *ven*·go de mooy *le*·khos

FAREWELLS

It's been great meeting you.	Me ha encantado conocerte. me a en·kan·*ta*·do ko·no·*ther*·te
Keep in touch!	¡Nos mantendremos en contacto! nos man·ten·*dre*·mos en kon·*tak*·to
Are you on Facebook?	¿Estás en Facebook? es·*tas* en *feys*·book

LANGUAGE TIP: SPANISH IDIOMS

Even idioms translate across languages. Here are a few golden oldies:

It's like casting pearls before swine.	Es como echar margaritas a los cerdos. (lit: it's like feeding daisies to the pigs) es *ko*·mo e·*char* mar·ga·*ree*·tas a los *ther*·dos
When it rains, it pours.	Éramos pocos y parió la abuela. (lit: there were a few of us then granny gave birth) e·ra·mos *po*·kos y pa·*ree*·o la a·*bwe*·la
This is like watching grass grow.	Es más largo que un día sin pan. (lit: it's longer than a day without bread) es mas *lar*·go ke oon *dee*·a seen pan

If you ever visit (South Africa), you can stay with me.	Si algún día visitas (Sudáfrica), te puedes quedar conmigo. see al·*goon dee*·a vee·*see*·tas (soo·*da*·free·ka) te *pwe*·des ke·*dar* kon·*mee*·go
Q **What's your (address)?**	¿Cuál es tu (dirección)? kwal es too (dee·rek·*thyon*)
A **Here's my ...**	Esta es mi ... m/f *es*·te/*es*·ta es mee ...
A **Here's my address.**	Esta es mi dirección. *es*·ta es mee dee·rek·*thyon*
A **Here's my email address.**	Esta es mi dirección de email. *es*·ta es mee dee·rek·*thyon* de *ee*·mayl

For more on addresses, see **directions** (p57).

BASQUE

Basque (*euskara,* in Basque), is spoken at the western end of the Pyrenees and along the Bay of Biscay – from Bayonne in France to Bilbao in Spain, and inland, almost to Pamplona. Dialects are also spoken, including Bizkaian, Gipuzkoan, High Navarrese, Aezkoan, Salazarese, Lapurdian, Low Navarrese and Suberoan. No one quite knows its origin, but the most likely theory is that Basque is the lone survivor of a language family that once extended across Europe, and was wiped out by the languages of the Celts, Germanic tribes and Romans.

Speaking Spanish in the Basque-speaking towns might be expected from a foreigner, but is not as warmly received as an attempt at one of the most ancient languages of Europe.

Hi!	Kaixo! *kai*·sho
Good morning.	Egun on. e·goon *on*
Good afternoon/evening.	Arratsalde on. a·*ra*·chyal·de *on*
Goodbye.	Agur. a·*goor*
Take care.	Ondo ibili. on·do ee·*beel*·ee
How are you?	Zer moduz? ser mo·*doos*
Fine, thank you.	Ongi, eskerrik asko. on·gee e·*ske*·reek as·ko

LISTEN FOR

Euskal Herrian beti jai!	e·oos·*kal* e·*ree*·an *be*·tee yai The Basque Country's always partying!
Gora gu 'ta gutarrak!	*go*·ra goo ta *goo*·ta·rak Hurray for us!

Excuse me.	Barkatu. bar·*ka*·too
Please.	Mesedez. me·se·des
Thank you.	Eskerrik asko. es·*ke*·reek *as*·ko
You're welcome.	Ez horregatik. es o·*re*·ga·teek
Do you speak English?	Ingelesez ba al dakizu? een·*ge*·le·ses ba al da·kee·*soo*
I know a little Basque.	Euskara apur bat badakit. e·*oos*·ka·ra a·*poor* bat ba·da·*keet*
I don't understand.	Ez dut ulertzen. es toot oo·*ler*·tzen
Could you speak in Spanish, please?	Erdaraz egingo al didazu, mesedez? *er*·da·ras e·*geen*·go al dee·*da*·soo me·se·des
How do you say that in Basque?	Nola esaten da hori euskara? *no*·la e·*sa*·ten da *o*·ree e·oo·ska·*ra*

☑ CULTURE TIP: SPANISH IN AMERICA

Columbus' arrival in the New World in 1492 launched the era of Spanish expansion in America, one which is also reflected in the language. *Patata*, *tomate*, *cacao* and *chocolate* are just a few examples of words that entered Spanish (and consequently English) from the indigenous American languages. Bear in mind that Spanish has evolved differently in the Americas, and it's a good idea to take Lonely Planet's *Latin American Spanish* phrasebook if that's your destination.

CATALAN

Catalan (*català,* in Catalan) is spoken by up to 10 million people in the northeast of Spain, a territory that comprises Catalonia, coastal Valencia and the Balearic Islands (Majorca, Minorca and Ibiza).

Outside Spain, Catalan is also spoken in Andorra, the south of France and the town of Alguer in Sardinia. Many famous creatives have been Catalan speakers: painters like Dalí, Miró and Picasso, architects like Gaudí, and writers like Mercè Rodoreda.

Despite the fact that almost all Catalan speakers from Spain are bilingual, they appreciate it when visitors attempt to communicate, if even in the simplest way, in Catalan.

Hello!	Hola! *o*·la
Good morning.	Bon dia. bon *dee*·a
Good afternoon.	Bona tarda. *bo*·na *tar*·da
Good evening.	Bon vespre. bon *ves*·pra
Goodbye.	Adéu. a·de·oo
How are you?	Com estàs? kom as·*tas*
(Very) Well.	(Molt) Bé. (mol) be
Excuse me.	Perdoni. par·do·nee
Sorry.	Ho sento. oo *sen*·to
Please.	Sisplau. sees·*pla*·oo
Thank you.	Gràcies. *gra*·see·as

LISTEN FOR

Això rai!	a·*sho* ra·ee	No problem!
Quin tip de riure!	kin tip da ri·a·*oo*·ra	What a laugh!

Yes/No.	Sí/No. see/no
Do you speak English?	Parla anglès? *par*·la an·*gles*
Could you speak in Castilian, please?	Pot parlar castellà sisplau? pot par·*la* kas·ta·*lya* sees·*pla*·oo
I (don't) understand.	(No) Ho entenc. (no) oo an·teng
How do you say ...?	Com es diu ...? kom az *dee*·oo ...

GALICIAN

Galician (*galego*, in Galician), is an official language of the Autonomous Community of Galicia and is also widely understood in the neighbouring regions of Asturias and Castilla-Léon. It's very similar to Portuguese, as the two languages have roots in Vulgar Latin.

Galicians are likely to revert to Spanish when addressing a stranger, especially a foreigner, but making a small effort to communicate in Galician will always be welcomed.

Hello!	Ola! *o*·la
Good day.	Bon dia. bon *dee*·a
Good afternoon/evening.	Boa tarde. *bo*·a *tar*·de

Goodbye.	Adeus. a·*de*·oos Até logo. a·*te* *lo*·go
Excuse me.	Perdón. per·*don*
Please.	Por favor. por fa·*vor*
Thank you.	Grazas. *gra*·sas
Many thanks.	Moitas grazas. *moy*·tas *gra*·sas
That's fine.	De nada. de *na*·da
Yes./No.	Si./Non. see/non
Do you speak English?	Fala inglés? *fa*·la een·*gles*
Could you speak in Spanish, please?	Pode falar en español, por favor? *po*·de fa·*la* en e·spa·*nyol* por fa·*bor*
I (don't) understand.	(Non) Entendo. (non) en·*ten*·do
What's this called in Galician?	Como se chama iso en galego? *ko*·mo se *cha*·ma ee·so en ga·*le*·go

Interests

KEY PHRASES

What do you do in your spare time?	¿Qué te gusta hacer en tu tiempo libre?	ke te *goos*·ta a·*ther* en too *tyem*·po *lee*·bre
Do you like (travel-ling)?	¿Te gusta (viajar)?	te *goos*·ta (vya·*khar*)
I (don't) like ...	(No) Me gusta ...	(no) me *goos*·ta ...

COMMON INTERESTS

What do you do in your spare time?	¿Qué te gusta hacer en tu tiempo libre? ke te *goos*·ta a·*ther* en too *tyem*·po *lee*·bre
Q **Do you like (travelling)?**	¿Te gusta (viajar)? te *goos*·ta (vya·*khar*)
A **I like (cooking).**	Me gusta (cocinar). me *goos*·ta (ko·thee·*nar*)
A **I don't like (hiking).**	No me gusta (el excursionismo). no me *goos*·ta (el eks·koor·syo·*nees*·mo)
I (don't) like photography.	(No) Me gusta la fotografía. (no) me *goos*·ta la fo·to·gra·*fee*·a
I (don't) like shopping.	(No) Me gusta ir de compras. (no) me *goos*·ta eer de *kom*·pras

For more activities, see **sports** (p142) and the **dictionary** (p205).

MUSIC

Do you like to ...?	¿Te gusta ...?	te *goos*·ta ...
dance	ir a bailar	eer a bai·*lar*
go to concerts	ir a conciertos	eer a kon·*thyer*·tos
listen to music	escuchar música	es·koo·*char* *moo*·see·ka
play an instrument	tocar algún instrumento	*to*·kar al·*goon* eens·troo·*men*·to
sing	cantar	*kan*·tar

What music do you like?

ke *moo*·see·ka te *goos*·ta

¿Qué música te gusta?

Which bands do you like?	¿Qué grupos te gustan? ke *groo*·pos te *goos*·tan
Which singers do you like?	¿Qué cantantes te gustan? ke kan·*tan*·tes te *goos*·tan
What music do you like?	¿Qué música te gusta? ke *moo*·see·ka te *goos*·ta
classical music	música f clásica *moo*·see·ka *kla*·see·ka
jazz	jazz m khath
pop	música f pop *moo*·see·ka pop
rock	música f rock *moo*·see·ka rok
world music	música f étnica *moo*·see·ka *et*·nee·ka

CINEMA & THEATRE

I feel like going to (a comedy).	Tengo ganas de ir a (una comedia). *ten*·go *ga*·nas de eer a (*oo*·na ko·*me*·dya)
What's showing at the cinema (tonight)?	¿Qué ponen en el cine (esta noche)? ke *pon*·en en el *thee*·ne (*es*·ta *no*·che)
Is it in (English)?	¿Es en (inglés)? es en (een·*gles*)
Is it dubbed?	¿Está doblada? es·*ta* dob·*la*·da
Does it have (English) subtitles?	¿Tiene subtítulos (en inglés)? *tye*·ne soob·*tee*·too·los (en een·*gles*)

Have you seen ...?	¿Has visto ...? as *vees*·to ...
Q **Who's in it?**	¿Quién actúa? kyen ak·*too*·a
A **It stars ...**	Actúa ... ak·*too*·a ...
Are those seats taken?	¿Están ocupados estos asientos? es·*tan* o·koo·pa·dos *es*·tos a·*syen*·tos
Q **Did you like the film/ play?**	¿Te gustó el cine/teatro? te goos·*to* el *thee*·ne/te·a·tro
A **I thought it was excellent/OK.**	Me pareció excelente/ regular. me pa·re·*thyo* eks·the·*len*·te/ re·goo·*lar*
A **I thought it was long.**	Me pareció largo. me pa·re·*thyo* *lar*·go
I (don't) like ...	(No) Me gusta/gustan ... sg/pl (no) me *goos*·ta/*goos*·tan ...

animated films	películas f pl de dibujos animados	pe·*lee*·koo·las de dee·*boo*·khos a·nee·*ma*·dos
comedy	comedia f	ko·*me*·dya
documentary	documentales m pl	do·koo·men·*ta*·les
drama	drama m	*dra*·ma
(Spanish) cinema	cine m (español)	*thee*·ne (es·pa·*nyol*)
horror movies	cine m de terror	*thee*·ne de te·*ror*
sci-fi	cine m de ciencia ficción	*thee*·ne de *thyen*·thya feek·*thyon*

Off to a show? See **buying tickets** (p44) and **going out** (p130).

BOOKS & READING

What kind of books do you read?	¿Qué tipo de libros lees? ke *tee*·po de *lee*·bros *le*·es
On this trip I'm reading ...	En este viaje estoy leyendo ... en *es*·te *vya*·khe es·*toy* le·*yen*·do ...
Have you read ...?	¿Has leído ...? as le·*ee*·do ...
Q **Which (Spanish) author do you recommend?**	¿Qué autor (español) recomiendas? ke ow·*tor* (es·pa·*nyol*) re·ko·*myen*·das
A **I'd recommend ...**	Recomiendo a ... re·ko·*myen*·do a ...
Where can I exchange books?	¿Dónde puedo cambiar libros? *don*·de *pwe*·do kam·*byar lee*·bros

For more on books and reading, see **shopping** (p80).

VOLUNTEERING

I'd like to volunteer my skills.	Me gustaría ofrecer mis conocimientos. me goos·ta·*ree*·a o·fre·*ther* mees ko·no·thee·*myen*·tos
Are there any volunteer programmes available in the area?	¿Hay programas de voluntariado en la zona? ai pro·*gra*·mas de vo·loon·ta·*rya*·do en la *tho*·na

Feelings & Opinions

KEY PHRASES

Are you ...?	¿Tienes/Estás ...?	*tye*·nes/es·*tas* ...
I'm (not) ...	(No) Tengo/ Estoy ...	(no) *ten*·go/ es·*toy* ...
What did you think of it?	¿Qué pensaste de eso?	ke pen·*sas*·te de *e*·so
I thought it was ...	Pienso que fue ...	*pyen*·so ke fwe ...
Did you hear about ...?	¿Has oído que ...?	as o·*ee*·do ke ...

FEELINGS

Feelings are described with either nouns or adjectives: the nouns use 'have' in Spanish (eg, 'I have hunger') and the adjectives use 'be' (like in English).

Q **Are you ...?**	¿Tienes ...? *tye*·nes ...
A **I'm (not) ...**	(No) Tengo ... (no) *ten*·go ...

cold	frío	*free*·o
hot	calor	ka·*lor*
hungry	hambre	*am*·bre
in a hurry	prisa	*pree*·sa
thirsty	sed	seth

Q **Are you ...?**	¿Estás ...?	es·*tas* ...
A **I'm (not) ...**	(No) Estoy ...	(no) es·*toy* ...

annoyed	fastidiado/a m/f	fas·tee·*dya*·do/a
embarrassed	avergonzado/a m/f	a·ver·gon·*tha*·do/a
happy	feliz m&f	fe·*leeth*
sad	triste m&f	*trees*·te
tired	cansado/a m/f	kan·*sa*·do/a
well	bien m&f	byen

I'm a little (sad).	Estoy un poco (triste). m&f es·*toy* oon *po*·ko (*trees*·te)
I'm quite (disappointed).	Estoy bastante (decepcionado/a). m/f es·*toy* bas·*tan*·te (de·thep·thyo *na*·do/a)
I feel very (lucky).	Me siento muy (afortunado/a). m/f me *syen*·to mooy (a·for·too·*na*·do/a)

If you're not feeling well, see **health** (p158).

OPINIONS

Q **Did you like it?**	¿Te gustó? te goos·*to*
Q **What did you think of it?**	¿Qué pensaste de eso? ke pen·*sas*·te de *e*·so

Ⓐ **I thought it was ...**	Pienso que fue ... *pyen*·so ke fwe ...
Ⓐ **It's ...**	Es ... es ...

beautiful	bonito/a m/f	bo·*nee*·to/a
bizarre	raro/a m/f	*ra*·ro/a
entertaining	entretenido/a m/f	en·tre·te·*nee*·do/a
excellent	fantástico/a m/f	fan·*tas*·tee·ko/a
horrible	horrible m&f	o·*ree*·ble

I thought it was OK.	Pienso que estaba bien. *pyen*·so ke es·*ta*·ba byen
He's/She's the best.	Es un trozo de pan. (lit: he's/she's a piece of bread) es oon *tro*·tho de pan
I disagree!	No estoy de acuerdo! no es·*toy* de a·*kwer*·do
Yes, but ...	Sí, pero ... see *pe*·ro ...
Whatever.	Lo que sea. lo ke *se*·a

POLITICS & SOCIAL ISSUES

Ⓠ **Who do you vote for?**	¿A quién votas? a kyen *vo*·tas
Ⓐ **I support the ... party.**	Apoyo al partido ... a·*po*·yo al par·*tee*·do ...
Did you hear about ...?	¿Has oído que ...? as o·*ee*·do ke ...
Are you in favour of ...?	¿Estás a favor de ...? es·*tas* a fa·*vor* de ...

LISTEN FOR

Claro.	*kla*·ro	Sure.
¡Claro que sí!	*kla*·ro ke see	Of course!
¡De ningún modo!	de neen·*goon* *mo*·do	No way!
Era broma.	e·ra *bro*·ma	Just joking.
Está bien.	es·*ta* byen	It's OK.
Estoy bien.	es·*toy* byen	I'm OK.
Quizás.	kee·*thas*	Maybe.
Sin problema.	seen pro·*ble*·ma	No problem.
Un momento.	oon mo·*men*·to	Just a minute.
Vale.	*va*·le	OK.
¡Ya lo creo!	ya lo *kre*·o	You bet!

How do people feel about ...?

¿Cómo se siente la gente sobre ...?
ko·mo se *syen*·te la *khen*·te *so*·bre ...

the economy	la economía f	la e·ko·no·*mee*·a
health care	sanidad f pública	san·ee·*dad* *poo*·blee·ka
immigration	inmigración f	een·mee·gra·*thyon*
war in ...	guerra f en ...	*ge*·ra en ...

THE ENVIRONMENT

Is there an environmental problem here?

¿Aquí hay un problema con el medio ambiente?
a·*kee* ai oon pro·*ble*·ma kon el *me*·dyo am·*byen*·te

Is this (forest) protected?	¿Está este (bosque) protegido? es·*ta* *es*·te (*bos*·ke) pro·te·*khee*·do
Where can I recycle this?	¿Dónde se puede reciclar esto? *don*·de se *pwe*·de re·thee·*klar* *es*·to
climate change	cambio m climático *kam*·byo klee·*ma*·tee·ko
pollution	contaminación f kon·ta·mee·na·*thyon*
recycling	reciclaje m re·thee·*kla*·khe

I'm happy.
es·*toy* fe·*leeth*
Estoy feliz.

Going Out

KEY PHRASES

What's on tonight?	¿Qué hay esta noche?	ke ai es·ta *no*·che
Where are the clubs?	¿Dónde están las discotecas?	*don*·de es·*tan* las dees·ko·*te*·kas
Would you like to go for a coffee?	¿Quieres que vayamos a tomar un café?	*kye*·res ke va·*ya*·mos a to·*mar* oon ka·*fe*
What time shall we meet?	¿A qué hora quedamos?	a ke o·ra ke·*da*·mos
Where will we meet?	¿Dónde quedamos?	*don*·de ke·*da*·mos

WHERE TO GO

What's there to do in the evenings?
¿Qué se puede hacer por las noches?
ke se *pwe*·de a·*ther* por las *no*·ches

What's on ...?
¿Qué hay ...?
ke ai ...

locally	en la zona	en la *tho*·na
this weekend	este fin de semana	es·te feen de se·*ma*·na
today	hoy	oy
tonight	esta noche	es·ta *no*·che

Where are there gay venues?
¿Dónde hay lugares gay?
don·de ai loo·*ga*·res gay

Where are there places to eat?	¿Dónde hay lugares para comer? *don*·de ai loo·*ga*·res *pa*·ra ko·*mer*
Where are the clubs?	¿Dónde están las discotecas? *don*·de es·*tan* las dees·ko·*te*·kas
Where are there pubs?	¿Dónde hay pubs? *don*·de ai poobs
Is there a local ... guide?	¿Hay una guía ... de la zona? ai *oo*·na *gee*·a ... de la *tho*·na

entertainment	del ocio	del *o*·thyo
film	de cine	de *thee*·ne
gay	de lugares gay	de loo·*ga*·res gay
music	de música	de *moo*·see·ka

I feel like going to a/the ...	Tengo ganas de ir ... *ten*·go *ga*·nas de eer ...

ballet	al ballet	al ba·*le*
bar	a un bar	a oon bar
cafe	a un café	a oon ka·*fe*
concert	a un concierto	a oon kon·*thyer*·to
karaoke bar	a un bar de karaoke	a oon bar de ka·ra·o·ke
movies	al cine	al *thee*·ne
nightclub	a una discoteca	a *oo*·na dees·ko·*te*·ka
party	a una fiesta	a *oo*·na *fyes*·ta
restaurant	a un restaurante	a oon res·tow·*ran*·te
theatre	al teatro	al te·*a*·tro

INVITATIONS

What are you doing this evening?	¿Qué haces esta noche? ke *a*·thes *es*·ta *no*·che
What are you up to (right now)?	¿Qué haces (ahora)? ke *a*·thes (a·*o*·ra)
Would you like to go for a ...?	¿Quieres que vayamos a ...? *kye*·res ke va·*ya*·mos a ...

coffee	tomar un café	to·*mar* oon ka·*fe*
drink	tomar algo	to·*mar* *al*·go
meal	comer	ko·*mer*
walk	pasear	pa·se·*ar*

I feel like going dancing.	Me apetece ir a bailar. me a·pe·*te*·the eer a bai·*lar*
I feel like going out somewhere.	Me apetece salir. me a·pe·*te*·the sa·*leer*
It's on me.	Invito yo. een·*vee*·to yo
Do you know a good restaurant?	¿Conoces algún buen restaurante? ko·*no*·thes al·*goon* bwen res·tow·*ran*·te
Do you want to come to the (...) concert with me?	¿Quieres venir conmigo al concierto (de ...)? *kye*·res ve·*neer* kon·*mee*·go al kon·*thyer*·to (de ...)
We're having a party.	Vamos a dar una fiesta. *va*·mos a dar *oo*·na *fyes*·ta
Do you want to come?	¿Por qué no vienes? por ke no *vye*·nes
Are you ready?	¿Estás listo/a? m/f es·*tas* *lees*·to/a

CULTURE TIP: MOVIE SUBTITLES

Foreign movies are usually dubbed into Spanish, but in bigger cities you'll find that some films have Spanish subtitles. Look out for *v.o.* (*version original* ver·*syon* o·ree·khee·*nal*, 'original version') or *v.o.s.* (*version original subtitulada* ver·*syon* o·ree·khee·*nal* soob·tee·too·*la*·da, 'original version with subtitles') in listings.

RESPONDING TO INVITATIONS

Sure!	¡Por supuesto! por soo·*pwes*·to
Yes, I'd love to.	Me encantaría. me en·kan·ta·*ree*·a
Where will we go?	¿A dónde vamos? a *don*·de va·*mos*
That's very kind of you.	Es muy amable por tu parte. es mooy a·*ma*·ble por too *par*·te
No, I'm afraid I can't.	Lo siento pero no puedo. lo *syen*·to *pe*·ro no *pwe*·do
Sorry, I can't sing/dance.	Lo siento, no sé cantar/bailar. lo *syen*·to no se kan·*tar*/bai·*lar*
What about tomorrow?	¿Qué tal mañana? ke tal ma·*nya*·na

LISTEN FOR

¡Eh, tú!	e *too*	Hey!
¡Escucha (esto)!	es·*koo*·cha (es·to)	Listen (to this)!
¡Mira!	*mee*·ra	Look!

ARRANGING TO MEET

Q **What time shall we meet?**	¿A qué hora quedamos? a ke *o*·ra ke·*da*·mos
A **Let's meet at (eight) o'clock.**	Quedamos a las (ocho). ke·*da*·mos a las (*o*·cho)
Q **Where will we meet?**	¿Dónde quedamos? *don*·de ke·*da*·mos
A **Let's meet at the (entrance).**	Quedamos en (la entrada). ke·*da*·mos en (la en·*tra*·da)
I'll pick you up.	Paso a recogerte. *pa*·so a re·ko·*kher*·te
I'll be coming later.	Iré más tarde. ee·*re* mas *tar*·de
Where will you be?	¿Dónde estarás? *don*·de es·ta·*ras*
OK!	¡Hecho! e·cho
I'll see you then.	Nos vemos. nos *ve*·mos
See you later/tomorrow.	Hasta luego/mañana. *as*·ta *lwe*·go/ma·*nya*·na
I'm looking forward to it.	Tengo muchas ganas de ir. *ten*·go *moo*·chas *ga*·nas de eer

Sorry I'm late.	Siento llegar tarde. *syen*·to lye·*gar tar*·de
Never mind.	No pasa nada. no *pa*·sa *na*·da

NIGHTCLUBS & BARS

Where can we go (salsa) dancing?	¿Dónde podemos ir a bailar (la salsa)? *don*·de po·*de*·mos eer a bai·*lar* (la *sal*·sa)
Ⓠ **What type of music do you like?**	¿Qué tipo de música prefieres? ke *tee*·po de *moo*·see·ka pre·*fye*·res
Ⓐ **I really like (reggae).**	Me encanta (el reggae). me en·*kan*·ta (el *re*·gai)
Come on!	¡Vamos! *va*·mos
This place is great!	¡Este lugar me encanta! *es*·te loo·*gar* me en·*kan*·ta

For more on bars and drinks, see **eating out** (p177).

DRUGS

I don't take drugs.	No consumo ningún tipo de drogas. no kon·*soo*·mo neen·*goon tee*·po de *dro*·gas
Do you want to have a smoke?	¿Nos fumamos un porro? nos foo·*ma*·mos oon *po*·ro

See also **police** (p156).

Romance

KEY PHRASES

Would you like to do something?	¿Quieres hacer algo?	*kye*·res a·*ther al*·go
I love you.	Te quiero.	te *kye*·ro
Leave me alone, please	Déjame en paz, por favor.	*de*·kha·me en path por fa·*vor*

ASKING SOMEONE OUT

Don't be surprised if invitations come late in the day. Social life in Spain continues well into the night: sometimes people begin to eat dinner at 10pm and many clubs open at midnight.

Q **Would you like to do something (tonight)?**	¿Quieres hacer algo (esta noche)? *kye*·res a·*ther al*·go (*es*·ta *no*·che)
A **Yes, I'd love to.**	Me encantaría. me en·kan·ta·*ree*·a
A **I'm busy.**	Estoy ocupado/a. m/f es·*toy* o·koo·*pa*·do/a

PICK-UP LINES

Would you like a drink?	¿Te apetece una copa? te a·pe·*te*·the *oo*·na *ko*·pa
Do you have a light?	¿Tienes fuego? *tye*·nes *fwe*·go

You're great.	Eres estupendo/a. m/f *e*·res es·too·*pen*·do/a
You mustn't come here much, because I would have noticed you sooner.	No debes venir mucho por aquí porque me habría fijado en ti antes. no *de*·bes ve·*neer moo*·cho por a·*kee por*·ke me a·*bree*·a fee·*kha*·do en tee *an*·tes

REJECTIONS

I'm here with my boyfriend/girlfriend.	Estoy aquí con mi novio/a. m/f es·*toy* a·*kee* kon mee *no*·vyo/a
Excuse me, I have to go now.	Lo siento, pero me tengo que ir. lo *syen*·to *pe*·ro me *ten*·go ke eer
Leave me alone, please.	Déjame en paz, por favor. *de*·kha·me en path por fa·*vor*
Go away!	¡Vete! *ve*·te
Hey, I'm not interested in talking to you.	Mira tío/a, es que no me interesa hablar contigo. m/f *mee*·ra *tee*·o/a es ke no me een·te·*re*·sa ab·*lar* kon·*tee*·go

GETTING CLOSER

Can I kiss you?	¿Te puedo besar? te *pwe*·do be·*sar*
Do you want to come inside for a drink?	¿Quieres entrar a tomar algo? *kye*·res en·*trar* a to·*mar al*·go

LANGUAGE TIP: MASCULINE & FEMININE

In this book, masculine forms appear before the feminine forms. If you see a word ending in *-o/a*, it means the masculine form ends in *-o* and the feminine form ends in *-a* (ie you replace the *-o* ending with the *-a* ending to make it feminine), eg *hijo/a ee*·kho/a m/f (son/daughter). The same goes for the plural endings *-os/as*, eg *hijos/as ee*·khos/as m/f (sons/daughters). If you see an *(a)* between brackets at the end of a word, it means you have to add it in order to make that word feminine, eg *español(a)* es·pa·*nyol*/es·pa·*nyo*·la m/f (Spanish). In other cases we spell out the whole word, eg *actor/actriz* ak·*tor*/ak·*treeth* m/f (actor/actress). See also **gender** (p19).

Do you want a massage?	¿Quieres un masaje? *kye*·res oon ma·sa·khe
Let's go to bed!	¡Vámonos a la cama! *va*·mo·nos a la *ka*·ma

SEX

Kiss me!	¡Dame un beso! *da*·me oon *be*·so
I want you.	Te deseo. te de·*se*·o
I want to make love to you.	Quiero hacerte el amor. *kye*·ro a·*ther*·te el a·*mor*
Do you have a condom?	¿Tienes un condón? *tye*·nes oon kon·*don*
Q **Do you like this?**	¿Esto te gusta? *es*·to te *goos*·ta
A **I (don't) like that.**	Eso (no) me gusta. *e*·so (no) me *goos*·ta

I think we should stop now.	Pienso que deberíamos parar. *pyen*·so ke de·be·*ree*·a·mos pa·*rar*
Oh yeah!	¡Así! a·*see*
That was amazing.	Eso fue increíble. e·so fwe een·kre·*ee*·ble
Can I stay over?	¿Puedo quedarme? *pwe*·do ke·*dar*·me

LOVE

Q **Do you love me?**	¿Me quieres? me *kye*·res
A **I love you.**	Te quiero. te *kye*·ro
I think we're good together.	Creo que estamos muy bien juntos. *kre*·o ke es·*ta*·mos mooy byen *khoon*·tos

LANGUAGE TIP: ENDEARMENTS

Here are a few terms of endearment you might use with the one you love.

heart	corazón m&f	ko·ra·*thon*
heaven	cielo m&f	*thye*·lo
little love	amorcito/a m/f	a·mor·*thee*·to/a
my life	mi vida m&f	mee *vee*·da
my love	mi amor m&f	mee a·*mor*
treasure	tesoro m&f	te·*so*·ro

Beliefs & Culture

KEY PHRASES

What's your religion?	¿Cuál es su/tu religión? pol/inf	kwal es soo/too re·lee·*khyon*
I'm ...	Soy ...	soy ...
I'm sorry, it's against my beliefs.	Lo siento, eso va en contra de mis creencias.	lo *syen*·to *e*·so va en *kon*·tra de mees kre·*en*·thyas

RELIGION

Q **What's your religion?**	¿Cuál es su/tu religión? pol/inf kwal es soo/too re·lee·*khyon*
A **I'm (not) ...**	(No) Soy ... (no) soy ...

agnostic	agnóstico/a m/f	ag·*nos*·tee·ko/a
Buddhist	budista m&f	boo·*dees*·ta
Catholic	católico/a m/f	ka·*to*·lee·ko/a
Christian	cristiano/a m/f	krees·*tya*·no/a
Hindu	hindú m&f	een·*doo*
Jewish	judío/a m/f	khoo·*dee*·o/a
Muslim	musulmán m musulmana f	moo·sool·*man* moo·sool·*ma*·na

I'm (not) religious.	(No) Soy religioso/a. m/f (no) soy re·lee·*khyo*·so/a

I (don't) believe in God.	(No) Creo en Dios. (no) *kre*·o en *dyos*
I (don't) believe in destiny/fate.	(No) Creo en el destino. (no) *kre*·o en el des·*tee*·no
Can I pray here?	¿Puedo rezar aquí? *pwe*·do re·*thar* a·*kee*

CULTURAL DIFFERENCES

Is this a local custom?	¿Esto es una costumbre local? *es*·to es *oo*·na kos·*toom*·bre lo·*kal*
This is fun.	Esto es divertido. *es*·to es dee·ver·*tee*·do
This is (very) interesting.	Esto es (muy) interesante. *es*·to es (mooy) een·te·re·*san*·te
This is (very) different.	Esto es (muy) diferente. *es*·to es (mooy) dee·fe·*ren*·te
I'm not used to this.	No estoy acostumbrado/a a esto. m/f no es·*toy* a·kos·toom·*bra*·do/a a *es*·to
I'm sorry, it's against my beliefs.	Lo siento, eso va en contra de mis creencias. lo *syen*·to e·so va en *kon*·tra de mees kre·*en*·thyas
I'll try it.	Lo probaré. lo pro·ba·*re*
Sorry, I didn't mean to do/say anything wrong.	Lo siento, lo hice/dije sin querer. lo *syen*·to lo *ee*·the/*dee*·khe seen ke·*rer*

Sports

KEY PHRASES

What sport do you play?	¿Qué deporte practicas?	ke de·*por*·te prak·*tee*·kas
What's your favourite team?	¿Cuál es tu equipo favorito?	kwal es too e·*kee*·po fa·vo·*ree*·to
What's the score?	¿Cómo van?	*ko*·mo van

SPORTING INTERESTS

Q **What sport do you play?**	¿Qué deporte practicas? ke de·*por*·te prak·*tee*·kas
Q **What sport do you follow?**	¿A qué deporte eres aficionado/a? m/f a ke de·*por*·te e·res a·fee·thyo·*na*·do/a
A **I play/do ...**	Practico ... prak·*tee*·ko ...
A **I follow ...**	Soy aficionado/a al ... m/f soy a·fee·thyo·*na*·do/a al ...

basketball	baloncesto m	ba·lon·*thes*·to
cycling	ciclismo m	thee·*klees*·mo
football (soccer)	fútbol m	*foot*·bol
tennis	tenis m	*te*·nis
volleyball	voleibol m	*vo*·ley·bol

For more sports, see the **dictionary** (p205).

Do you like sport?	¿Te gustan los deportes? te *goos*·tan los de·*por*·tes
I like watching it.	Me gusta mirar. me *goos*·ta mee·*rar*
Who's your favourite sportsperson?	¿Quién es tu deportista favorito/a? m/f kyen es too de·por·*tees*·ta fa·vo·*ree*·to/a
What's your favourite team?	¿Cuál es tu equipo favorito? kwal es too e·*kee*·po fa·vo·*ree*·to

GOING TO A GAME

Would you like to go to a (basketball) game?	¿Te gustaría ir a un partido de (baloncesto)? te goos·ta·*ree*·a eer a oon par·*tee*·do de (ba·lon·*thes*·to)
Who are you supporting?	¿Con qué equipo vas? kon ke e·*kee*·po vas
Who's playing?	¿Quién juega? kyen *khwe*·ga
Who's winning?	¿Quién gana? kyen *ga*·na
That was a (boring) game.	Ese partido fue (aburrido). e·se par·*tee*·do fwe (a·boo·*ree*·do)
That was a (great) game!	¡Ese partido fue (cojonudo)! e·se par·*tee*·do fwe (ko·kho·*noo*·do)
What's the score?	¿Cómo van? *ko*·mo van

☑ CULTURE TIP: LOCAL SPORTS

If you hear the sounds of bat, ball and exertion, it may be *pelotari* (pelota players) enjoying the traditional game of *pelota vasca*, Basque handball. It's also known as *jai-alai* in Basque.

ball	pelota f	pe·*lo*·ta
striker	delantero/a m/f	de·lan·*te*·ro/a
wall	frontón m	fron·*ton*

PLAYING SPORT

Q **Do you want to play?**	¿Quieres jugar? *kye*·res khoo·*gar*
A **Yeah, that'd be great.**	Sí, me encantaría. see me en·kan·ta·*ree*·a
A **Not at the moment, thanks.**	Ahora mismo no, gracias. a·o·ra *mees*·mo no *gra*·thyas
A **I have an injury.**	Tengo una lesión. *ten*·go *oo*·na le·*syon*
Can I join in?	¿Puedo jugar? *pwe*·do khoo·*gar*
Where's the best place to run around here?	¿Cuál es el mejor sitio para hacer footing por aquí cerca? kwal es el me·*khor see*·tyo *pa*·ra a·*ther foo*·teen por a·*kee ther*·ka
Where's the nearest gym?	¿Dónde está el gimnasio más cercano? *don*·de es·*ta* el kheem·*na*·syo mas ther·*ka*·no
Do I have to be a member to attend?	¿Hay que ser socio/a para entrar? m/f ai ke ser *so*·thyo/a *pa*·ra en·*trar*

Where's the nearest swimming pool?	¿Dónde está la piscina más cercana? *don*·de es·*ta* la pees·*thee*·na mas ther·*ka*·na
Where's the nearest tennis court?	¿Dónde está la pista de tenis más cercana? *don*·de es·*ta* la *pees*·ta de *te*·nees mas ther·*ka*·na
Where are the changing rooms?	¿Dónde están los vestuarios? *don*·de es·*tan* los ves·*twa*·ryos
What's the charge per ...?	¿Cuánto cobran por ...? *kwan*·to *ko*·bran por ...

day	día	*dee*·a
game	partida	par·*tee*·da
hour	hora	*o*·ra
visit	visita	vee·*see*·ta

Can I hire a ...?	¿Es posible alquilar una ...? es po·*see*·ble al·kee·*lar oo*·na ...

ball	pelota	pe·*lo*·ta
bicycle	bicicleta	bee·thee·*kle*·ta
court	cancha	*kan*·cha
racquet	raqueta	ra·*ke*·ta

What a goal/pass!	¡Qué gol/pase! ke gol/*pa*·se
Your/My point.	Tu/Mi punto. too/mee *poon*·to
Kick it to me!	¡Pásamelo! *pa*·sa·me·lo

LISTEN FOR

fuera de juego	*fwe*·ra de *khwe*·go	offside
penalty m	pe·*nal*·tee	penalty
portero m	por·*te*·ro	goalkeeper
saque m **de esquina**	*sa*·ke de es·*kee*·na	corner
tiro m **libre**	*tee*·ro *lee*·bre	free kick

You're a good player.	Juegas bien. *khwe*·gas byen
Thanks for the game.	Gracias por el partido. *gra*·thyas por el par·*tee*·do

SOCCER/FOOTBALL

Who plays for (Real Madrid)?	¿Quién juega en el (Real Madrid)? kyen *khwe*·ga en el (re·*al* ma·*dreeth*)
What a terrible team!	¡Qué equipo más espantoso! ke e·*kee*·po mas es·pan·*to*·so
He's a great player.	Es un gran jugador. es oon gran khoo·ga·*dor*
He played brilliantly in the match against (Italy).	Jugó fenomenal en el partido contra (Italia). khoo·*go* fe·no·me·*nal* en el par·*tee*·do *kon*·tra (ee·*ta*·lya)
Which team is at the top of the league?	¿Qué equipo está en primera posición en la liga? ke e·*kee*·po es·*ta* en pree·*me*·ra po·see·*thyon* en la *lee*·ga

Outdoors

KEY PHRASES

Do we need a guide?	¿Se necesita un guía?	se ne·the·see·ta oon *gee*·a
I'm lost.	Estoy perdido/a. m/f	es·*toy* per·*dee*·do/a
What's the weather like?	¿Qué tiempo hace?	ke *tyem*·po a·the

HIKING

There's plenty of walking, hiking and mountaineering to do in Spain. A recognised cross-country walking trail is known as *Gran Recorrido (GR)* gran re·ko·*ree*·do, while the shorter walking paths scattered throughout the country are called *Pequeños Recorridos (PR)* pe·*ke*·nyos re·ko·*ree*·dos.

Where can I find out about hiking trails?	¿Dónde hay información sobre caminos rurales de la zona? *don*·de ai een·for·ma·*thyon* so·bre ka·*mee*·nos roo·*ra*·les de la *tho*·na
Do we need a guide?	¿Se necesita un guía? se ne·the·see·ta oon *gee*·a
Are there guided treks?	¿Se organizan excursiones guiadas? se or·ga·*nee*·than eks·koor·*syo*·nes gee·a·das

Where can I ...?	¿Dónde puedo ...? *don*·de *pwe*·do ...	
buy supplies	comprar víveres	kom·*prar* vee·ver·es
find someone who knows this area	encontrar a alguien que conozca el área	en·kon·*trar* a *al*·gyen ke ko·*noth*·ka el a·re·a
get a map	obtener un mapa	ob·te·*ner* oon *ma*·pa
hire hiking gear	alquilar un equipo para ir de excursion	al·kee·*lar* oon e·*kee*·po *pa*·ra eer de eks·koor·*syon*

How long is the trail?	¿Cuántos kilómetros tiene el camino? *kwan*·tos kee·*lo*·me·tros *tye*·ne el ka·*mee*·no
How high is the climb?	¿A qué altura se escala? a ke al·*too*·ra se es·*ka*·la
Do we need to take bedding?	¿Se necesita llevar algo en qué dormir? se ne·the·*see*·ta lye·*var* *al*·go en ke dor·*meer*
Do we need to take food/water?	¿Se necesita llevar comida/agua? se ne·the·*see*·ta lye·*var* ko·*mee*·da/*a*·gwa
Is the track (well-)marked?	¿Es (bien) marcado el sendero? es (byen) mar·*ka*·do el sen·*de*·ro
Is the track open?	¿Es abierto el sendero? es a·*byer*·to el sen·*de*·ro

LOOK FOR

Por Aquí a ...	por a·*kee* a ...	This Way To ...
Prohibido Acampar	pro·ee·*bee*·do a·kam·*par*	No Camping
Terreno de Cámping	te·*re*·no de *kam*·peen	Camping Ground

Is the track scenic?
¿Es pintoresco el sendero?
es peen·to·*res*·ko el sen·*de*·ro

Which is the easiest/shortest route?
¿Cuál es el camino más fácil/corto?
kwal es el ka·*mee*·no mas *fa*·theel/*kor*·to

Which is the most interesting route?
¿Cuál es el camino más interesante?
kwal es el ka·*mee*·no mas een·te·re·*san*·te

Where's a/the ...?
¿Dónde hay ...?
don·de ai ...

camping site	un cámping	oon *kam*·peen
village	un pueblo	oon *pwe*·blo
showers	duchas	*doo*·chas
toilets	servicios	ser·*vee*·thyos

Where have you come from?
¿De dónde vienes?
de *don*·de *vye*·nes

How long did it take?
¿Cuánto ha tardado?
kwan·to a tar·*da*·do

Does this path go to ...?
¿Este camino va a ...?
es·te ka·*mee*·no va a ...

Can we go through here?
¿Se puede pasar por aquí?
se *pwe*·de pa·*sar* por a·*kee*

LOOK FOR

¡Prohibido Nadar! pro·ee·*bee*·do na·*dar* No Swimming!

Is the water OK to drink?	¿Se puede beber el agua? se *pwe*·de be·*ber* el *a*·gwa
Is it safe?	¿Es seguro? es se·*goo*·ro
Is there a hut there?	¿Hay una cabaña allí? ai *oo*·na ka·*ba*·nya a·*lyee*
When does it get dark?	¿A qué hora oscurece? a ke *o*·ra os·koo·*re*·the
I'm lost.	Estoy perdido/a. m/f es·*toy* per·*dee*·do/a

AT THE BEACH

Where's the best beach?	¿Dónde está la playa mejor? *don*·de es·*ta* la *pla*·ya me·*khor*
Where's the nearest beach?	¿Dónde está la playa más cercana? *don*·de es·*ta* la *pla*·ya mas ther·*ka*·na
Is it safe to dive/swim here?	¿Es seguro bucear/nadar aquí? es se·*goo*·ro boo·the·*ar*/na·*dar* a·*kee*
What time is high/low tide?	¿A qué hora es la marea alta/baja? a ke *o*·ra es la ma·*re*·a *al*·ta/*ba*·kha
How much to rent a chair?	¿Cuánto por alquilar una silla? *kwan*·to por al·kee·*lar* *oo*·na *see*·lya

How much to rent an umbrella? (for sun)	¿Cuánto por alquilar un parasol? *kwan*·to por al·kee·*lar* oon pa·ra·*sol*

WEATHER

Q **What's the weather like?**	¿Qué tiempo hace? ke *tyem*·po a·the
A **Today it's ...**	Hoy hace ... oy a·the ...

cold	frío	*free*·o
freezing	un frío que pela	oon *free*·o ke *pe*·la
hot	mucho calor	*moo*·cho ka·*lor*
sunny	sol	sol
warm	calor	ka·*lor*
windy	viento	*vyen*·to

A **(Today) It's raining.**	(Hoy) Está lloviendo. (oy) es·*ta* lyo·*vyen*·do
A **(Today) It's snowing.**	(Hoy) Está nevando. (oy) es·*ta* ne·*van*·do
Q **What's the weather forecast?**	¿Cuál es el pronóstico del tiempo? kwal es el pro·*nos*·tee·ko del *tyem*·po
A **(Tomorrow) It will be raining.**	(Mañana) Lloverá. (ma·*nya*·na) lyo·ve·*ra*
Where can I buy a rain jacket?	¿Dónde puedo comprar un impermeable? *don*·de *pwe*·do kom·*prar* oon eem·per·me·a·ble

Where can I buy sunblock?	¿Dónde puedo comprar crema solar? *don*·de *pwe*·do kom·*prar kre*·ma so·*lar*
Where can I buy an umbrella? (for rain)	¿Dónde puedo comprar un paraguas? *don*·de *pwe*·do kom·*prar* oon pa·*ra*·gwas
hail	granizo m gra·*nee*·tho
storm	tormenta f tor·*men*·ta
sun	sol m sol

FLORA & FAUNA

What ... is that?	¿Qué ... es ése/ésa? m/f ke ... es *e*·se/*e*·sa

animal	animal m	a·nee·*mal*
bird	pájaro m	*pa*·kha·ro
flower	flor f	flor
plant	planta f	*plan*·ta
tree	árbol m	*ar*·bol

Can you eat the fruit?	¿Se puede comer la fruta? se *pwe*·de ko·*mer* la *froo*·ta
Is it endangered?	¿Está en peligro de extinción? es·*ta* en pe·*lee*·gro de eks·teen·*thyon*
Is it common?	¿Es común? es ko·*moon*

For geographical and agricultural terms, and names of animals and plants, see the **dictionary** (p205).

SAFE TRAVEL

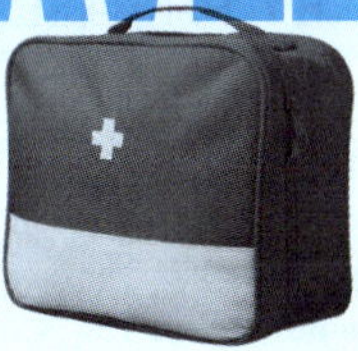

Emergencies

KEY PHRASES

Help!	¡Socorro!	so·*ko*·ro
There's been an accident.	Ha habido un accidente.	a a·*bee*·do oon ak·thee·*den*·te
It's an emergency!	¡Es una emergencia!	es *oo*·na e·mer·*khen*·thee·ya

Help!	¡Socorro! so·*ko*·ro
Stop!	¡Pare! *pa*·re
Go away!	¡Váyase! *va*·ya·se
Leave me alone!	¡Déjame en paz! *de*·kha·me en path
Thief!	¡Ladrón! lad·*ron*
Fire!	¡Fuego! *fwe*·go
It's an emergency!	¡Es una emergencia! es *oo*·na e·mer·*khen*·thee·ya
There's been an accident.	Ha habido un accidente. a a·*bee*·do oon ak·thee·*den*·te
Do you have a first-aid kit?	¿Tiene un botiquín de primeros auxilios? *tye*·ne oon bo·tee·*keen* de pree·*me*·ros owk·*see*·lyos

LISTEN FOR

¡Es peligroso!	es pe·lee·*gro*·so	It's dangerous!

Call the police!	¡Llame a la policía! *lya*·me a la po·lee·*thee*·a
Call a doctor!	¡Llame a un médico! *lya*·me a oon *me*·dee·ko
Call an ambulance!	¡Llame a una ambulancia! *lya*·me a *oo*·na am·boo·*lan*·thya
Could you help me, please?	¿Me puede ayudar, por favor? me *pwe*·de a·yoo·*dar* por fa·*vor*
I have to use the telephone.	Necesito usar el teléfono. ne·the·*see*·to oo·*sar* el te·*le*·fo·no
I'm lost.	Estoy perdido/a. m/f es·*toy* per·*dee*·do/a
Where are the toilets?	¿Dónde están los servicios? *don*·de es·*tan* los ser·*vee*·thyos

Police

KEY PHRASES

Where's the police station?	¿Dónde está la comisaría?	*don*·de es·*ta* la ko·mee·sa·*ree*·a
I want to contact my embassy/ consulate.	Quiero ponerme en contacto con mi embajada/ consulado.	*kye*·ro po·*ner*·me en kon·*tak*·to kon mee em·ba·*kha*·da/ kon·soo·*la*·do
My bag was stolen.	Mi bolso fue robado.	mee *bol*·so fwe ro·*ba*·do

In an emergency, call the police (dial 112). They will then put you through to other emergency services (fire and ambulance). For more on making a call, see **communications** (p85).

Where's the police station?	¿Dónde está la comisaría? *don*·de es·*ta* la ko·mee·sa·*ree*·a
I want to report an offence.	Quiero denunciar un delito. *kye*·ro de·noon·*thyar* oon de·*lee*·to
I've been robbed.	Me han robado. me an ro·*ba*·do
I've been raped.	He sido violado/a. m/f e *see*·do vee·o·*la*·do/a
It was him/her.	Fue él/ella. fwe el/*e*·lya
My (money) was stolen.	Mi (dinero) fue robado. mee (dee·*ne*·ro) fwe ro·*ba*·do
My (bag/handbag) was stolen.	Mi (bolso) fue robado. mee (*bol*·so) fwe ro·*ba*·do

My (bags/suitcases) were stolen.	Mis (maletas) fueron robadas. mee (ma·*le*·tas) fwe·*ron* ro·*ba*·das
I've lost (my passport).	He perdido (mi pasaporte). e per·*dee*·do (mee pa·sa·*por*·te)
What am I accused of?	¿De qué me acusan? de ke me a·*ku*·san
I didn't realise I was doing anything wrong.	No sabía que estaba haciendo algo mal. no sa·*bee*·a ke es·*ta*·ba a·*thyen*·do *al*·go mal
I'm innocent.	Soy inocente. soy ee·no·*then*·te
I want to contact my embassy/consulate.	Quiero ponerme en contacto con mi embajada/ consulado. *kye*·ro po·*ner*·me en kon·*tak*·to kon mee em·ba·*kha*·da/ kon·soo·*la*·do
Can I call a lawyer?	¿Puedo llamar a un abogado? *pwe*·do lya·*mar* a oon a·bo·*ga*·do
I need a lawyer who speaks (English).	Necesito un abogado que hable (inglés). ne·the·*see*·to oon a·bo·*ga*·do ke a·ble (een·*gles*)
Can I have a copy, please?	¿Puede darme una copia, por favor? *pwe*·de *dar*·me *oo*·na *ko*·pya por fa·*vor*
This drug is for personal use.	Esta droga es para uso personal. es·ta *dro*·ga es *pa*·ra *oo*·so per·so·*nal*
I have a prescription for this drug.	Tengo receta para esta droga. *ten*·go re·*the*·ta *pa*·ra es·ta *dro*·ga

Health

KEY PHRASES

Where's the nearest hospital?	¿Dónde está el hospital más cercano?	*don*·de es·*ta* el os·*pee*·tal mas ther·*ka*·no
I'm sick.	Estoy enfermo/a. m/f	es·*toy* en·*fer*·mo/a
I need a doctor.	Necesito un doctor.	ne·the·*see*·to oon dok·*tor*
I'm on regular medication for ...	Estoy bajo medicación para ...	es·*toy* *ba*·kho me·dee·ka·*thyon* *pa*·ra ...
I'm allergic to ...	Soy alérgico/a a... m/f	soy a·*ler*·khee·ko/a a ...

DOCTOR

Where's the nearest ...?
¿Dónde está ... más cercano/a? m/f
don·de es·*ta* ... mas ther·*ka*·no/a

chemist/pharmacy	la farmacia f	la far·*ma*·thya
dentist	el dentista m	el den·*tees*·ta
doctor	el médico m	el *me*·dee·ko
hospital	el hospital m	el os·pee·*tal*
medical centre	el ambulatorio m	el am·boo·la·*to*·ryo
optometrist	el oculista m	el o·koo·*lees*·ta

CULTURE TIP: ETIQUETTE TIP

A polite way to respond to someone sneezing is by saying *¡Salud!* sa·*lood* (health) or *¡Jesús!* khe·*soos* (lit: 'Jesus').

I need a doctor (who speaks English).	Necesito un médico (que hable inglés). ne·the·*see*·to oon *me*·dee·ko (ke a·ble een·*gles*)
Could I see a female doctor?	¿Puede examinarme una doctora? *pwe*·de ek·sa·mee·*nar*·me *oo*·na dok·*to*·ra
I've run out of my medication.	Se me terminaron los medicamentos. se me ter·mee·*na*·ron los me·dee·ka·*men*·tos
This is my usual medicine.	Este es mi medicamento habitual. *es*·te es mee me·dee·ka·*men*·to a·bee·too·*al*
I don't want a blood transfusion.	No quiero que me hagan una transfusión de sangre. no *kye*·ro ke me *a*·gan *oo*·na trans·foo·*syon* de *san*·gre
Please use a new syringe.	Por favor, use una jeringa nueva. por fa·*vor oo*·se *oo*·na khe·*reen*·ga *nwe*·va
I need new contact lenses.	Necesito lentillas nuevas. ne·the·*see*·to len·*tee*·yas *nwe*·vas
I need new glasses.	Necesito gafas nuevas. ne·the·*see*·to *ga*·fas *nwe*·vas

I've been vaccinated for ...	Estoy vacunado/a contra ... m/f es·*toy* va·koo·*na*·do/a *kon*·tra ...
He's/She's been vaccinated for ...	Está vacunado/a contra ... m/f es·*ta* va·koo·*na*·do/a *kon*·tra ...

tetanus	el tétano	el *te*·ta·no
typhus	el tifus	el *tee*·foos
hepatitis A/B/C	la hepatitis A/B/C	la e·pa·*tee*·tees a/be/the
... fever	la fiebre ...	la *fye*·bre ...

For women's medical issues, see **women's health** (p162).

SYMPTOMS & CONDITIONS

I'm sick.	Estoy enfermo/a. m/f es·*toy* en·*fer*·mo/a
I have ...	Tengo ... *ten*·go ...
I've recently had ...	Hace poco he tenido ... a·the *po*·ko e te·*nee*·do ...
I'm on regular medication for ...	Estoy bajo medicación para ... es·*toy ba*·kho me·dee·ka·*thyon pa*·ra ...
It hurts here.	Me duele aquí. me *dwe*·le a·*kee*
I've been injured.	He sido herido/a. m/f e *see*·do e·*ree*·do/a
I've been vomiting.	He estado vomitando. e es·*ta*·do vo·mee·*tan*·do

LISTEN FOR

¿Qué le pasa?	*ke le pa·sa* What's the problem?
¿Dónde le duele?	*don·de le dwe·le* Where does it hurt?
¿Tiene fiebre?	*tye·ne fye·bre* Do you have a temperature?
¿Desde cuándo se siente así?	*des·de kwan·do se syen·te a·see* How long have you been like this?
¿Ha tenido esto antes?	*a te·nee·do es·to an·tes* Have you had this before?

I can't sleep.	No puedo dormir. *no pwe·do dor·meer*
I have a rash.	Tengo una erupción cutánea. *ten·go oo·na e·roop·thyon koo·ta·ne·a*
I have an infection.	Tengo una infección. *ten·go oo·na in·fek·thyon*
I feel ...	Me siento ... *me syen·to ...*

better	mejor m&f	*me·khor*
depressed	deprimido/a m/f	*de·pree·mee·do/a*
dizzy	mareado/a m/f	*ma·re·a·do/a*
shivery	destemplado/a m/f	*des·tem·pla·do/a*
weak	débil m&f	*de·beel*
worse	peor m&f	*pe·or*

asthma	asma m *as*·ma
diarrhoea	diarrea f dee·a·*re*·a
fever	fiebre f *fye*·bre
headache	dolor m de cabeza do·*lor* de ka·*be*·tha
sprain	torcedura f tor·the·*doo*·ra

For more symptoms & conditions, see the **dictionary** (p205).

WOMEN'S HEALTH

(I think) I'm pregnant.	(Creo que) Estoy embarazada. (*kre*·o ke) es·*toy* em·ba·ra·*tha*·da
I haven't had my period for ... weeks.	Hace ... semanas que no me viene la regla. *a*·the ... se·*ma*·nas ke no me *vye*·ne la *reg*·la
I'm on the pill.	Tomo la píldora. *to*·mo la *peel*·do·ra
I've noticed a lump here.	He notado un bulto aquí. e no·*ta*·do oon *bool*·to a·*kee*
I have period pain.	Tengo dolor menstrual. *ten*·go do·*lor* mens·troo·*al*
contraception	anticonceptivos m pl an·tee·kon·thep·*tee*·vos
pregnancy test	prueba f de embarazo *prwe*·ba de em·ba·*ra*·tho
the morning-after pill	píldora f del día siguiente *peel*·do·ra del *dee*·a see·*gyen*·te

LISTEN FOR

¿Usted bebe?	oos·*ted be*·be Do you drink?
¿Usted fuma?	oos·*ted foo*·ma Do you smoke?
¿Usted toma drogas?	oos·*ted to*·ma *dro*·gas Do you take drugs?
¿Tiene usted alergias?	*tye*·ne oos·*ted* a·*ler*·khyas Are you allergic to anything?
¿Se encuentra bajo medicación?	se en·*kwen*·tra *ba*·kho me·dee·ka·*thyon* Are you on medication?

ALLERGIES

I'm allergic to ...	Soy alérgico/a ... m/f soy a·*ler*·khee·ko/a ...
He/She is allergic to ...	Es alérgico/a ... m/f es a·*ler*·khee·ko/a ...

antibiotics	a los antibióticos	a los an·tee·*byo*·tee·kos
anti-inflammatories	a los anti-inflamatorios	a los an·tee·een·fla·ma·*to*·ryos
aspirin	a la aspirina	a la as·pee·*ree*·na
bees	a las abejas	a las a·*be*·khas
codeine	a la codeína	a la ko·de·ee·na
penicillin	a la penicilina	a la pe·nee·thee·*lee*·na
pollen	al polon	al *po*·len

I have a skin allergy.	Tengo una alergia en la piel. *ten*·go *oo*·na a·*ler*·khya en la pyel

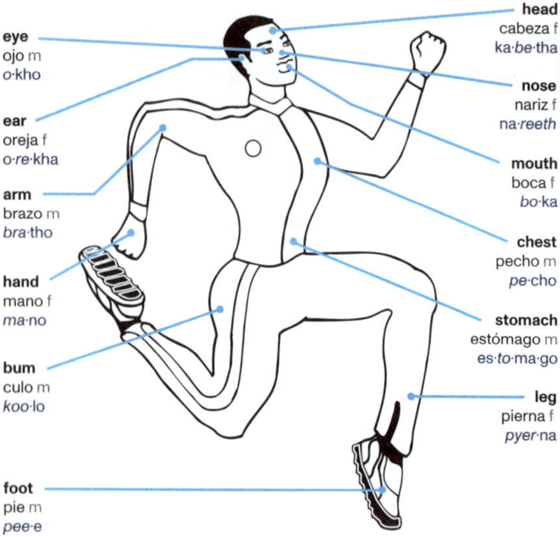

I'm on a special diet.	Estoy a régimen especial. es·*toy* a *re*·khee·men es·pe·*thyal*
antihistamines	antihistamínicos m pl *an*·tee·ees·ta·*mee*·nee·kos
inhaler	inhalador m een·a·la·*dor*
sulphur-based drugs	drogas con base de azufre f pl *dro*·gas kon *ba*·se de a·*thoo*·fre

For food-related allergies, see **vegetarian & special meals** (p187).

PARTS OF THE BODY

My ... hurts.	Me duele ... me *dwe*·le ...
I can't move my ...	No puedo mover ... no *pwe*·do mo·*ver* ...
I have a cramp in my ...	Tengo calambres en ... *ten*·go ka·*lam*·bres en ...
My ... is swollen.	Mi ... está hinchado. mee ... es·*ta* een·*cha*·do

For more parts of the body, see the **dictionary** (p205).

CHEMIST/PHARMACY

I need something for ...	Necesito algo para ... ne·the·*see*·to *al*·go *pa*·ra ...
I have a prescription.	Tengo receta médica. *ten*·go re·*the*·ta *me*·dee·ka
Do I need a prescription for ...?	¿Necesito receta para ...? ne·the·*see*·to re·*the*·ta *pa*·ra ...
How many times a day?	¿Cuántas veces al día? *kwan*·tas *ve*·thes al *dee*·a

For pharmaceutical items, see the **dictionary** (p205).

LISTEN FOR

¿Ha tomado esto antes?	a to·*ma*·do *es*·to *an*·tes Have you taken this before?
Dos veces al día (con la comida).	dos *ve*·thes al *dee*·a (kon la ko·*mee*·da) Twice a day (with food).

LISTEN FOR

Abra.	a·bra	Open wide.
No se mueva.	no se *mwe*·va	Don't move.
¡Enjuague!	en·*khwa*·ge	Rinse!

DENTIST

I have a broken tooth.	Se me ha roto un diente. se me a *ro*·to oon *dyen*·te
I have a toothache.	Me duele una muela. me *dwe*·le *oo*·na *mwe*·la
I've lost a filling.	Se me ha caído un empaste. se me a ka·*ee*·do oon em·*pas*·te
My orthodontic braces broke/fell off.	Se me rompió/cayó el aparato dental. se me rom·*pyo*/ka·*yo* el a·pa·*ra*·to den·*tal*
My gums hurt.	Me duelen las encías. me *dwe*·len las en·*thee*·as
I don't want it extracted.	No quiero que me lo saquen. no *kye*·ro ke me lo *sa*·ken
I need an anaesthetic.	Necesito una anestesia. ne·the·*see*·to *oo*·na a·nes·*te*·sya
I need a filling.	Necesito un empaste. ne·the·*see*·to oon em·*pas*·te

FOOD

Eating Out

KEY PHRASES

Can you recommend a restaurant?	¿Puede recomendar un restaurante?	*pwe*·de re·ko·men·*dar* oon res·tow·*ran*·te
I'd like a table for two, please.	Quería una mesa para dos, por favor.	ke·*ree*·a *oo*·na *me*·sa *pa*·ra dos por fa·*vor*
I'd like the menu, please.	Quería la carta, por favor.	ke·*ree*·a la *kar*·ta por fa·*vor*
I'd like ...	Quería ...	ke·*ree*·a ...
Please bring the bill.	Nos trae la cuenta, por favor.	nos *tra*·e la *kwen*·ta por fa·*vor*

BASICS

The main meal in Spain, 'lunchtime' is called *la hora de comer* la *o*·ra de ko·*mer*. It's served between 1.30pm and 4.30pm.

breakfast	desayuno m de·sa·*yoo*·no
lunch	comida f ko·*mee*·da
dinner	cena f *the*·na
snack	tentempié m ten·tem·*pye*
eat/drink	comer/beber ko·*mer*/be·*ber*

I'd like ...	Quería ... *ke·ree·a ...*
I'm starving!	¡Tengo mucha hambre! m/f *ten·go moo·cha ham·bre*
Enjoy your meal!	¡Buen provecho! *bwen pro·ve·cho*

FINDING A PLACE TO EAT

Can you recommend a ...?	¿Puede recomendar un/una ...? m/f *pwe·de re·ko·men·dar oon/oo·na ...*

bar	bar m	*bar*
cafe	café m	*ka·fe*
coffee bar	cafetería f	*ka·fe·te·ree·a*
restaurant	restaurante m	*res·tow·ran·te*

Are you still serving food?	¿Siguen sirviendo comida? *see·gen seer·vyen·do ko·mee·da*
How long is the wait?	¿Cuánto hay que esperar? *kwan·to ai ke es·pe·rar*
Where would you go for a cheap meal?	¿Dónde se puede comer barato? *don·de se pwe·de ko·mer ba·ra·to*
Where would you go for local specialities?	¿Dónde se puede comer comida típica? *don·de se pwe·de ko·mer ko·mee·da tee·pee·ka*

LISTEN FOR

Lo siento, hemos cerrado.	lo *syen*·to e·mos the·*ra*·do Sorry, we're closed.
No tenemos mesa.	no te·*ne*·mos *me*·sa We have no free tables.
Un momento.	oon mo·*men*·to One moment.

I'd like to reserve a table for (two) people.	Quería reservar una mesa para (dos) personas. ke·*ree*·a re·ser·*var* *oo*·na *me*·sa *pa*·ra (dos) per·*so*·nas
I'd like to reserve a table for (eight) o'clock.	Quería reservar una mesa para las (ocho). ke·*ree*·a re·ser·*var* *oo*·na *me*·sa *pa*·ra las (*o*·cho)

AT THE RESTAURANT

I'd like a table for (two), please.	Quería una mesa para (dos), por favor. ke·*ree*·a *oo*·na *me*·sa *pa*·ra (dos) por fa·*vor*

For two, please.	Para dos, por favor.	*pa*·ra dos por fa·*vor*

I'd like the drink list, please.	Quería la lista de bebidas, por favor. ke·*ree*·a la *lees*·ta de be·*bee*·das por fa·*vor*

Eating Out

CAN I SEE THE MENU, PLEASE?
¿Puedo ver la carta, por favor?
pwe·do ver la *kar*·ta por fa·*vor*

WHAT WOULD YOU RECOMMEND FOR ...?
¿Qué me recomendaría para ...?
ke me re·ko·men·da·*ree*·a *pa*·ra ...

THE MAIN COURSE
el plato principal
el *pla*·to preen·thee·*pal*

DESSERT
postre
pos·tre

DRINKS
bebidas
be·*bee*·das

CAN YOU BRING ME SOME ..., PLEASE?
Me trae ..., por favor?
me *tra*·e ... por fa·*vor*

I'D LIKE THE BILL, PLEASE.
Quería la cuenta, por favor.
ke·*ree*·a la *kwen*·ta por fa·*vor*

I'd like the menu, please.	Quería la carta, por favor. ke·*ree*·a la *kar*·ta por fa·*vor*

The menu, please.	La carta, por favor.	la *kar*·ta por fa·*vor*

Do you have children's meals?	¿Tienen comidas para niños? *tye*·nen ko·*mee*·das *pa*·ra *nee*·nyos
Do you have a menu in English?	¿Tienen una carta en inglés? *tye*·nen *oon*·a *kar*·ta en een·*gles*
Is service included in the bill?	¿La cuenta incluye servicio? la *kwen*·ta een·*kloo*·ye ser·*vee*·thyo
What would you recommend?	¿Qué recomienda? ke re·ko·*myen*·da
Can you tell me which traditional foods I should try?	¿Qué platos típicos debería probar? ke *pla*·tos *tee*·pee·kos de·be·*ree*·a pro·*bar*

LISTEN FOR

¿Le gusta ...?	le *goos*·ta ... Do you like ...?
Recomiendo ...	re·ko·*myen*·do ... I suggest the ...
¿Cómo lo quiere preparado?	*ko*·mo lo *kye*·re pre·pa·*ra*·do How would you like that cooked?

I'll have what they're having.
Tomaré lo mismo que ellos.
to·ma·*re* lo *mees*·mo ke e·lyos

Does it take long to prepare?
¿Tarda mucho en prepararse?
tar·da *moo*·cho en pre·pa·*rar*·se

What's in that dish?
¿Que lleva ese plato?
ke *lye*·va e·se *pla*·to

Are these complimentary?
¿Estos son gratis?
es·tos son *gra*·tees

We're just having drinks.
Sólo queremos tomar algo.
so·lo ke·*re*·mos to·*mar al*·go

Just drinks. Sólo bebidas. *so*·lo be·*bee*·das

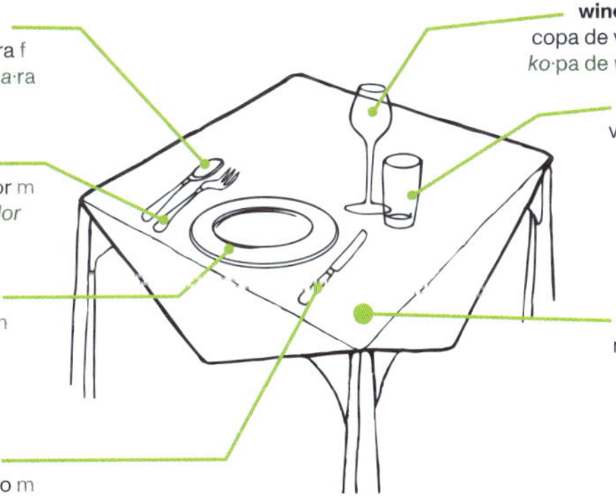

REQUESTS

Please bring a glass.	Nos trae un vaso, por favor. nos *tra*·e oon *va*·so por fa·*vor*
Please bring a napkin.	Nos trae una servilleta, por favor. nos *tra*·e *oo*·na ser·vee·*lye*·ta por fa·*vor*
I'd like it ...	Lo quiero ... lo *kye*·ro ...
I don't want it ...	No lo quiero ... no lo *kye*·ro ...

deep fried	frito	*free*·to
medium	al punto	al *pun*·to
rare	poco hecha	*po*·ko e·cho
re-heated	recalentado	re·ka·len·*ta*·do
steamed	al vapor	al va·*por*
well-done	muy hecho	mooy e·cho
with the dressing on the side	con el aliño aparte	kon el a·*lee*·nyo a·*par*·te
without ...	sin ...	seen ...

For other specific meal requests, see **vegetarian & special meals** (p187).

COMPLIMENTS & COMPLAINTS

I love this dish.	Me encanta este plato. me en·*kan*·ta *es*·te *pla*·to
I didn't order this.	No he pedido esto. No e pe·*dee*·do *es*·to

LOOK FOR

Aperitivos	a·pe·ree·*tee*·vos	Appetisers
Cervezas	ther·*ve*·thas	Beers
Sopas	*so*·pas	Soups
Entrantes	en·*tran*·tes	Starters
Ensaladas	en·sa·*la*·das	Salads
Postres	*pos*·tres	Desserts
Refrescos	re·*fres*·kos	Soft Drinks
Segundos Platos	se·*goon*·dos *pla*·tos	Main Courses

That was delicious!	¡Estaba buenísimo! es·*ta*·ba bwe·*nee*·see·mo
My compliments to the chef.	Mi enhorabuena al cocinero. mee en·o·ra·*bwe*·na al ko·thee·*ne*·ro
I'm full.	Estoy lleno/a. m/f es·*toy lye*·no/a
This is burnt.	Esto está quemado. es·to es·*ta* ke·*ma*·do
This is (too) cold.	Esto está (demasiado) frío. es·to es·*ta* (de·ma·*sya*·do) *free*·o
This is superb.	Esto está muy rico. es·to es·*ta* mooy·*ree*·ko
We love the local cuisine.	Nos encanta la comida típica de la zona. nos en·*kan*·ta la ko·*mee*·da *tee*·pee·ka de la *tho*·na

PAYING THE BILL

Please bring the bill.	Nos trae la cuenta, por favor. nos *tra*·e la *kwen*·ta por fa·*vor*
Bill, please.	La cuenta, por favor. la *kwen*·ta por fa·*vor*
There's a mistake in the bill.	Hay un error en la cuenta. ai oon e·*ror* en la *kwen*·ta

For methods of payment, see **money & banking** (p91).

NONALCOHOLIC DRINKS

I don't drink alcohol.	No bebo alcohol. no *be*·bo al·*kol*
(cup of) coffee ...	(taza de) café ... (*ta*·tha de) ka·*fe* ...
(cup of) tea ...	(taza de) té ... (*ta*·tha de) te ...
with milk	con leche kon *le*·che
without sugar	sin azúcar seen a·*thoo*·kar
soft drink	refresco m re·*fres*·ko
(boiled) water	agua (hervida) *a*·gwa (er·*vee*·da)
(sparkling) mineral water	agua mineral (con gas) *a*·gwa mee·ne·*ral* (kon gas)

ALCOHOLIC DRINKS

... beer	cerveza f ... ther·*ve*·tha ...	
draught	de barril	de ba·*ril*
dark	negra	*neg*·ra
light	rubia	*roo*·bee·a
nonalcoholic	sin alcohol	sin al·*kol*

small bottle of beer (250 ml)	botellín m bo·te·*lyin*
litre bottle of beer	litrona f lee·*tro*·na
bottle of beer (300 ml)	mediana f me·*dya*·na

What would you recommend?
ke re·ko·*myen*·da
¿Qué recomienda?

a glass/pint of beer	una caña/pinta de cerveza *oo*·na *ka*·nya/*peen*·ta de ther·*ve*·tha
a jug of beer	una jarra de cerveza *oo*·na *kha*·ra de ther·*ve*·tha
brandy	coñac m *ko*·nyak
Champagne	champán m cham·*pan*
cocktail	coctél m *cok*·tel
sangria (red-wine punch)	sangría f san·*gree*·a
a shot of (rum)	un chupito de (ron) oon choo·*pee*·to de (ron)
a shot of (gin)	un chupito de (ginebra) oon choo·*pee*·to de (khee·*ne*·bra)
a shot of (whisky)	un chupito de (güisqui) oon choo·*pee*·to de (*gwees*·kee)
a bottle/glass of ... wine	una botella/copa de vino ... *oo*·na bo·*te*·lya/*ko*·pa de *vee*·no ...

dessert	dulce	*dool*·the
red	tinto	*teen*·to
rosé	rosado	ro·*sa*·do
sparkling	espumoso	es·poo·*mo*·so
white	blanco	*blan*·ko

CULTURE TIP: TAPAS

Tapas are scrumptious cooked bar snacks, available pretty much around the clock at bars and some clubs. You'll find they're free in some areas of Spain, particularly in the south, laid out along the bar for you to choose from.

banderilla f/ **moruno** m/ **pinchito** m	ban·de·*ree*·lya/ mo·*roo*·no/ peen·*chee*·to	small tapa serving on bread or a toothpick
ración f	ra·*thyon*	large tapa serving
montadito m	mon·ta·*dee*·to	bread-topped tapa
pan tumaca m	pan too·*ma*·ka	tapa of toasted bread rubbed with tomatoes and garlic, served with oil
queso m **en aceite**	*ke*·so en a·*they*·te	cheese in olive oil, served as a tapa

IN THE BAR

Excuse me!	¡Oiga! *oy*·ga
I'm next.	Ahora voy yo. a·*o*·ra voy yo
Q **What would you like?**	¿Qué quieres tomar? ke *kye*·res to·*mar*
A **I'll have ...**	Para mí ... *pa*·ra mee ...
Same again, please.	Otra de lo mismo. *o*·tra de lo *mees*·mo
No ice, thanks.	Sin hielo, gracias. seen *ye*·lo *gra*·thyas
I'll buy you a drink.	Te invito a una copa. te een·*vee*·to a *oo*·na *ko*·pa

LISTEN FOR

¿Dónde le gustaría sentarse?	*don*·de le gus·ta·*ree*·a sen·*tar*·se Where would you like to sit?
¿En qué le puedo ayudar?	en ke le *pwe*·do a·yoo·*dar* What can I get for you?
¡Aquí tiene!	a·*kee* *tye*·ne Here you go!

It's my round.	Es mi ronda. es mee *ron*·da
You can get the next one.	La próxima la pagas tú. la *prok*·see·ma la *pa*·gas too
Do you serve meals here?	¿Sirven comidas aquí? *seer*·ven ko·*mee*·das a·*kee*

DRINKING UP

Cheers!	¡Salud! sa·*lood*
Thanks, but I don't feel like it.	Lo siento, pero no me apetece. lo *syen*·to *pe*·ro no me a·pe·*te*·the
No thanks, I'm driving.	No gracias, tengo que conducir. no *gra*·thyas *ten*·go ke kon·doo·*theer*
This is hitting the spot.	Me lo estoy pasando muy bien. me lo es·*toy* pa·*san*·do mooy byen

CULTURE TIP: MINIS

Many Spanish bars provide massive plastic beakers of beer to cater for young revellers. It's cut with water and average tasting - but cheap and free flowing! These fountains of froth are called *minis*.

I feel fantastic!	¡Me siento fenomenal! me *syen*·to fe·no·me·*nal*
I'm feeling drunk.	Esto me está subiendo mucho. es·to me es·*ta* soo·*byen*·do *moo*·cho
I think I've had one too many.	Creo que he tomado demasiado. *kre*·o ke e to·*ma*·do de·ma·*sya*·do
I'm tired, I'd better go home.	Estoy cansado/a, mejor me voy a casa. m/f es·*toy* kan·*sa*·do/a me·*khor* me voy a *ka*·sa
I don't think you should drive.	No creo que deberías conducir. no *kre*·o ke de·be·*ree*·as kon·doo·*theer*
Can you call a taxi for me?	¿Me puedes pedir un taxi? me *pwe*·des pe·*deer* oon *tak*·see

Self-Catering

KEY PHRASES

What's the local speciality?	¿Cuál es la especialidad de la zona?	kwal es la es·pe·thya·lee·*dad* de la *tho*·na
Where can I find the ... section?	¿Dónde está la sección de ...?	*don*·de es·*ta* la sek·*thyon* de ...
I'd like ...	Póngame ...	*pon*·ga·me ...

BUYING FOOD

Where can I find the ... section?
¿Dónde está la sección de ...?
don·de es·*ta* la sek·*thyon* de ...

dairy	productos lácteos	pro·*dook*·tos *lak*·te·os
frozen goods	productos congelados	pro·*dook*·tos kon·khe·*la*·dos
fruit and vegetable	frutas y verduras	*froo*·tas ee ver·*doo*·ras
meat	carne	*kar*·ne

Where's the health-food section/store?
¿Dónde esta la sección/tienda de comida dietética?
don·de es·*ta* la sek·*thyon*/*tyen*·da de ko·*mee*·da dye·*te*·tee·ka

What's that?
¿Qué es eso?
ke es *e*·so

LISTEN FOR

¿En qué le puedo ayudar?	en ke le *pwe*·do a·yoo·*dar* Can I help you?
¿Qué quería?	ke ke·*ree*·a What would you like?
No tengo.	no *ten*·go I don't have any.
No queda más.	no *ke*·da mas There's none left.

Can I taste it?	¿Puedo probarlo/a? m/f *pwe*·do pro·*bar*·lo/a
What's the local speciality?	¿Cuál es la especialidad de la zona? kwal es la es·pe·thya·lee·*dad* de la *tho*·na
How much?	¿Cuánto? *kwan*·to
How many?	¿Cuántos/as? m/f *kwan*·tos/as
How much is (a kilo of cheese)?	¿Cuánto vale (un kilo de queso)? *kwan*·to *va*·le (oon *kee*·lo de *ke*·so)
Do you have anything cheaper?	¿Tiene algo más barato? *tye*·ne *al*·go mas ba·*ra*·to
Do you have any other kinds?	¿Tiene otros tipos? *tye*·ne *ot*·ros *tee*·pos
Do you sell locally produced food?	¿Se venden productos de la zona? se *ven*·den pro·*dook*·tos de la *tho*·na

Do you sell organic produce?	¿Se venden productos agrícolas biológicos? se *ven*·den pro·*dook*·tos a·*gree*·ko·las bee·o·*lo*·khee·kos
I'd like ...	Póngame ... *pon*·ga·me ...

(three) pieces	(tres) piezas	(tres) *pye*·thas
(six) slices	(seis) lonchas	(seys) *lon*·chas
(two) kilos	(dos) kilos	(dos) *kee*·los
(200) grams	(doscientos) gramos	(dos·*thyen*·tos) *gra*·mos

half a dozen	una media docena *oo*·na *me*·dya do·*the*·na
half a kilo	medio kilo *me*·dyo *kee*·lo
a kilo	un kilo oon *kee*·lo
a bottle (of ...)	una botella (de ...) *oo*·na bo·*te*·lya (de ...)
a jar	un frasco oon *fras*·ko
a packet	un paquete oon pa·*ke*·te
(just) a little	(sólo) un poquito (*so*·lo) oon po·*kee*·to
many	muchos/as **m/f** *moo*·chos/as
(a bit) more	(un poco) más (oon *po*·ko) mas
some	algunos/as **m/f** al·*goo*·nos/as

LISTEN FOR

Eso es (un manchego).	*e*·so es (oon man·*che*·go) That's (a manchego).
Eso es (cinco euros).	*e*·so es (*theen*·ko e·*oo*·ros) That's (five euros).
¿Algo más?	*al*·go mas Anything else?

less	menos *me*·nos
that one	ese *e*·se
this	esto *es*·to
Enough!	¡Basta! *ba*·sta

For food items, see the **menu decoder** (p190) and the **dictionary** (p205).

COOKING

cooked	cocido/a **m/f** ko·*thee*·do/a
dried	seco/a **m/f** *se*·ko/a
fresh	fresco/a **m/f** *fres*·ko/a
frozen	congelado/a **m/f** kon·khe·*la*·do/a
raw	crudo/a **m/f** *kroo*·do/a
smoked	ahumado/a **m/f** a·oo·*ma*·do/a

Could I please borrow a/an ...?	¿Me puede prestar un/una ...? m/f	me *pwe*·de pres·*tar* oon/*oo*·na ...
Where's a/an ...?	¿Dónde hay un/una ...? m/f	*don*·de ai oon/*oo*·na ...

bottle opener	abrebotellas m	a·bre·bo·*te*·lyas
can opener	abrelatas m	a·bre·*la*·tas
chopping board	tabla f para cortar	*tab*·la *pa*·ra kor·*tar*
corkscrew	sacacorchos m	sa·ka·*kor*·chos
cup	taza f	*ta*·tha
fork	tenedor m	te·ne·*dor*
frying pan	sartén f	sar·*ten*
glass	vaso m	*va*·so
knife	cuchillo m	koo·*chee*·lyo
plate	plato m	*pla*·to
saucepan	cazo m	*ka*·tho
spoon	cuchara f	koo·*cha*·ra
toaster	tostadora f	tos·ta·*do*·ra

For more cooking terminology, see the **dictionary** (p205).

Vegetarian & Special Meals

KEY PHRASES

Do you have vegetarian food?	¿Tienen comida vegetariana?	*tye*·nen ko·*mee*·da ve·khe·ta·*rya*·na
Could you prepare a meal without ...?	¿Me puede preparar una comida sin ...?	me *pwe*·de pre·pa·*rar oo*·na ko·*mee*·da seen ...
I'm allergic to ...	Soy alérgico/a a ... m/f	soy a·*ler*·khee·ko/a a ...

SPECIAL DIETS & ALLERGIES

I'm vegetarian.	Soy vegetariano/a. m/f soy ve·khe·ta·*rya*·no/a
I'm on a special diet.	Estoy a régimen especial. es·*toy* a *re*·khee·men es·pe·*thyal*
I'm allergic to ...	Soy alérgico/a ... m/f soy a·*ler*·khee·ko/a ...

dairy produce	a los productos lácteos	a los pro·*dook*·tos *lak*·te·os
honey	a la miel	a la myel
MSG	al glutamato monosódico	al gloo·ta·*ma*·to mo·no·*so*·dee·ko
nuts	a los frutos secos	a los *froo*·tos *se*·kos
seafood	a los mariscos	a los ma·*rees*·kos
shellfish	a los crustáceos	a los kroos·*ta*·thyos

ORDERING FOOD

Is there a (vegetarian) restaurant near here?	¿Hay un restaurante (vegetariano) por aquí? ai oon res·tow·*ran*·te (ve·khe·ta·*rya*·no) por a·*kee*
Do you have vegetarian food?	¿Tienen comida vegetariana? *tye*·nen ko·*mee*·da ve·khe·ta·*rya*·na
Do you have halal food?	¿Tienen comida halal? *tye*·nen ko·*mee*·da a·*lal*
Do you have kosher food?	¿Tienen comida kosher? *tye*·nen ko·*mee*·da *ko*·sher
Do you have vegan food?	¿Tienen comida vegana? *tye*·nen ko·*mee*·da ve·*gan*·a
I don't eat red meat.	No como carne roja. no *ko*·mo *kar*·ne *ro*·kha
Is it cooked in/with butter?	¿Está cocinado en/con mantequilla? es·ta ko·thee·*na*·do en/kon man·te·*kee*·lya
Could you prepare a meal without ...?	¿Me puede preparar una comida sin ...? me *pwe*·de pre·pa·*rar oo*·na ko·*mee*·da seen ...

eggs	huevo	*we*·vo
fish	pescado	pes·*ka*·do
meat/fish stock	caldo de carne/ pescado	*kal*·do de *kar*·ne/ pes·*ka*·do
pork	cerdo	*ther*·do
poultry	aves	*a*·ves

LISTEN FOR

¿Puede comer ...?	*pwe*·de ko·*mer* ... Can you eat ...?
Le preguntaré al cocinero.	le pre·goon·ta·*re* al ko·thee·*ne*·ro I'll check with the cook.
Todo lleva (carne).	*to*·do *lye*·va (*kar*·ne) It all has (meat) in it.

Is this ...?	¿Esto es ...? *es*·to es ...

free of animal produce	sin productos de animales	seen pro·*dook*·tos de a·nee·*ma*·les
free-range	de corral	de *ko*·ral
genetically modified	transgénico	trans·*khe*·nee·ko
gluten-free	sin gluten	seen *gloo*·ten
low in sugar	bajo en azúcar	*ba*·kho en a·*thoo*·kar
low-fat	bajo en grasas	*ba*·kho en *gra*·sas
organic	orgánico	or·*ga*·nee·ko
salt-free	sin sal	seen sal

MENU Decoder

LÉXICO CULINARIO

This miniguide to Spanish cuisine lists dishes and ingredients in Spanish alphabetical order (see **alphabet**, p12). Spanish nouns have their gender indicated by ⓜ or ⓕ. If it's a plural noun, you'll also see pl.

A

acedía ⓕ a·the·*dee*·a wedge sole (flatfish)
aceite ⓜ a·*they*·te oil
— de coco de *ko*·ko coconut oil
— de girasol de khee·ra·*sol* sunflower oil
— de oliva de o·*lee*·va olive oil
— de oliva virgen extra de o·*lee*·va *veer*·khen *eks*·tra extra virgin olive oil
aceituna ⓕ a·they·*too*·na olive
— negra *ne*·gra black olive
— rellena re·*lye*·na stuffed olive
— verde *ver*·de green olive
ácido/a ⓜ/ⓕ a·thee·do/a tart (flavour)
adobo ⓜ a·*do*·bo marinade
aguacate ⓜ a·gwa·*ka*·te avocado
ajiaco ⓜ a·*khya*·ko potato soup from Colombia
(al) ajoarriero (al) a·kho·a·*rye*·ro 'mule-driver's garlic' – anything cooked in a sauce of onions, garlic & chili
alajú ⓜ a·la·*khoo* honey & almond cake
albaricoque ⓜ al·ba·ree·*ko*·ke apricot
— seco *se*·ko dried apricot
albóndigas ⓕ pl al·*bon*·dee·gas meatballs
— de pescado de pes·*ka*·do fish balls
alcachofas ⓕ pl al·ka·*cho*·fas artichokes
— guisadas a la española gee·sa·das a la es·pa·*nyo*·la artichokes in wine
— rellenas re·*lye*·nas stuffed artichokes
alcaparra ⓕ al·ka·*pa*·ra caper
alioli ⓜ a·lee·o·lee garlic & oil sauce • garlic mayonnaise
alita ⓕ a·*leet*·ta (chicken) wing
almejas ⓕ pl al·*me*·khas clams – superb eaten raw
— a la marinera a la ma·ree·*ne*·ra clams in white wine
— al horno al *or*·no baked clams
almendrado ⓜ al·men·*dra*·do almond cake or biscuit • chocolate covered ice cream bar
almendras ⓕ pl al·*men*·dras almonds
alubia ⓕ a·*loo*·bya haricot bean
alubia blanca ⓕ a·*loo*·bya blan·*ka* white bean
anacardo ⓜ a·na·*kar*·do cashew nut

anchoas ⓕ pl an·*cho*·as cured anchovy fillets
anguila ⓕ an·*gee*·la adult eel
angulas ⓕ pl an·*goo*·las baby eels – prized as a delicacy, they resemble vermicelli
— en all i pebre en al ee *pe*·bre baby eels with pepper & garlic
apio ⓜ *a*·pyo celery
arándano ⓜ a·*ran*·da·no blueberry • redcurrant • blackcurrant • cranberry
arenque ⓜ a·*ren*·ke herring
— ahumado a·oo·*ma*·do kipper
arroz ⓜ a·*roth* rice
— a banda (de València) a *ban*·da (de va·*len*·thya) fish paella
— a la Alcireña a la al·thee·*re*·nya baked rice dish
— blanco blan·*ko* white rice
— con leche kon *le*·che rice pudding
— con pollo kon *po*·lyo chicken & rice
— integral een·te·*gral* brown rice
— marinera ma·ree·*ne*·ra seafood & rice
— salvaje sal·*va*·khe wild rice
asadillo ⓜ a·sa·*dee*·lyo roasted red peppers
asados ⓜ pl a·*sa*·dos roast meats
atún ⓜ a·*toon* tuna – often served marinated & raw
— al horno al *or*·no baked tuna
avellana ⓕ a·ve·*lya*·na hazelnut
aves ⓕ pl *a*·ves poultry
azúcar ⓜ a·*thoo*·kar sugar

B

bacalao ⓜ ba·ka·*low* cod – usually salted & dried
— a la vizcaína a la veeth·ka·ee·na cod with chilies & bell peppers
— del convento del kon·*ven*·to cod with potatoes & spinach in broth
bacón ⓜ ba·*kon* bacon
barbo ⓜ *bar*·bo barbel
barra ⓕ *ba*·ra long stick of bread
batata ⓕ ba·*ta*·ta type of sweet potato
beicon ⓜ *bey*·kon streaky bacon rashers
berberechos ⓜ pl ber·be·*re*·chos cockles
— en vinagre en vee·*na*·gre cockles in vinegar
berenjenas ⓕ pl be·ren·*khe*·nas aubergines • eggplants
— a la mallorquina a la ma·lyor·*kee*·na with garlic mayonnaise
— con setas kon *se*·tas with mushrooms
berza ⓕ *ber*·tha cabbage
— a la andaluza a la an·da·*loo*·tha cabbage & meat hotpot
besugo ⓜ be·*soo*·go red bream
— a la Donostiarra a la do·nos·*tya*·ra barbecued red bream with garlic & paprika
— estilo San Sebastián es·*tee*·lo san se·bas·*tyan* barbecued red bream with garlic & paprika
bienmesabe ⓜ byen·me·*sa*·be egg yolk & almond confection
bisbe ⓜ *bees*·be black & white blood sausage
bistec ⓜ bees·*tek* steak
— con patatas kon pa·*ta*·tas steak with chips
bizcocha ⓕ **manchega** beeth·*ko*·cha man·*che*·ga cake soaked in milk, sugar, vanilla & cinnamon
bizcocho ⓜ beeth·*ko*·cho sponge cake
— de almendra de al·*men*·dra almond cake
— de avellana de a·ve·*lya*·na hazelnut cake
bizcochos ⓜ pl **borrachos** beeth·*ko*·chos bo·*ra*·chos cake soaked in liqueur
bocadillo ⓜ bo·ka·*dee*·lyo sandwich made with a baguette

bocas Ⓕ pl **de la isla** *bo*·kas de la *ees*·la large crab claws
bogavante Ⓜ bo·ga·*van*·te lobster
bollo Ⓜ *bo*·lyo crusty bread roll
boniato Ⓜ bon·ee·*a*·to type of sweet potato
bonito Ⓜ bo·*nee*·to white fleshy tuna
boquerones Ⓜ pl bo·ke·*ro*·nes anchovies marinated in wine vinegar – mostly eaten fresh, grilled or fried
— **fritos** *free*·tos fried anchovies
brócoli Ⓜ *bro*·ko·lee broccoli
bull Ⓜ **de atún** bool de a·*toon* tuna tripe
buñuelitos Ⓜ pl boo·nywe·*lee*·tos small cheese or ham fritters
— **de San José** de san kho·*se* lemon & vanilla fritters
buñuelo Ⓜ boo·*nywe*·lo fried pastry
burrida Ⓕ **de ratjada** boo·*ree*·da de rat·*kha*·da fish soup with almonds
butifarra Ⓕ **(blanca)** boo·tee·*fa*·ra (*blan*·ka) pork sausage
— **con setas** kon *se*·tas Catalan sausage with mushrooms

C

caballa Ⓕ ka·*ba*·lya mackerel
cabra Ⓕ *ka*·bra goat
cabracho Ⓜ ka·*bra*·cho scorpion fish
cacahuete Ⓜ ka·ka·*we*·te peanut
cachelos Ⓜ pl ka·*che*·los potatoes with spicy sausage & pork
calabacín Ⓜ ka·la·ba·*theen* courgette • zucchini
calabaza Ⓕ ka·la·*ba*·tha pumpkin
calamares Ⓜ pl ka·la·*ma*·res calamari – popular fried or stuffed
— **fritos a la romana** *free*·tos a la ro·*ma*·na squid rings fried in batter
— **rellenos** re·*lye*·nos stuffed squid
calçots Ⓜ pl kal·*sots* spring onion-like vegetables chargrilled and eaten with a **romesco** dipping sauce
caldeirada Ⓕ kal·dey·*ra*·da fish & potatoes in a paprika sauce • fish soup
caldereta Ⓕ kal·de·*re*·ta stew
— **asturiana** as·too·*rya*·na fish stew
— **de cordero** de kor·*de*·ro lamb stew
caldillo Ⓜ **de perro** kal·*dee*·lyo de *pe*·ro fish soup with onions & orange juice
caldo Ⓜ *kal*·do broth • clear soup • stock
— **al estilo del Mar Menor** al es·*tee*·lo del mar me·*nor* fish stew from the Mar Menor
— **gallego** ga·*lye*·go broth with haricot beans, ham & sausage
callos Ⓜ pl *ka*·lyos tripe
camagroc Ⓜ ka·ma·*grok* yellowfoot mushroom
camarones fritos Ⓜ pl ka·ma·*ro*·nes *free*·tos deep-fried prawns
cañaillas Ⓕ pl **de la Isla** ka·*nyay*·lyas de la *ees*·la boiled sea snails
canelones Ⓜ pl ka·na·*lo*·nes cannelloni
— **con espinaca** kon es·pee·*na*·ka cannelloni with spinach, anchovies & bechamel
— **con pescado** kon pes·*ka*·do cannelloni with cod, eggs & mushrooms
canapés Ⓜ pl **de fiambres** ka·na·*pes* de fee·*am*·bres mini hors d'oeuvres with ham, anchovies or cheese
cangrejo Ⓜ kan·*gre*·kho large-clawed crab usually eaten steamed or boiled
cantalupo Ⓜ kan·ta·*loo*·po cantaloupe
canutillos Ⓜ pl ka·noo·*tee*·lyos cream biscuits
capones Ⓜ pl **de Villalba** ka·*po*·nes de vee·*lyal*·ba Christmas dish of chicken marinated in brandy

caracoles ⓜ ka·ra·*ko*·les snails
caramelos ⓜ pl ka·ra·*me*·los sweets • candy
cardos ⓜ pl **fritos** *kar*·dos *free*·tos fried thistles
carne ⓕ *kar*·ne meat
— molida mo·*lee*·da minced meat
cassolada ⓕ ka·so·*la*·da potato & vegetable stew with bacon & ribs
castaña ⓕ kas·*ta*·nya chestnut
caviar ⓜ ka·*vyar* caviar
caza ⓕ *ka*·tha game
cazón ⓜ ka·*thon* dogfish or shark with a sweet scallop-like flavour
cazuelitas ⓕ pl **de langostinos San Rafael** ka·thwe·*lee*·tas de lan·gos·*tee*·nos san ra·fa·*el* baked rice with seafood
cebolla ⓕ the·*bo*·lya onion
cecina ⓕ the·*thee*·na cured meat
cerdo ⓜ *ther*·do pork
cereales ⓜ pl the·re·a·les cereal
cereza ⓕ the·*re*·tha cherry
— silvestre seel·*ves*·tre wild cherry
ciervo ⓜ *thyer*·vo deer
cigala ⓕ thee·*ga*·la langoustine
ciruela ⓕ thee·*rwe*·la plum
— pasa *pa*·sa prune
civet ⓜ **de llebre** see·*vet* de *le*·bre hare stew
chalote ⓜ cha·*lo*·te shallot
champiñones ⓜ pl cham·pee·*nyo*·nes cultivated white mushrooms
chanquetes ⓜ pl chan·*ke*·tes whitebait
(al) chilindrón (al) chee·leen·*dron* cooked in a tomato & red pepper sauce
chipirón ⓜ chee·pee·*ron* baby squid
chocolate ⓜ cho·ko·*la*·te chocolate
— blanco *blan*·ko white chocolate
— caliente ka·lee·*en*·te thick hot chocolate
— con leche kon *le*·che milk chocolate
chocos ⓜ pl *cho*·kos cuttlefish

chorizo ⓜ cho·*ree*·tho spicy red cured sausage
— de Pamplona de pam·*plo*·na fine-textured, hard chorizo
— de Salamanca de sa·la·*man*·ka chunky chorizo from Salamanca
chuletas ⓕ pl choo·*le*·tas chops • cutlets
— al sarmiento al sar·*myen*·to chops prepared over wood from vines
— de buey de bwey ox chops
— de cerdo de *ther*·do pork chops
— de cerdo a la aragonesa de *ther*·do a la a·ra·go·*ne*·sa baked pork chops with wine & onion
— de cordero de kor·*de*·ro lamb chops
— de ternera de ter·*ne*·ra veal chops • veal cutlets
chuletón ⓜ choo·*le*·ton T-bone steak
churros ⓜ *choo*·ros fried doughnut strips
cochifrito ⓜ **de cordero** ko·chee·*free*·to de kor·*de*·ro lamb fried with garlic & lemon
cochinillo ⓜ ko·chee·*nee*·lyo suckling pig
— asado a·*sa*·do roast suckling pig
— de pelotas de pe·*lo*·tas meatball stew
coco ⓜ *ko*·ko coconut
codornices ⓕ pl **a la plancha** ko·dor·*nee*·thes a la *plan*·cha grilled quail
codorniz ⓕ ko·dor·*neeth* quail
— con pimientos kon pee·*myen*·tos peppers stuffed with quail
col ⓕ kol cabbage
— lombarda lom·*bar*·da red cabbage
coles ⓕ pl **de bruselas** *ko*·les de broo·*se*·las Brussels sprouts
coliflor ⓕ ko·lee·*flor* cauliflower
conejo ⓜ ko·*ne*·kho rabbit
— de monte de *mon*·te wild rabbit
coquina ⓕ ko·*kee*·na wedge clam
corazón ⓜ ko·ra·*thon* heart

cordero ⓜ kor·de·ro lamb
— al chilindrón al chee·leen·*dron* lamb in tomato & bell pepper sauce
— con almendras kon al·*men*·dras lamb in almond sauce
costillas ⓕ pl kos·*tee*·lyas ribs
crema ⓕ *kre*·ma cream
— catalana ka·ta·*la*·na crème brûlée
— de espinacas de es·pee·*na*·kas cream of spinach soup
— de naranja de na·*ran*·kha orange cream dessert
— de San José de san kho·*se* egg custard flavoured with cinnamon
— de verduras de ver·*doo*·ras cream of vegetable soup
crocante ⓜ kro·*kan*·te ice cream with chopped nuts & chocolate

D

de soja de *so*·kha of/with soya
despojos ⓜ pl des·*po*·khos offal
dorada ⓕ do·*ra*·da gilthead bream
— a la sal a la sal salted gilthead bream
dulce ⓜ *dool*·the sweet
— de batata de ba·*ta*·ta sweet potato pudding from South America
dulces ⓜ pl *dool*·thes sweets
— de las monjas *dool*·thes de las *mon*·khas confectionery made by nuns & sold in convents or cake shops

E

embutidos ⓜ pl em·boo·*tee*·dos generic name for cured sausages
empanada ⓕ em·pa·*na*·da savoury pie
— de carne de *kar*·ne meat pie
— de espinaca de es·pee·*na*·ka spinach pie
empanadilla ⓕ em·pa·na·*dee*·lya small pastry, either sweet or savoury
empanado ⓜ em·pa·*na*·do coated in bread crumbs
empiñonado ⓜ em·pee·nyo·*na*·do small marzipan-filled pastry with pinenuts
encurtidos ⓜ pl en·koor·*tee*·dos pickles
ensaimada ⓕ en·sai·*ma*·da spiral-shaped bun made with lard
ensalada ⓕ en·sa·*la*·da salad
— de frutas de *froo*·tas fruit salad
— de patatas de pa·*ta*·tas potato salad
— del tiempo del *tyem*·po seasonal salad
— mixta *meeks*·ta mixed salad
escalivada ⓕ es·ka·lee·*va*·da roasted red peppers, aubergine & onions in olive oil
escalopes ⓜ pl **de ternera rellenos** es·ka·*lo*·pes de ter·*ne*·ra re·*lye*·nos deep fried veal cutlets stuffed with egg & cheese
espaguetis ⓜ pl es·pa·*ge*·tees spaghetti
espárragos ⓜ pl es·*pa*·ra·gos asparagus
— con dos salsas kon dos *sal*·sas asparagus & tomato or paprika mayonnaise
— en vinagreta en vee·na·*gre*·ta asparagus in vinaigrette
espinacas ⓕ pl es·pee·*na*·kas spinach
— a la catalana a la ka·ta·*la*·na spinach with pinenuts & raisins
esqueixada ⓕ es·kee·*sha*·da cod dressed with olives, tomato & onion
etxeko kopa e·*che*·ko *ko*·pa Basque ice cream dessert

F

fabada ⓕ **asturiana** fa·*ba*·da as·too·*rya*·na stew made with pork, blood sausage & white beans

faisán ⓜ fai·*san* pheasant
faves ⓕ pl **a la catalana** *fa*·ves a la ka·ta·*la*·na broad beans with ham
fiambres ⓜ pl fee·*am*·bres cold meats
— surtidos soor·*tee*·dos selection of cold meats
fideos ⓜ pl fee·*de*·os pasta noodles
fideuà ⓕ fee·*de*·wa short noodles with fish & shellfish
fideus ⓜ pl **a la cassola** fee·*de*·oos a la ka·*so*·la Catalan noodle dish
filete ⓜ fee·*le*·te steak • any boneless slice of meat
— a la parrilla a la pa·*ree*·lya grilled beef steak
— de ternera de ter·*ne*·ra beef steak
filloas ⓕ pl fee·*lyo*·as Galician pancakes, savoury or sweet
flan ⓜ flan creme caramel
flaó ⓕ fla·*o* sweet cheese flan
flor manchega ⓕ flor man·*che*·ga deep-fried pastry shaped like flower
frambuesa ⓕ fram·*bwe*·sa raspberry
frangellos ⓜ pl fran·*khe*·lyos sweet made from cornmeal, milk & honey
fresa ⓕ *fre*·sa strawberry
fricandó ⓜ free·kan·*do* Catalan beef stew
frite ⓜ *free*·te lamb stew, served on festive occasions
fritos ⓜ pl *free*·tos fried
— con miel kon myel honey-roasted fritters
fritura ⓕ free·*too*·ra mixed fried fish
fruta ⓕ *froo*·ta fruit
— variada va·*ree*·a·da selection of fresh fruit
frutas ⓕ pl **en almibar** *froo*·tas en al·*mee*·bar fruit in syrup
frutos ⓜ pl **secos** *froo*·tos *se*·kos nuts
fuet ⓕ foo·*et* thin cured sausage

G

gachas ⓕ pl **manchegas** *ga*·chas man·*che*·gas porridge made from flour, garlic & paprika
galleta ⓕ ga·*lye*·ta biscuit • cookie
gambas ⓕ pl *gam*·bas prawns
— a la plancha a la *plan*·cha grilled prawns
— en gabardina en ga·bar·*dee*·na prawns in batter
Gamonedo ⓜ ga·mo·*ne*·do sharp-tasting cheese, smoked & cured
garbanzos ⓜ pl gar·*ban*·thos chickpeas
— con cebolla kon the·*bo*·lya chickpeas in onion sauce
— tostados tos·*ta*·dos roasted chickpeas (sold as a snack)
Gata-Hurdes ga·ta·*oor*·des cheese
gazpacho ⓜ gath·*pa*·cho cold tomato soup
— andaluz an·da·*looz* cold tomato soup with chopped salad vegetables
— pastoril pas·to·*reel* rabbit stew with tomato & garlic
gazpachos ⓜ pl **manchegos** gath·*pa*·chos man·*che*·gos game & vegetable hotpot
Gaztazarra ⓜ gath·ta·*tha*·ra cheese
gofio ⓜ *go*·fyo toasted cornmeal or barley
grano ⓜ *gra*·no grain
— largo *lar*·go long grain (rice)
gratinado ⓜ **de berenjenas** gra·tee·*na*·do de be·ren·*khe*·nas aubergine gratin • eggplant gratin
Grazalema ⓕ gra·tha·*le*·ma semi-cured sheep's milk cheese
guindilla ⓕ geen·*dee*·lya mild green chili
guisado ⓜ gee·*sa*·do stew
— de cordero de kor·*de*·ro lamb ragout
— de ternera de ter·*ne*·ra veal ragout

guisante ⓜ gee·*san*·te pea
— seco *se*·ko split pea
guisantes ⓜ pl **con jamón** gee·*san*·tes kon kha·*mon* pea & ham dish
guisat ⓜ **de marisco** gee·*sat* de ma·*rees*·ko stew made with seafood
guiso ⓜ **de conejo estilo canario** *gee*·so de ko·*ne*·kho es·*tee*·lo ka·*na*·ryo rabbit stew
guiso ⓜ **de rabo de toro** *gee*·so de *ra*·bo de *to*·ro oxtail stew

H

habas ⓕ pl *a*·bas broad beans
— a la granadina a la gra·na·*dee*·na broad beans with eggs & ham
— fritas *free*·tas fried broad beans (sold as a snack)
hamburguesa ⓕ am·boor·*ge*·sa hamburger
harina ⓕ a·*ree*·na flour
— integral een·te·*gral* wholemeal flour
helado ⓜ e·*la*·do ice cream
hígado ⓜ *ee*·ga·do liver
higo ⓜ *ee*·go fig
— seco *se*·ko dried fig
hogaza ⓕ o·*ga*·tha dense round loaf
hoja ⓕ **de parra** o·kha de *pa*·ra vine leaf
hojaldres ⓜ pl o·*khal*·dres small flaky pastries covered in sugar
hojas ⓕ pl **verdes** o·khas *ver*·des green vegetables
hornazo ⓜ or·*na*·tho bread stuffed with sausage
hortalizas ⓕ pl or·ta·*lee*·thas vegetables
huevo ⓜ *we*·vo egg
— cocido ko·*thee*·do boiled egg
— de chocolate de cho·ko·*la*·te chocolate egg
— frito *free*·to fried egg
huevos ⓜ pl *we*·vos egg dishes
— a la flamenca a la fla·*men*·ka baked vegetables with egg & ham
— al estilo Sóller al es·*tee*·lo *so*·lyer fried eggs served with a milk & vegetable sauce
— escalfados es·kal·*fa*·dos poached eggs
— revueltos re·*vwel*·tos scrambled eggs

J

jabalí ⓜ kha·ba·*lee* wild boar
— con salsa de castaños kon *sal*·sa de kas·*ta*·nyos wild boar in chestnut sauce
jamón ⓜ kha·*mon* ham
— cocido ko·*thee*·do cooked ham
— ibérico ee·*ber*·ik·o ham from the Iberian pig, said to be the best in Spain
— serrano se·*ra*·no cured mountain ham
jengibre ⓜ khen·*gee*·bre ginger
jerez (al) khe·*reth* (al) in a sherry sauce
judía ⓕ khoo·*dee*·a bean
judías ⓕ pl **del tío Lucas** khoo·*dee*·as del *tee*·o *loo*·kas bean stew with garlic & bacon
judías ⓕ pl **verdes a la castellana** khoo·*dee*·as *ver*·des a la kas·te·*lya*·na fried peppers, garlic & green beans
judiones ⓜ pl **de la granja** kho·dee·o·nes de la *gran*·kha pork & bean stew

K

kiskilla kees·*kee*·lya shrimp (also spelled **quisquilla**)

L

langosta ⓕ lan·*gos*·ta lobster
— a la ibicenca a la ee·bee·*then*·ka lobster with stuffed squid

langostinos ⓜ pl lan·gos·*tee*·nos king prawns
— a la plancha a la *plan*·cha grilled king prawns
lechuga ⓕ le·*choo*·ga lettuce
legumbres ⓕ pl le·*goom*·bres pulses
— secas *se*·kas dried pulses
lengua ⓕ *len*·gwa tongue
— a la aragonesa a la a·ra·go·*ne*·sa tongue in tomato & bell pepper sauce
lenguado ⓜ len·*gwa*·do sole
— al chacolí con hongos al cha·ko·*lee* kon *on*·gos sole with white wine & mushrooms
lenguados ⓜ pl **al plato** len·*gwa*·dos al *pla*·to sole & mushroom casserole
lenguas ⓕ pl **con salsa de almendras** *len*·gwas kon *sal*·sa de al·*men*·dras tongue in almond sauce
lentejas ⓕ pl len·*te*·khas lentils
liebre ⓕ *lye*·bre hare
— con castañas kon kas·*ta*·nyas hare with chestnuts
— estofada es·to·*fa*·da stewed hare
lima ⓕ *lee*·ma lime
limón ⓜ lee·*mon* lemon
llagostí ⓜ **a l'allioli** lyan·gos·*tee* a la·lyee·o·lee grilled prawns in garlic mayonnaise
llenguado ⓜ **a la nyoca** lyen·*gwa*·do a la *nyo*·ka sole with pine nuts & raisins
lomo ⓜ *lo*·mo fillet • loin • sirloin
— curado koo·*ra*·do cured pork sausage
— de cerdo de *ther*·do loin of pork
longaniza ⓕ lon·ga·*nee*·tha long & skinny cured sausage
lubina ⓕ loo·*bee*·na sea bass
— a la marinera a la ma·ree·*ne*·ra sea bass in parsley sauce

M

macedonia ⓕ **de frutas** ma·the·*do*·nya de *froo*·tas fruit salad
macedonia ⓕ **de verduras** ma·the·*do*·nya de ver·*doo*·ras mixed vegetables
magdalena ⓕ ma·da·*le*·na small cake to dunk in coffee
magras ⓕ pl *ma*·gras fried eggs, ham, cheese & tomato
maíz ⓜ ma·*eeth* maize • corn
— dulce *dool*·the sweetcorn
mandarina ⓕ man·da·*ree*·na tangerine • mandarin • satsuma
mango ⓜ *man*·go mango
manitas ⓕ pl **de cerdo** ma·*nee*·tas de *ther*·do pig's trotters
manteca ⓕ man·*te*·ka lard
mantecado ⓜ man·te·*ka*·do a soft lard biscuit • dairy ice cream
mantequilla ⓕ man·te·*kee*·lya butter
— sin sal seen sal unsalted butter
manzana ⓕ man·*tha*·na apple
manzanas ⓕ **asadas** man·*tha*·nas a·*sa*·das baked apples
maracuyá ⓜ mar·ra·koo·*ya* passion fruit
margarina ⓕ mar·ga·*ree*·na margarine
marinera (a la) ma·ree·*ne*·ra (a la) cooked or served in a white wine sauce
mariscos ⓜ ma·*rees*·kos shellfish • seafood
marmitako mar·mee·*ta*·ko fresh tuna & potato casserole
mar y cel ⓜ mar ee sel dish of sausages, rabbit, shrimp & angler fish
masa ⓕ *ma*·sa pastry (dough)
mayonesa ⓕ ma·yo·*ne*·sa mayonnaise
medallones ⓜ pl **de merluza** me·da·*lyo*·nes de mer·*loo*·tha hake steaks

mejillones ⓜ pl me·khee·*lyo*·nes mussels
— **al vino blanco** al *vee*·no *blan*·ko mussels in white wine
— **con salsa** kon *sal*·sa mussels with tomato sauce
mel ⓕ **i mató** mel ee ma·*to* dessert of curd cheese with honey
melocotón ⓜ me·lo·ko·*ton* peach
melocotones ⓜ pl **al vino** me·lo·ko·*to*·nes al *vee*·no peaches in red wine
melón ⓜ me·*lon* melon
membrillo ⓜ mem·*bree*·lyo quince jelly
menestra ⓕ me·*nes*·tra mixed vegetable stew
— **de pollo** de *po*·lyo chicken & vegetable stew
merengue ⓜ me·*ren*·ge meringue
merluza ⓕ mer·*loo*·tha hake
mermelada ⓕ mer·me·*la*·da marmalade
mero ⓜ *me*·ro grouper
miel ⓕ myel honey
— **de azahar** de a·tha·*ar* orange blossom honey
— **de caña** de *ka*·nya treacle
migas ⓕ pl *mee*·gas fried cubes of bread with bell peppers
— **a la aragonesa** a la a·ra·go·*ne*·sa fried bread with bacon rashers in tomato sauce
moje ⓜ **manchego** *mo*·khe man·*che*·go cold broth with black olives
mojete ⓜ mo·*khe*·te dipping sauce for bread, made from potatoes, garlic, tomatoes & paprika
— **murciano** moor·*thya*·no fish & bell pepper dish
mojo ⓜ *mo*·kho spicy bell pepper sauce
mollejas ⓕ pl mo·*lye*·khas sweetbreads
mollete ⓜ mo·*lye*·te soft round bap roll
monas ⓕ pl **de pascua** *mo*·nas de *pas*·kwa Easter cakes • figures made of chocolate
mongetes ⓕ pl **seques i butifarra** mon·*zhe*·tes *se*·kes ee boo·tee·*fa*·ra haricot beans with roasted pork sausage
mora ⓕ *mo*·ra blackberry
moraga ⓕ **de sardina** mo·*ra*·ga de sar·*dee*·na sardines cooked over a fire
morcilla ⓕ mor·*thee*·lya black pudding, often stewed with beans & vegetables
mortadela ⓕ mor·ta·*de*·la mortadella sausage
morteruelo ⓜ mor·te·*rwe*·lo pate dish containing offal, game & spices
mostachones ⓜ pl mos·ta·*cho*·nes small cakes for dipping in coffee or hot chocolate (also spelled **mostatxones**)
mostaza ⓕ mos·*ta*·tha mustard
— **en grano** en *gra*·no mustard seed
mousse ⓜ **de chocolate** moos de cho·ko·*la*·te chocolate mousse
múgil ⓜ *moo*·kheel grey mullet
mujol ⓜ moo·*khol* mullet
múrgolas ⓕ pl *mur*·go·las morel mushrooms
muslo ⓜ *moos*·lo (chicken) leg & thigh

N

nabo ⓜ *na*·bo root vegetable • turnip
naranja ⓕ na·*ran*·kha orange
nata ⓕ *na*·ta cream
— **agria** a·grya sour cream
— **montada** mon·*ta*·da whipped cream
natillas ⓕ pl na·*tee*·lyas creamy custard dessert
— **de chocolate** de cho·ko·*la*·te chocolate custard

navaja (f) na·*va*·kha razor clam
nécora (f) *ne*·ko·ra small crab
nueces (f) pl *new*·thes nuts
nuez (f) nweth walnut
— de América de a·*me*·ree·ka pecan nut

Ñ

ñora (f) *nyo*·ra sweet red pepper (usually dried)

O

oca (f) *o*·ka goose
olla (f) *o*·lya meat & vegetable stew • cooking pot
oreja (f) **de mar** o·*re*·kha de mar abalone
ostiones (m) pl **a la gaditana** os·*tyo*·nes a la ga·dee·*ta*·na Cádiz oysters with garlic, parsley & bread crumbs
ostra (f) *os*·tra oyster
oveja (f) o·*ve*·kha mutton

P

pa (m) **amb oli** pa amb *o*·lee toasted bread with garlic & olive oil
pacana (f) pa·*ka*·na pecan
paella (f) pa·*e*·lya rice dish which has many regional variations
— marinera ma·ree·*ne*·ra paella with fish & seafood
— zamorana tha·mo·*ra*·na paella with meat
palitos (m) pl **de queso** pa·*lee*·tos de *ke*·so cheese straws
palmera (f) pal·*me*·ra leaf-shaped flaky pastry, often coated in chocolate
palomitas (f) pl pa·lo·*mee*·tas popcorn
pan (m) pan bread
— aceite a·*they*·te flat round bread
— árabe *a*·ra·be pita bread
— de Alá de a·*la* 'Allah's Bread' – dessert
— de boda de *bo*·da sculpted bread traditionally made for weddings
— de centeno de then·*te*·no rye bread
— duro *doo*·ro stale bread, used for toasting & eating with olive oil
— integral een·te·*gral* wholemeal bread
panaché (m) pa·na·*che* mixed vegetable stew
panceta (f) pan·*the*·ta salt-cured, streaky bacon
panchineta (f) pan·chee·*ne*·ta puff pastry with cream
panecillo (m) pa·ne·*thee*·lyo small bread roll
panellets (m) pl pa·ne·*lyets* small marzipan-filled balls rolled in pine nuts
papas (f) pl **arrugadas** *pa*·pas a·roo·*ga*·das small unpeeled & salted boiled potatoes
pargo (m) *par*·go sea bream
parrillada (f) pa·ree·*lya*·da grilled meat
— de mariscos de ma·*rees*·kos seafood grill
pastel (m) pas·*tel* cake
— de atún de a·*toon* baked tuna loaf
— de boda de *bo*·da wedding cake
— de chocolate de cho·ko·*la*·te chocolate cake
— de cierva de *thyer*·va meat pie
— de cumpleaños de koom·ple·*a*·nyos birthday cake
pastelitos (m) pl **de miel** pas·te·*lee*·tos de myel honey fritters
pataco (m) pa·*ta*·ko tuna & potato stew
patatas (f) pl pa·*ta*·tas potatoes
— a la riojana a la ree·o·*kha*·na potatoes with chorizo & paprika
— alioli a·lee·o·lee potatoes in garlic mayonnaise

— **bravas** *bra*·vas potatoes in spicy tomato sauce
— **con chorizo** kon cho·*ree*·tho potatoes with chorizo
— **estofadas** es·to·*fa*·das stewed potatoes
pato ⓜ *pa*·to duck
— **a la sevillana** a la se·vee·*lya*·na duck with orange sauce
— **alcaparrada** al·ka·pa·*ra*·da duck with capers & almonds
pavo ⓜ *pa*·vo turkey
pececillos ⓜ pl pe·the·*thee*·lyos small fish
pechina ⓕ pe·*chee*·na scallop
pecho ⓜ *pe*·cho breast of lamb
pechuga ⓕ pe·*choo*·ga breast of poultry
pepinillo ⓜ pe·pee·*nee*·lyo gherkin • pickle
pepino ⓜ pe·*pee*·no cucumber
pepitoria ⓕ pe·pee·*to*·rya sauce made with egg & almond
pera ⓕ *pe*·ra pear
La Peral ⓕ la pe·*ral* soft cheese
perca ⓕ *per*·ka perch
perdices ⓕ pl per·*dee*·thes partridges
— **a la manchega** a la man·*che*·ga partridge in red wine & bell peppers
— **con chocolate** kon cho·ko·*la*·te partridge with chocolate
perdiz ⓕ per·*deeth* partridge
peregrina ⓕ pe·re·*gree*·na scallop
pericana ⓕ pe·ree·*ka*·na dish of dried peppers, salt cod, olives & olive oil
perrito ⓜ **caliente** pe·*ree*·to ka·lee·*en*·te hot dog
pescada ⓕ **á galega** pes·*ka*·da a ga·*le*·ga hake fried in olive oil & served with garlic & paprika sauce
pescadilla ⓕ pes·ka·*dee*·lya young hake
pescaditos ⓜ pl **rebozados** pes·ka·*dee*·tos re·bo·*tha*·dos small fish fried in batter
pescado ⓜ pes·*ka*·do fish
— **a l'all cremat** a lal kre·*mat* fish in burnt garlic
pescaíto ⓜ **frito** pes·ka·*ee*·to *free*·to tiny fried fish
pestiños ⓜ pl pes·*tee*·nyos honey-coated aniseed pastries, fried with filling
pez ⓕ **espada** peth es·*pa*·da swordfish
picada ⓕ pee·*ka*·da mixture of garlic, parsley, toasted almonds & nuts, often used to thicken sauces
picadillo ⓜ pee·ka·*dee*·lyo ground meat or salad with diced vegetables
— **de atún** de a·*toon* salad made with diced tuna & bell peppers
— **de ternera** de ter·*ne*·ra minced or ground beef
pichón ⓜ pee·*chon* pigeon
pichones ⓜ pl **asados** pee·*cho*·nes a·*sa*·dos roast pigeons
pilotes ⓕ pl pee·*lo*·tes Catalan meatballs
pimiento ⓜ pee·*myen*·to bell pepper
— **amarillo** a·ma·*ree*·lyo yellow pepper
— **rojo** *ro*·kho red pepper
— **verde** *ver*·de green pepper
pimientos ⓜ pl pee·*myen*·tos peppers (the ones from El Bierzo are especially good)
— **a la riojana** a la ree·o·*kha*·na roast red pepper fried in oil & garlic
— **al chilindrón** al chee·leen·*dron* pepper casserole
piña ⓕ *pee*·nya pineapple
pinchito ⓜ **moruno** peen·*chee*·to mo·*roo*·no lamb & chicken kebabs
piñón ⓜ pee·*nyon* pinenut
pinta ⓕ *peen*·ta pinto bean
pintada ⓕ peen·*ta*·da guinea fowl
piquillo ⓜ pee·*kee*·lyo sweet & spicy peppers
pistacho ⓜ pees·*ta*·cho pistachio nut

pisto ⓜ **manchego** *pees*·to man·*che*·go courgette (zucchini) with bell peppers & tomato, fried or stewed
plátano ⓜ *pla*·ta·no banana
pochas ⓕ pl *po*·chas beans
— a la riojana a la ree·o·*kha*·na beans with chorizo in spicy paprika sauce
— con almejas kon al·*me*·khas beans with clams
pollo ⓜ *po*·lyo chicken
— asado a·*sa*·do roast chicken
— con samfaina kon sam·*fai*·na chicken with mixed vegetables
— en escabeche en es·ka·*be*·che marinated chicken
— en salsa de ajo en *sal*·sa de *a*·kho chicken in garlic sauce
— granadina gra·na·*dee*·na chicken with wine & ham
— y langosta ee lan·*gos*·ta chicken with crayfish
polvorón ⓜ pol·vo·*ron* almond shortbread, often eaten at Christmas
pomelo ⓜ po·*me*·lo grapefruit
postre ⓜ *pos*·tre dessert
— de naranja de na·*ran*·kha cream-filled oranges
potaje ⓜ po·*ta*·khe stew
— castellano kas·te·*lya*·no broth with beans & sausages
— de garbanzos de gar·*ban*·thos broth with chickpeas
— de lentejas de len·*te*·khas lentil broth
— gitano ⓜ khee·*ta*·no Andalucian chickpea & tripe stew
pote ⓜ **gallego** *po*·te ga·*lye*·go pork, bean & greens stew
potito ⓜ po·*tee*·to jar of baby food
pringada ⓕ preen·*ga*·da bread dipped in sauce • sandwich made with meat left over from cocido
productos ⓜ pl **ecológicos** pro·*dook*·tos e·ko·*lo*·khee·kos organic produce
productos ⓜ pl **del mar** pro·*dook*·tos del mar seafood products
productos ⓜ pl **lácteos** pro·*dook*·tos *lak*·te·os dairy products
puchero ⓜ poo·*che*·ro casserole
pudin ⓜ *poo*·din pudding
puerro ⓜ *pwe*·ro leek
pulpo ⓜ *pool*·po octopus
— ⓜ **a feira** *pool*·po a *fey*·ra spicy boiled octopus with paprika
punta ⓕ **de diamante** *poon*·ta de dya·*man*·te confection from Valencia
porrusalda ⓕ po·roo·*sal*·da cod & potato stew

Q

queso ⓜ *ke*·so cheese
— azul a·*thool* blue cheese
— crema *kre*·ma cream cheese
quisquilla ⓕ kees·*kee*·lya shrimp (also spelled **kiskilla**)

R

rábano ⓜ *ra*·ba·no radish
rabas ⓕ **en salsa verde** *ra*·bas en *sal*·sa *ver*·de squid in green sauce
rape ⓜ *ra*·pe monkfish
— a la gallega a la ga·*lye*·ga monkfish with potatoes & garlic sauce
— a la Monistrol a la mo·nees·*trol* monkfish with bechamel sauce
redondo ⓜ re·*don*·do round (of beef)
— al horno al *or*·no roast beef
regañaos ⓜ pl re·ga·*nya*·os flatbread topped with sardines & red pepper
relleno ⓜ re·*lye*·no stuffing
remolacha ⓕ re·mo·*la*·cha beetroot • beet
reo ⓜ *re*·o sea trout
repollo ⓜ re·*po*·lyo cabbage
repostería ⓕ re·pos·te·*ree*·a confectionery
requesón ⓜ re·ke·*son* cottage cheese

riñón ⓜ *ree·nyon* kidney
róbalo ⓜ *ro·ba·lo* sea bass
rodaballo ⓜ *ro·da·ba·lyo* turbot
romero ⓜ *ro·me·ro* rosemary
romesco ⓜ *ro·mes·ko* sweet red pepper, almond & garlic sauce
rosca ⓕ **de carne** *ros·ka de kar·ne* ring-shaped meatloaf
rosco ⓜ *ros·ko* small sweet bun
rossejat ⓜ *ro·se·dyat* rice or noodles with fish & shellfish
rovellons ⓜ pl **a la plancha** *ro·ve·lyons a la plan·cha* garlic mushrooms
ruibarbo ⓜ *roo·ee·bar·bo* rhubarb

S

salchicha ⓕ *sal·chee·cha* pork sausage
salchichón ⓜ *sal·chee·chon* cured & peppery white sausage
salmón ⓜ *sal·mon* salmon
— a la ribereña *a la ree·be·re·nya* salmon in a cider sauce
— ahumado *a·oo·ma·do* smoked salmon
salmonete ⓜ *sal·mo·ne·te* red mullet
salmorejo ⓜ *sal·mo·re·kho* thick gazpacho soup made from tomato, bread, olive oil, vinegar, garlic & green pepper
— de Córdoba *de kor·do·ba* gazpacho soup made with more vinegar than usual
salpicón ⓜ *sal·pee·kon* fish or meat salad
salsa ⓕ *sal·sa* sauce
— alioli *a·lee·o·lee* garlic mayonnaise
— de holandesa *de o·lan·de·sa* hollandaise sauce
— de mayonesa *de ma·yo·ne·sa* mayonnaise sauce
— de tomate *de to·ma·te* tomato sauce
— inglesa *een·gle·sa* Worcestershire sauce
— tártara *tar·ta·ra* tartar sauce
— verde *ver·de* parsley & garlic sauce
samfaina ⓕ *sam·fai·na* slow-cooked vegetables, similar to ratatouille
sancocho ⓜ *san·ko·cho* fish dish served with potatoes
— canario *ka·na·ryo* baked monkfish with potatoes
sandía ⓕ *san·dee·a* watermelon
sándwich ⓜ *san·dweech* sandwich
— mixto *meeks·to* toasted ham & cheese sandwich
sardinas ⓕ *sar·dee·nas* sardines
— a la parrilla *a la pa·ree·lya* sardines grilled
— en cazuela *en ka·thwe·la* sardines served in a clay pot
sargo ⓜ *sar·go* bream
sepia ⓕ *se·pya* cuttlefish
sesos ⓜ pl *se·sos* brains
setas ⓕ pl *se·tas* wild mushrooms
— a la kashera *a la ka·she·ra* sauteed wild mushrooms
— rellenas *re·lye·nas* stuffed mushrooms
sofrit pagés ⓜ *so·freet pa·zhes* vegetable stew
sofrito ⓜ *so·free·to* sautéed base of onion, garlic, tomato
soja ⓕ *so·kha* soya bean
soldaditos ⓜ pl **de Pavía** *sol·da·dee·tos de pa·vee·a* cod fritters
solomillo ⓜ *so·lo·mee·lyo* fillet
sopa ⓕ *so·pa* soup
— del día *del dee·a* soup of the day
sopas ⓕ pl **de leche** *so·pas de le·che* pieces of bread soaked in milk & cinnamon
sopas ⓕ pl **engañadas** *so·pas en·ga·nya·das* soup made from bell pepper, onion shoots, vinegar, figs & grapes

sorbete ⓜ sor·*be*·te sorbet
sorroputún ⓜ so·ro·poo·*toon* tuna casserole
suizo ⓜ *swee*·tho sugared bun
sukaldi soo·*kal*·dee beef stew
suquet ⓜ soo·*ket* fish stew
suspiros ⓜ pl **de monja** soos·*pee*·ros de *mon*·kha 'nun's sighs' – custard sweets

T

tallarines ⓜ pl ta·lya·*ree*·nes pasta noodles • wedge clams
tarta ⓕ *tar*·ta cake • tart
— de almendra de al·*men*·dra almond tart
— de manzana de man·*tha*·na apple tart
tartaleta ⓕ tar·ta·*le*·ta tartlet
tartaletas ⓕ pl **de huevos revueltos** tar·ta·*le*·tas de *we*·vos re·*vwel*·tos scrambled egg tartlets
ternera ⓕ ter·*ne*·ra veal
— a la sevillana a la se·vee·*lya*·na veal served with wine & olives
— en cazuela con berenjenas en ka·*thwe*·la kon be·ren·*khe*·nas veal & aubergine (eggplant) casserole
tirabeque ⓜ tee·ra·*be*·ke mangetout
tocino ⓜ to·*thee*·no salted pork • bacon
— del cielo del *thye*·lo creamy dessert made with egg yolk & sugar, with a caramel topping
tomate ⓜ to·*ma*·te tomato
— (de) pera (de) *pe*·ra plum tomato
— frito *free*·to tinned tomato sauce
tomates ⓜ pl to·*ma*·tes tomatoes
— enteros y pelados en·*te*·ros ee pe·*la*·dos tinned whole tomatoes
— rellenos de atún re·*lye*·nos de a·*toon* tomatoes stuffed with tuna
topinambur ⓜ top·een·am·*boor* Jerusalem artichoke
toro ⓜ *to*·ro bull meat
torrefacto ⓜ to·re·*fak*·to sugar-roasted coffee beans
torrija ⓕ to·*ree*·kha French toast
torta ⓕ *tor*·ta pie • tart • flat bread
— de aceite de a·*they*·te sweet, flat cake or biscuit made with oil
— pascualina pas·kwa·*lee*·na spinach & egg pie, eaten at Easter
tortilla ⓕ tor·*tee*·lya omelette
— española es·pa·*nyo*·la potato & onion omelette
— francesa fran·*the*·sa plain omelette
tortillas ⓕ pl **de camarones** tor·*tee*·lyas de ka·ma·*ro*·nes prawn fritters
tortita ⓕ tor·*tee*·ta small pancake
tostada ⓕ tos·*ta*·da toasted bread
tripas ⓕ pl *tree*·pas intestines • tripe
trucha ⓕ *troo*·cha trout
— a la marinera a la ma·ree·*ne*·ra trout in a white wine sauce
truchas ⓕ pl *troo*·chas trout
— a la navarra a la na·*va*·ra trout with ham
— con vino y romero kon *vee*·no ee ro·*me*·ro trout with red wine & rosemary
trufa ⓕ *troo*·fa truffle
— tarta *tar*·ta chocolate truffle cake
tumbet (de peix) ⓜ toom·*bet* (de peysh) layered onion, aubergine (eggplant), pepper, & potato (with fish)
turrón ⓜ too·*ron* Spanish nougat

U

uva ⓕ *oo*·va grape
— de corinto de ko·*reen*·to currant
— pasa *pa*·sa raisin
— sultana sool·*ta*·na sultana

V

vacuno ⓜ va·*koo*·no beef
venado ⓜ ve·*na*·do venison
verduras ⓕ ver·*doo*·ras vegetables
vieira ⓕ vee·*ey*·ra scallop
villagodio ⓜ vee·lya·*go*·dyo large steak
vinagre ⓜ vee·*na*·gre vinegar

Y

yemas ⓕ pl *ye*·mas small round cakes • egg yolks
yogur ⓜ yo·*goor* yoghurt

Z

zanahoria ⓕ tha·na·o·rya carrot
zarangollo ⓜ tha·ran·*go*·lyo fried courgette (zucchini) & onion, often with egg
zarzamora ⓕ thar·tha·*mo*·ra blackberry
zarzuela ⓕ **de mariscos** thar·*thwe*·la de ma·*rees*·kos shellfish stew
zarzuela ⓕ **de pescado** thar·*thwe*·la de pes·*ka*·do fish in stew
zurrukutano ⓜ thoo·roo·koo·*ta*·no cod & green pepper soup

DICTIONARY

English to Spanish

INGLÉS–ESPAÑOL

Nouns in the dictionary have their gender indicated by ⓜ or ⓕ. If it's a plural noun, you'll also see pl. Where a word that could be either a noun or a verb has no gender indicated, it's a verb.

A

(to be) able poder po·*der*
aboard a bordo a *bor*·do
abortion aborto ⓜ a·*bor*·to
about sobre *so*·bre
above arriba a·*ree*·ba
abroad en el extranjero en el eks·tran·*khe*·ro
accept aceptar a·thep·*tar*
accident accidente ⓜ ak·thee·*den*·te
accommodation alojamiento ⓜ a·lo·kha·*myen*·to
across a través a tra·*ves*
activist activista ⓜ&ⓕ ak·tee·*vees*·ta
acupuncture acupuntura ⓕ a·koo·poon·*too*·ra
adaptor adaptador ⓜ a·dap·ta·*dor*
address dirección ⓕ dee·rek·*thyon*
administration administración ⓕ ad·mee·nees·tra·*thyon*
admission price precio ⓜ de entrada *pre*·thyo de en·*tra*·da
admit admitir ad·mee·*teer*
adult adulto ⓜ a·*dool*·to
advertisement anuncio ⓜ a·*noon*·thyo
advice consejo ⓜ kon·*se*·kho
aerobics aeróbics ⓜ ai·*ro*·beeks
Africa África ⓕ *a*·free·ka
after después de des·*pwes* de
aftershave aftershave *ahf*·ter·sha·eev
again otra vez *o*·tra veth
age edad ⓕ e·*dad*
aggressive agresivo/a ⓜ/ⓕ a·gre·*see*·vo/a
agree estar de acuerdo es·*tar* de a·*kwer*·do
agriculture agricultura ⓕ a·gree·kul·*too*·ra
AIDS SIDA ⓜ *see*·da
air aire ⓜ *ai*·re
air mail por vía aérea por *vee*·a a·*e*·re·a
air-conditioned con aire acondicionado kon *ai*·re a·kon·dee·thyo·*na*·do
air-conditioning aire ⓜ acondicionado *ai*·re a·kon·dee·thyo·*na*·do
airline aerolínea ⓕ ai·ro·*lee*·nya
airport aeropuerto ⓜ ai·ro·*pwer*·to
alarm clock despertador ⓜ des·per·ta·*dor*
alcohol alcohol ⓜ al·*kol*
all todo *to*·do
allergy alergia ⓕ a·*ler*·khya
allow permitir per·mee·*teer*
almonds almendras ⓕ pl al·*men*·dras
almost casi *ka*·see

alone solo/a ⓜ/ⓕ so·lo/a
already ya ya
also también tam·*byen*
altar altar ⓜ al·*tar*
altitude altura ⓕ al·*too*·ra
always siempre *syem*·pre
amateur aficionado/a ⓜ/ⓕ a·fee·thyo·*na*·do/a
ambassador embajador/embajadora ⓜ/ⓕ em·ba·kha·*dor*/em·ba·kha·*do*·ra
among entre *en*·tre
anarchist anarquista ⓜ&ⓕ a·nar·*kees*·ta
ancient antiguo/a ⓜ/ⓕ an·*tee*·gwo/a
and y ee
angry enfadado/a ⓜ/ⓕ en·fa·*da*·do/a
animal animal ⓜ a·nee·*mal*
ankle tobillo ⓜ to·*bee*·lyo
annoying pesado/a ⓜ/ⓕ pe·*sa*·do/a
answer respuesta ⓕ res·*pwes*·ta
ant hormiga ⓕ or·*mee*·ga
anthology antología ⓕ an·to·lo·*khee*·a
antibiotics antibióticos ⓜ pl an·tee·*byo*·tee·kos
antique antigüedad ⓕ an·tee·gwe·*dad*
antiseptic antiséptico ⓜ an·tee·*sep*·tee·ko
any (some) alguno/a ⓜ/ⓕ al·*goo*·no/a
any (whichever) cualquier ⓜ&ⓕ kwal·*kyer*
appendix apéndice ⓜ a·*pen*·dee·the
apple manzana ⓕ man·*tha*·na
appointment cita ⓕ *thee*·ta
apricot albaricoque ⓜ al·ba·ree·*ko*·ke
archaeological arqueológico/a ⓜ/ⓕ ar·keo·*lo*·khee·ko/a
architect arquitecto/a ⓜ/ⓕ ar·kee·*tek*·to/a
architecture arquitectura ⓕ ar·kee·tek·*too*·ra
argue discutir dees·koo·*teer*
arm brazo ⓜ *bra*·tho
army ejército ⓜ e·*kher*·thee·to
arrest detener de·te·*ner*
arrivals llegadas ⓕ pl lye·*ga*·das
arrive llegar lye·*gar*
art arte ⓜ *ar*·te
art gallery museo ⓜ de arte moo·*se*·o de *ar*·te
artichoke alcachofa ⓕ al·ka·*cho*·fa
artist artista ⓜ&ⓕ ar·*tees*·ta
ashtray cenicero ⓜ the·nee·*the*·ro
Asia Asia ⓕ *a*·sya
ask (a question) preguntar pre·goon·*tar*
ask (for something) pedir pe·*deer*
aspirin aspirina ⓕ as·pee·*ree*·na
assault asalto ⓜ a·*sal*·to
asthma asma ⓜ *as*·ma
athletics atletismo ⓜ at·le·*tees*·mo
atmosphere atmósfera ⓕ at·*mos*·fe·ra
aubergine berenjenas ⓕ be·ren·*khe*·nas
aunt tía ⓕ *tee*·a
Australia Australia ⓕ ow·*stra*·lya
autumn otoño ⓜ o·*to*·nyo
avenue avenida ⓕ a·ve·*nee*·da
avocado aguacate ⓜ a·gwa·*ka*·te

B

B&W (film) blanco y negro *blan*·ko ee *ne*·gro
baby bebé ⓜ be·*be*
baby food comida ⓕ de bebé ko·*mee*·da de be·*be*
baby powder talco ⓜ *tal*·ko
babysitter canguro ⓜ kan·*goo*·ro
back (of body) espalda ⓕ es·*pal*·da
back (of chair) respaldo ⓜ res·*pal*·do
backpack mochila ⓕ mo·*chee*·la
bacon beicón ⓜ bay·*kon*
bad malo/a ⓜ/ⓕ *ma*·lo/a
bag bolso ⓜ *bol*·so
baggage equipaje ⓜ e·kee·*pa*·khe
baggage allowance ⓜ límite de equipaje *lee*·mee·te de e·kee·*pa*·khe
baggage claim recogida ⓕ de equipajes re·ko·*khee*·da de e·kee·*pa*·khes

bakery panadería (f) pa·na·de·ree·a
balance (account) saldo (m) sal·do
balcony balcón (m) bal·kon
ball pelota (f) pe·lo·ta
ballet ballet (m) ba·le
banana plátano (m) pla·ta·no
band grupo (m) groo·po
bandage vendaje (m) ven·da·khe
bank banco (m) ban·ko
bank account cuenta (f) bancaria kwen·ta ban·ka·rya
banknote billete (m) (de banco) bee·lye·te (de ban·ko)
baptism bautizo (m) bow·tee·tho
bar bar (m) bar
bar (with music) pub (m) poob
bar work trabajo (m) de camarero/a (m)/(f) tra·ba·kho de ka·ma·re·ro/a
basket canasta (f) ka·nas·ta
basketball baloncesto (m) ba·lon·thes·to
bath bañera (f) ba·nye·ra
bathing suit bañador (m) ba·nya·dor
bathroom baño (m) ba·nyo
battery (car) batería (f) ba·te·ree·a
battery (small) pila (f) pee·la
be ser ser · estar es·tar
beach playa (f) pla·ya
bean sprouts brotes (m) pl de soja bro·tes de so·kha
beans judías khoo·dee·as
beautiful hermoso/a (m)/(f) er·mo·so/a
beauty salon salón (m) de belleza sa·lon de be·lye·tha
because porque por·ke
bed cama (f) ka·ma
bedding ropa (f) de cama ro·pa de ka·ma
bedroom habitación (f) a·bee·ta·thyon
bee abeja (f) a·be·kha
beef carne (f) de vaca kar·ne de va·ka
beer cerveza (f) ther·ve·tha
beetroot remolacha (f) re·mo·la·cha
before antes an·tes
beggar mendigo/a (m)/(f) men·dee·go/a
begin comenzar ko·men·thar
behind detrás de de·tras de
Belgium Bélgica (f) bel·khee·ka
below abajo a·ba·kho
best lo mejor lo me·khor
bet apuesta (f) a·pwes·ta
better mejor me·khor
between entre en·tre
Bible Biblia (f) bee·blya
bicycle bicicleta (f) bee·thee·kle·ta
big grande gran·de
bike bici (f) bee·thee
bike chain cadena (f) de bici ka·de·na de bee·thee
bike path camino (m) de bici ka·mee·no de bee·thee
bill cuenta (f) kwen·ta
biodegradable biodegradable bee·o·de·gra·da·ble
biography biografía (f) bee·o·gra·fee·a
bird pájaro (m) pa·kha·ro
birth certificate partida (f) de nacimiento par·tee·da de na·thee·myen·to
birthday cumpleaños (m) koom·ple·a·nyos
birthday cake pastel (m) de cumpleaños pas·tel de koom·ple·a·nyos
biscuit (f) galleta ga·lye·ta
bite (dog) mordedura (f) mor·de·doo·ra
bite (food) bocado (m) bo·ka·do
bite (insect) picadura (f) pee·ka·doo·ra
black negro/a (m)/(f) ne·gro/a
blanket manta (f) man·ta
bleed sangrar san·grar
blind ciego/a (m)/(f) thye·go/a
blister ampolla (f) am·po·lya
blocked atascado/a (m)/(f) a·tas·ka·do/a
blood sangre (f) san·gre
blood group grupo (m) sanguíneo groo·po san·gee·neo

ENGLISH – SPANISH B

blood pressure presión ⓕ arterial pre·syon ar·te·ryal
blood test análisis ⓜ de sangre a·na·lee·sees de san·gre
blue azul a·thool
board (ship, etc) embarcarse em·bar·kar·se
boarding pass tarjeta ⓕ de embarque tar·khe·ta de em·bar·ke
bone hueso ⓜ we·so
book libro ⓜ lee·bro
book (make a reservation) reservar re·ser·var
booked out lleno/a ⓜ/ⓕ lye·no/a
bookshop librería ⓕ lee·bre·ree·a
boots botas ⓕ pl bo·tas
border frontera ⓕ fron·te·ra
boring aburrido/a ⓜ/ⓕ a·boo·ree·do/a
borrow tomar prestado to·mar pres·ta·do
botanic garden jardín ⓜ botánico khar·deen bo·ta·nee·ko
both ambos/as ⓜ/ⓕ pl am·bos/bas
bottle botella ⓕ bo·te·lya
bottle opener abrebotellas ⓜ a·bre·bo·te·lyas
bowl bol ⓜ bol
box caja ⓕ ka·kha
boxer shorts calzones ⓜ pl kal·tho·nes
boxing boxeo ⓜ bo·se·o
boy chico ⓜ chee·ko
boyfriend novio ⓜ no·vyo
bra sujetador ⓜ soo·khe·ta·dor
brakes frenos ⓜ pl fre·nos
branch (office) sucursal ⓕ soo·koor·sal
brandy coñac ⓜ ko·nyak
brave valiente va·lyen·te
bread pan ⓜ pan
bread rolls bollos bo·lyos
bread (rye) pan de centeno pan de then·te·no
bread (sourdough) pan de masa fermentada pan de ma·sa fer·men·ta·da
bread (white) pan blanco pan blan·ko
bread (wholemeal) pan integral pan een·te·gral
break romper rom·per
break down descomponerse des·kom·po·ner·se
breakfast desayuno ⓜ des·a·yoo·no
breasts senos ⓜ pl se·nos
breathe respirar res·pee·rar
brewery fábrica ⓕ de cerveza fab·ree·ka de ther·ve·tha
bribe soborno ⓜ so·bor·no
bribe sobornar so·bor·nar
bridge puente ⓜ pwen·te
briefcase maletín ⓜ ma·le·teen
brilliant estupendo/a ⓜ/ⓕ es·too·pen·do/a
bring traer tra·er
brochure folleto ⓜ fo·lye·to
broken roto/a ⓜ/ⓕ ro·to/a
bronchitis bronquitis ⓕ bron·kee·tees
brother hermano ⓜ er·ma·no
brown marrón ma·ron
bruise moratón ⓜ mor·a·ton
Brussels sprouts coles ⓜ pl de Bruselas ko·les de broo·se·las
bucket cubo ⓜ koo·bo
Buddhist budista ⓜ&ⓕ boo·dees·ta
buffet bufé ⓜ boo·fe
bug bicho ⓜ bee·cho
build construir kons·troo·eer
building edificio ⓜ e·dee·fee·thyo
bull toro ⓜ to·ro
bullfight corrida ⓕ ko·ree·da
bullring plaza ⓕ de toros pla·tha de to·ros
bum (of body) culo ⓜ koo·lo
burn quemadura ⓕ ke·ma·doo·ra
bus autobús ⓜ ow·to·boos
bus (intercity) autocar ⓜ ow·to·kar
bus station estación de autobuses/autocares ⓕ es·ta·thyon de ow·to·boo·ses/ow·to·ka·res
bus stop parada ⓕ de autobús pa·ra·da de ow·to·boos
business negocios ⓜ pl ne·go·thyos

business class clase ⓕ preferente kla·se pre·fe·ren·te
business person empresario/a ⓜ/ⓕ em·pre·sa·ryo/a
busker artista callejero/a ⓜ/ⓕ ar·tees·ta ka·lye·khe·ro/a
busy ocupado/a ⓜ/ⓕ o·koo·pa·do/a
but pero pe·ro
butcher's shop carnicería ⓕ kar·nee·the·ree·a
butter mantequilla ⓕ man·te·kee·lya
butterfly mariposa ⓕ ma·ree·po·sa
buttons botónes ⓜ pl bo·to·nes
buy comprar kom·prar

C

cabbage col kol
cable cable ⓜ ka·ble
cable car teleférico ⓜ te·le·fe·ree·ko
cafe café ⓜ ka·fe
cake pastel ⓜ pas·tel
cake shop pastelería ⓕ pas·te·le·ree·a
calculator calculadora ⓕ kal·koo·la·do·ra
calendar calendario ⓜ ka·len·da·ryo
calf ternero ⓜ ter·ne·ro
camera cámara ⓕ (fotográfica) ka·ma·ra (fo·to·gra·fee·ka)
camera shop tienda ⓕ de fotografía tyen·da de fo·to·gra·fee·a
camp acampar a·kam·par
camping store tienda ⓕ de cámping tyen·da de kam·peen
campsite cámping ⓜ kam·peen
can lata ⓕ la·ta
can (be able) poder po·der
can opener abrelatas ⓜ a·bre·la·tas
Canada Canadá ⓕ ka·na·da
cancel cancelar kan·the·lar
cancer cáncer ⓜ kan·ther
candle vela ⓕ ve·la
candy dulces ⓜ pl dool·thes
cantaloupe cantalupo ⓜ kan·ta·loo·po
capsicum (red/green) pimiento ⓜ rojo/verde pee·myen·to ro·kho/ver·de
car coche ⓜ ko·che
car hire alquiler ⓜ de coche al·kee·ler de ko·che
car owner's title papeles ⓜ pl del coche pa·pe·les del ko·che
car registration matrícula ⓕ ma·tree·koo·la
caravan caravana ⓕ ka·ra·va·na
cards cartas ⓕ pl kar·tas
care (about something) preocuparse por pre·o·koo·par·se por
care (for someone) cuidar de kwee·dar de
caring bondadoso/a ⓜ/ⓕ bon·da·do·so/a
carpark aparcamiento ⓜ a·par·ka·myen·to
carpenter carpintero/a ⓜ/ⓕ kar·peen·te·ro/a
carrot zanahoria ⓕ tha·na·o·rya
carry llevar lye·var
carton cartón ⓜ kar·ton
cash dinero ⓜ en efectivo dee·ne·ro en e·fek·tee·vo
cash (a cheque) cobrar (un cheque) ko·brar (oon che·ke)
cash register caja ⓕ (registradora) ka·kha (re·khees·tra·do·ra)
cashew nut anacardo ⓜ a·na·kar·do
cashpoint cajero ⓜ automático ka·khe·ro ow·to·ma·tee·ko
casino casino ⓜ ka·see·no
cassette casete ⓜ ka·se·te
castle castillo ⓜ kas·tee·lyo
casual work trabajo ⓜ eventual tra·ba·kho e·ven·twal
cat gato/a ⓜ/ⓕ ga·to/a
cathedral catedral ⓕ ka·te·dral
Catholic católico/a ⓜ/ⓕ ka·to·lee·ko/a
cauliflower coliflor ⓕ ko·lee·flor
cautious prudente proo·den·te
caves cuevas ⓕ pl kwe·vas
CD compact ⓜ kom·pakt

celebrate (an event) celebrar the·le·brar
celebration celebración ⓕ the·le·bra·thyon
cemetery cementerio ⓜ the·men·te·ryo
cent céntimo ⓜ then·tee·mo
centimetre centímetro ⓜ then·tee·me·tro
central heating calefacción ⓕ ka·le·fak·thyon
centre centro ⓜ then·tro
ceramic cerámica ⓕ the·ra·mee·ka
cereal cereales ⓜ pl the·re·a·les
certificate certificado ⓜ ther·tee·fee·ka·do
chair silla ⓕ see·lya
Champagne champán ⓜ cham·pan
chance oportunidad ⓕ o·por·too·nee·dad
change (money) cambio ⓜ kam·byo
change cambiar kam·byar
changing rooms vestuarios ⓜ pl ves·twa·ryos
chapel capilla ⓕ ka·pee·lya
charming encantador/encantadora ⓜ/ⓕ en·kan·ta·dor/en·kan·ta·do·ra
chat up (a person) ligar lee·gar
cheap barato/a ⓜ/ⓕ ba·ra·to/a
cheat tramposo/a ⓜ/ⓕ tram·po·so/a
check revisar re·vee·sar
check-in facturación ⓕ de equipajes fak·too·ra·thyon de e·kee·pa·khes
checkpoint control ⓜ kon·trol
cheese queso ⓜ ke·so
chef cocinero ⓜ ko·thee·ne·ro
chemist (person) farmacéutico/a ⓜ/ⓕ far·ma·the·oo·ti·ko/a
chemist (shop) farmacia ⓕ far·ma·thya
cheque (bank) cheque ⓜ che·ke
chess ajedrez ⓜ a·khe·dreth
chess board tablero ⓜ de ajedrez ta·ble·ro de a·khe·dreth
chest pecho ⓜ pe·cho
chewing gum chicle ⓜ chee·kle
chicken pollo ⓜ po·lyo
chicken breast pechuga ⓕ pe·choo·ga
chickpeas garbanzos ⓜ pl gar·ban·thos
child niño/a ⓜ/ⓕ nee·nyo/a
child seat asiento ⓜ de seguridad para bebés a·syen·to de se·goo·ree·dad pa·ra be·bes
childminding service guardería ⓕ gwar·de·ree·a
children hijos ⓜ pl ee·khos
chili guindilla ⓕ geen·dee·lya
chili sauce salsa ⓕ de guindilla sal·sa de geen·dee·lya
chocolate chocolate ⓜ cho·ko·la·te
choose escoger es·ko·kher
Christian cristiano/a ⓜ/ⓕ krees·tya·no/a
Christmas Navidad ⓕ na·vee·dad
Christmas Eve Nochebuena ⓕ no·che·bwe·na
church iglesia ⓕ ee·gle·sya
cider sidra ⓕ see·dra
cigar cigarro ⓜ thee·ga·ro
cigarette cigarrillo ⓜ thee·ga·ree·lyo
cigarette lighter mechero ⓜ me·che·ro
cigarette machine máquina ⓕ de tabaco ma·kee·na de ta·ba·ko
cigarette paper papel ⓜ de fumar pa·pel de foo·mar
cinema cine ⓜ thee·ne
circus circo ⓜ theer·ko
citizenship ciudadanía ⓕ thyu·da·da·nee·a
city ciudad ⓕ thyu·dad
city centre centro ⓜ de la ciudad then·tro de la thyu·dad
city walls murallas ⓕ pl moo·ra·lyas
civil rights derechos civiles ⓜ pl de·re·chos thee·vee·les
classical clásico/a ⓜ/ⓕ kla·see·ko/a
clean limpio/a ⓜ/ⓕ leem·pyo/a
cleaning limpieza ⓕ leem·pye·tha
client cliente/a ⓜ/ⓕ klee·en·te/a
cliff acantilado ⓜ a·kan·tee·la·do

climb subir soo·beer
clinic clínica ⓕ klee·nee·ka
cloak capa ⓕ ka·pa
cloakroom guardarropa ⓜ gwar·da·ro·pa
clock reloj ⓜ re·lokh
close cerrar the·rar
closed cerrado/a ⓜ/ⓕ the·ra·do/a
clothes line cuerda ⓕ para tender la ropa kwer·da pa·ra ten·der la ro·pa
clothing ropa ⓕ ro·pa
clothing store tienda ⓕ de ropa tyen·da de ro·pa
cloud nube ⓕ noo·be
cloudy nublado noo·bla·do
clove (garlic) diente ⓜ (de ajo) dyen·te (de a·kho)
cloves clavos ⓜ pl kla·vos
club discoteca ⓕ dees·ko·te·ka
clutch embrague ⓕ em·bra·ge
coach entrenador/entrenadora ⓜ/ⓕ en·tre·na·dor/en·tre·na·do·ra
coast costa ⓕ kos·ta
cocaine cocaína ⓕ ko·ka·ee·na
cockroach cucaracha ⓕ koo·ka·ra·cha
cocoa cacao ⓜ ka·kow
coconut coco ⓜ ko·ko
codeine codeína ⓕ ko·de·ee·na
coffee café ⓜ ka·fe
coins monedas ⓕ pl mo·ne·das
cold frío/a ⓜ/ⓕ free·o/a
cold (illness) resfriado ⓜ res·free·a·do
colleague colega ⓜ&ⓕ ko·le·ga
colour color ⓜ ko·lor
colour (film) película ⓕ en color pe·lee·koo·la en ko·lor
comb peine ⓜ pey·ne
come venir ve·neer
come (arrive) llegar lye·gar
comedy comedia ⓕ ko·me·dya
comfortable cómodo/a ⓜ/ⓕ ko·mo·do/a
communion comunión ⓕ ko·moo·nyon
communist comunista ⓜ&ⓕ ko·moo·nees·ta
companion compañero/a ⓜ/ⓕ kom·pa·nye·ro/a
company compañía ⓕ kom·pa·nyee·a
compass brújula ⓕ broo·khoo·la
complain quejarse ke·khar·se
computer ordenador ⓜ or·de·na·dor
computer games videojuegos ⓜ pl vee·de·o·khwe·gos
concert concierto ⓜ kon·thyer·to
conditioner acondicionador ⓜ a·kon·dee·thyo·na·dor
condoms condones ⓜ pl kon·do·nes
confession confesión ⓕ kon·fe·syon
confirm confirmar kon·feer·mar
connection conexión ⓕ ko·ne·ksyon
conservative conservador/conservadora ⓜ/ⓕ kon·ser·va·dor/kon·ser·va·do·ra
constipation estreñimiento ⓜ es·tre·nyee·myen·to
consulate consulado ⓜ kon·soo·la·do
contact lenses lentes ⓜ pl de contacto len·tes de kon·tak·to
contraceptives anticonceptivos ⓜ pl an·tee·kon·thep·tee·vos
contract contrato ⓜ kon·tra·to
convenience store supermercado ⓜ pequeño soo·per·mer·ka·do pe·ke·nyo
convent convento ⓜ kon·ven·to
cook cocinero ⓜ ko·thee·ne·ro
cook cocinar ko·thee·nar
corn maíz ⓜ ma·eeth
corn flakes copos ⓜ pl de maíz ko·pos de ma·eeth
corner esquina ⓕ es·kee·na
corrupt corrupto/a ⓜ/ⓕ ko·roop·to/a
cost costar kos·tar
cottage cheese requesón ⓜ re·ke·son
cotton algodón ⓜ al·go·don
cotton balls bolas ⓕ pl de algodón bo·las de al·go·don
cough tos ⓕ tos
cough medicine jarabe ⓜ kha·ra·be

count contar kon·tar
counter mostrador ⓜ mos·tra·dor
country país ⓜ pa·ees
countryside campo ⓜ kam·po
coupon cupón ⓜ koo·pon
courgette calabacín ⓜ ka·la·ba·theen
court (tennis) pista ⓕ pees·ta
couscous cuscús ⓜ koos·koos
cover charge precio ⓜ del cubierto pre·thyo del koo·byer·to
cow vaca ⓕ va·ka
crab cangrejo ⓜ kan·gre·kho
crackers galletas ⓕ pl saladas ga·lye·tas sa·la·das
crafts artesanía ⓕ ar·te·sa·nee·a
crash choque ⓜ cho·ke
crazy loco/a ⓜ/ⓕ lo·ko/a
cream (food) crema kre·ma
cream (moisturising) crema ⓕ hidratante kre·ma ee·dra·tan·te
cream cheese queso ⓜ crema ke·so kre·ma
crèche guardería ⓕ gwar·de·ree·a
credit card tarjeta ⓕ de crédito tar·khe·ta de kre·dee·to
cricket críquet ⓜ kree·ket
crop cosecha ⓕ ko·se·cha
crowded abarrotado/a ⓜ/ⓕ a·ba·ro·ta·do/a
cucumber pepino ⓜ pe·pee·no
cuddle abrazo ⓜ a·bra·tho
cup taza ⓕ ta·tha
cupboard armario ⓜ ar·ma·ryo
currency exchange cambio ⓜ (de dinero) kam·byo (de dee·ne·ro)
current (electricity) corriente ⓕ ko·ryen·te
current affairs actualidad ⓕ ak·twa·lee·dad
curry curry ⓜ koo·ree
curry powder curry ⓜ en polvo koo·ree en pol·vo
customs aduana ⓕ a·dwa·na
cut cortar kor·tar
cutlery cubiertos ⓜ pl koo·byer·tos
CV currículum ⓜ koo·ree·koo·loom
cycle andar en bicicleta an·dar en bee·thee·kle·ta
cycling ciclismo ⓜ thee·klees·mo
cyclist ciclista ⓜ&ⓕ thee·klees·ta
cystitis cistitis ⓕ thees·tee·tees

D

dad papá ⓜ pa·pa
daily diariamente dya·rya·men·te
dance bailar bai·lar
dangerous peligroso/a ⓜ/ⓕ pe·lee·gro·so/a
dark oscuro/a ⓜ/ⓕ os·koo·ro/a
date citarse thee·tar·se
date (a person) salir con sa·leer kon
date (time) fecha ⓕ fe·cha
date of birth fecha ⓕ de nacimiento fe·cha de na·thee·myen·to
daughter hija ⓕ ee·kha
dawn alba ⓕ al·ba
day día ⓜ dee·a
day after tomorrow pasado mañana pa·sa·do ma·nya·na
day before yesterday anteayer an·te·a·yer
dead muerto/a ⓜ/ⓕ mwer·to/a
deaf sordo/a ⓜ/ⓕ sor·do/a
deal (cards) repartir re·par·teer
decide decidir de·thee·deer
deep profundo/a ⓜ/ⓕ pro·foon·do/a
deforestation deforestación ⓕ de·fo·res·ta·thyon
degree título ⓜ tee·too·lo
delay demora ⓕ de·mo·ra
delirious delirante de·lee·ran·te
deliver entregar en·tre·gar
democracy democracia ⓕ de·mo·kra·thya
demonstration manifestación ⓕ ma·nee·fes·ta·thyon
Denmark Dinamarca ⓕ dee·na·mar·ka
dental floss hilo ⓜ dental ee·lo den·tal
dentist dentista ⓜ&ⓕ den·tees·ta

deny negar ne·gar
deodorant desodorante (m) de·so·do·ran·te
depart salir de sa·leer de
department store grandes almacenes (m) pl gran·des al·ma·the·nes
departure salida (f) sa·lee·da
deposit depósito (m) de·po·see·to
descendant descendiente (m) des·then·dyen·te
desert desierto (m) de·syer·to
design diseño (m) dee·se·nyo
destination destino (m) des·tee·no
destroy destruir des·troo·eer
detail detalle (m) de·ta·lye
diabetes diabetes (f) dee·a·be·tes
diaper pañal (m) pa·nyal
diaphragm diafragma (m) dee·a·frag·ma
diarrhoea diarrea (f) dee·a·re·a
diary agenda (f) a·khen·da
dice (die) dados (m) pl da·dos
dictionary diccionario (m) deek·thyo·na·ryo
die morir mo·reer
diet régimen (m) re·khee·men
different diferente (m)/(f) dee·fe·ren·te
difficult difícil (m)/(f) dee·fee·theel
dinner cena (f) the·na
direct directo/a (m)/(f) dee·rek·to/a
director director/directora (m)/(f) dee·rek·tor/dee·rek·to·ra
dirty sucio/a (m)/(f) soo·thyo/a
disabled discapacitado/a (m)/(f) dees·ka·pa·thee·ta·do/a
discount descuento (m) des·kwen·to
discover descubrir des·koo·breer
discrimination discriminación (f) dees·kree·mee·na·thyon
disease enfermedad (f) en·fer·me·dad
disk disco (m) dees·ko
dive bucear boo·the·ar
diving buceo (m) boo·the·o
diving (scuba) submarinismo (m) soob·ma·ree·nees·mo
diving equipment equipo (m) de inmersión (f) e·kee·po de een·mer·syon
dizzy mareado/a (m)/(f) ma·re·a·do/a
do hacer a·ther
doctor doctor/doctora (m)/(f) dok·tor/dok·to·ra
documentary documental (m) do·koo·men·tal
dog perro/a (m)/(f) pe·ro/a
dole paro (m) pa·ro
doll muñeca (f) moo·nye·ka
domestic flight vuelo (m) doméstico vwe·lo do·mes·tee·ko
donkey burro (m) boo·ro
door puerta (f) pwer·ta
double doble (m)/(f) do·ble
double bed cama (f) de matrimonio ka·ma de ma·tree·mo·nyo
double room habitación (f) doble a·bee·ta·thyon do·ble
down abajo a·ba·kho
downhill cuesta abajo kwes·ta a·ba·kho
dozen docena (f) do·the·na
draw dibujar dee·boo·khar
dream soñar so·nyar
dress vestido (m) ves·tee·do
dried fruit fruta (f) seca froo·ta se·ka
drink bebida (f) be·bee·da
drink beber be·ber
drive conducir kon·doo·theer
driving licence carnet (m) de conducir kar·ne de kon·doo·theer
drug droga (f) dro·ga
drug addiction drogadicción (f) dro·ga·deek·thyon
drug dealer traficante (m) de drogas tra·fee·kan·te de dro·gas
drums batería (f) ba·te·ree·a
drumstick (chicken) muslo (m) moos·lo
drunk borracho/a (m)/(f) bo·ra·cho/a
dry secar se·kar
duck pato (m) pa·to
dummy (pacifier) chupete (m) choo·pe·te

E

each cada *ka*·da
ear oreja ⓕ o·*re*·kha
early temprano tem·*pra*·no
earn ganar ga·*nar*
earplugs tapones ⓜ pl para los oídos ta·*po*·nes *pa*·ra los o·*ee*·dos
earrings pendientes ⓜ pl pen·*dyen*·tes
earth tierra ⓕ *tye*·ra
earthquake terremoto ⓜ te·re·*mo*·to
east este *es*·te
Easter Pascua ⓕ *pas*·kwa
Easter Week Semana ⓕ Santa se·*ma*·na *san*·ta
easy fácil *fa*·theel
eat comer ko·*mer*
economy class clase ⓕ turística *kla*·se too·*rees*·tee·ka
eczema eczema ⓕ ek·*the*·ma
editor editor/editora ⓜ/ⓕ e·dee·*tor*/e·dee·*to*·ra
education educación ⓕ e·doo·ka·*thyon*
egg huevo ⓜ *we*·vo
eggplant berenjenas ⓕ pl be·ren·*khe*·nas
elections elecciones ⓕ pl e·lek·*thyo*·nes
electrical store tienda ⓕ de productos eléctricos *tyen*·da de pro·*dook*·tos e·*lek*·tree·kos
electricity electricidad ⓕ e·lek·tree·thee·*dad*
elevator ascensor ⓜ as·then·*sor*
embarrassed avergonzado/a ⓜ/ⓕ a·ver·gon·*tha*·do/a
embassy embajada ⓕ em·ba·*kha*·da
emergency emergencia ⓕ e·mer·*khen*·thya
emotional emocional e·mo·thyo·*nal*
employee empleado/a ⓜ/ⓕ em·ple·*a*·do/a
employer jefe/a ⓜ/ⓕ *khe*·fe/a
empty vacío/a ⓜ/ⓕ va·*thee*·o/a
end fin ⓜ feen
end acabar a·ka·*bar*
endangered species especies ⓕ pl en peligro de extinción es·*pe*·thyes en pe·*lee*·gro de eks·teen·*thyon*
engagement compromiso ⓜ kom·pro·*mee*·so
engine motor ⓜ mo·*tor*
engineer ingeniero/a ⓜ/ⓕ een·khe·*nye*·ro/a
engineering ingeniería ⓕ een·khe·nye·*ree*·a
England Inglaterra ⓕ een·gla·*te*·ra
English inglés ⓜ een·*gles*
enjoy (oneself) divertirse dee·ver·*teer*·se
enough suficiente ⓜ/ⓕ soo·fee·*thyen*·te
enter entrar en·*trar*
entertainment guide guía ⓕ de ocio *gee*·a de *o*·thyo
envelope sobre ⓜ *so*·bre
environment medio ⓜ ambiente *me*·dyo am·*byen*·te
epilepsy epilepsia ⓕ e·pee·*lep*·sya
equal opportunity igualdad ⓕ de oportunidades ee·gwal·*dad* de o·por·too·nee·*da*·des
equality igualdad ⓕ ee·gwal·*dad*
equipment equipo ⓜ e·*kee*·po
escalator escalera ⓕ mecánica es·ka·*le*·ra me·*ka*·nee·ka
estate agent agente inmobiliario ⓜ a·*khen*·te een·mo·bee·*lya*·ryo
euro euro ⓜ *e*·oo·ro
Europe Europa ⓕ e·oo·*ro*·pa
euthanasia eutanasia ⓕ e·oo·ta·*na*·sya
evening tarde ⓕ *tar*·de
everything todo *to*·do
example ejemplo ⓜ e·*khem*·plo
excellent excelente ⓜ/ⓕ eks·the·*len*·te
exchange cambio ⓜ *kam*·byo
exchange (money) cambiar kam·*byar*
exchange rate tipo ⓜ de cambio *tee*·po de *kam*·byo
exchange (give gifts) regalar re·ga·*lar*
excluded no incluido no

een·kloo·ee·do
exhaust tubo ⓜ de escape *too*·bo de es·*ka*·pe
exhibit exponer eks·po·*ner*
exhibition exposición ⓕ eks·po·see·*thyon*
exit salida ⓕ sa·*lee*·da
expensive caro/a ⓜ/ⓕ *ka*·ro/a
experience experiencia ⓕ eks·pe·*ryen*·thya
express expreso/a ⓜ/ⓕ eks·*pre*·so/a
express mail correo ⓜ urgente ko·*re*·o oor·*khen*·te
extension (visa) prolongación ⓕ pro·lon·ga·*thyon*
eye ojo ⓜ *o*·kho
eye drops gotas ⓕ pl para los ojos *go*·tas *pa*·ra los *o*·khos

F

fabric tela ⓕ *te*·la
face cara ⓕ *ka*·ra
face cloth toallita ⓕ to·a·*lyee*·ta
factory fábrica ⓕ *fa*·bree·ka
fall caída ⓕ ka·*ee*·da
family familia ⓕ fa·*mee*·lya
family name apellido ⓜ a·pe·*lyee*·do
famous famoso/a ⓜ/ⓕ fa·*mo*·so/a
fan (hand held) abanico ⓜ a·ba·*nee*·ko
fan (electric) ventilador ⓜ ven·tee·la·*dor*
fanbelt correa del alternador ⓕ ko·*re*·a del al·ter·na·*dor*
fantastic fantástico/a ⓜ/ⓕ fan·*tas*·tee·ko/a
far lejos *le*·khos
farm granja ⓕ *gran*·kha
farmer agricultor/agricultora ⓜ/ⓕ a·gree·kool·*tor*/a·gree·kool·*to*·ra
fast rápido/a ⓜ/ⓕ *ra*·pee·do/a
fat gordo/a ⓜ/ⓕ *gor*·do/a
father padre ⓜ *pa*·dre
father-in-law suegro ⓜ *swe*·gro
fault (mechanical) falta ⓕ *fal*·ta
faulty defectuoso/a ⓜ/ⓕ de·fek·*two*·so/a
feed dar de comer dar de ko·*mer*
feel sentir sen·*teer*
feelings sentimientos ⓜ pl sen·tee·*myen*·tos
fence cerca ⓕ *ther*·ka
fencing esgrima ⓕ es·*gree*·ma
festival festival ⓜ fes·tee·*val*
fever fiebre ⓕ *fye*·bre
few pocos/as ⓜ/ⓕ *po*·kos/as
fiancé prometido ⓜ pro·me·*tee*·do
fiancée prometida ⓕ pro·me·*tee*·da
fiction ficción ⓕ feek·*thyon*
field campo ⓜ *kam*·po
fig higo ⓜ *ee*·go
fight pelea ⓕ pe·*le*·a
fight luchar loo·*char*
fill llenar lye·*nar*
fillet filete ⓜ fee·*le*·te
film película ⓕ pe·*lee*·koo·la
filtered con filtro kon *feel*·tro
find encontrar en·kon·*trar*
fine (penalty) multa ⓕ *mool*·ta
finger dedo ⓜ *de*·do
finish terminar ter·mee·*nar*
fire fuego ⓜ *fwe*·go
firewood leña ⓕ *le*·nya
first primero/a ⓜ/ⓕ pree·*me*·ro/a
first-aid kit botiquín ⓜ de primeros auxilios bo·tee·*keen* de pree·*me*·ros ow·*ksee*·lyos
first class primera clase pree·*me*·ra *kla*·se
first name nombre ⓜ de pila *nom*·bre de *pee*·la
fish pez ⓜ peth
fish (as food) pescado ⓜ pes·*ka*·do
fish shop pescadería ⓕ pes·ka·de·*ree*·a
fishing pesca ⓕ *pes*·ka
flag bandera ⓕ ban·*de*·ra
flannel toallita ⓕ to·a·*lyee*·ta
flashlight linterna ⓕ leen·*ter*·na
flat llano/a ⓜ/ⓕ *lya*·no/a
flea pulga ⓕ *pool*·ga
flooding inundación ⓕ

ee·noon·da·*thyon*
floor suelo ⓜ *swe*·lo
florist florista ⓜ&ⓕ flo·*rees*·ta
flour harina ⓕ a·*ree*·na
flower flor ⓕ flor
flower seller vendedor/vendedora ⓜ/ⓕ de flores ven·de·*dor*/ ven·de·*do*·ra de *flo*·res
fly volar vo·*lar*
foggy brumoso/a ⓜ/ⓕ broo·*mo*·so
follow seguir se·*geer*
food comida ⓕ ko·*mee*·da
food supplies víveres ⓜ pl *vee*·ve·res
foot pie ⓜ pye
football fútbol ⓜ *foot*·bol
footpath acera ⓕ a·*the*·ra
foreign extranjero/a ⓜ/ⓕ eks·tran·*khe*·ro/a
foreign tourist (slang) guiri ⓜ *gee*·ree
forest bosque ⓜ *bos*·ke
forever para siempre *pa*·ra *syem*·pre
forget olvidar ol·vee·*dar*
forgive perdonar per·do·*nar*
fork tenedor ⓜ te·ne·*dor*
fortnight quincena ⓕ keen·*the*·na
foul (dirty) sucio/a ⓜ/ⓕ *soo*·thyo/a
four-wheel drive vehicle todoterreno ⓜ to·do·te·*rre*·no
foyer vestíbulo ⓜ ves·*tee*·boo·lo
fragile frágil *fra*·kheel
France Francia ⓕ *fran*·thya
free (not bound) libre *lee*·bre
free (of charge) gratis *gra*·tees
freeze congelar kon·khe·*lar*
friend amigo/a ⓜ/ⓕ a·*mee*·go/a
frost escarcha ⓕ es·*kar*·cha
frozen foods productos congelados ⓜ pl pro·*dook*·tos kon·khe·*la*·dos
fruit fruta ⓕ *froo*·ta
fruit picking recolección ⓕ de fruta re·ko·lek·*thyon* de *froo*·ta
fry freír fre·*eer*
frying pan sartén ⓕ sar·*ten*
full lleno/a ⓜ/ⓕ *lye*·no/a
full-time a tiempo completo a *tyem*·po kom·*ple*·to
fun diversión ⓕ dee·ver·*syon*
funeral funeral ⓜ foo·ne·*ral*
funny gracioso/a ⓜ/ⓕ gra·*thyo*·so/a
furniture muebles ⓜ pl *mwe*·bles
future futuro ⓜ foo·*too*·ro

G

gay gay gay
general general khe·ne·*ral*
Germany Alemania ⓕ a·le·*ma*·nya
gift regalo ⓜ re·*ga*·lo
gig bolo ⓜ *bo*·lo
gin ginebra ⓕ khee·*ne*·bra
ginger jengibre ⓜ khen·*khee*·bre
girl (teenage) chica ⓕ *chee*·ka
girlfriend novia ⓕ *no*·vya
give dar dar
glandular fever fiebre ⓕ glandular *fye*·bre glan·doo·*lar*
glass (material) vidrio ⓜ *vee*·dryo
glass (drinking) vaso ⓜ *va*·so
glasses gafas ⓕ pl *ga*·fas
gloves guantes ⓜ pl *gwan*·tes
go ir eer
go out with salir con sa·*leer* kon
go shopping ir de compras eer de *kom*·pras
goal gol ⓜ gol
goalkeeper portero/a ⓜ/ⓕ por·*te*·ro/a
goat cabra ⓕ *ka*·bra
goat's cheese queso ⓜ de cabra *ke*·so de *ka*·bra
god Dios ⓜ dyos
goggles gafas ⓕ pl de submarinismo *ga*·fas de soob·ma·ree·*nees*·mo
golf ball pelota ⓕ de golf pe·*lo*·ta de golf
golf course campo ⓜ de golf *kam*·po de golf
good bueno/a ⓜ/ⓕ *bwe*·no/a
government gobierno ⓜ go·*byer*·no
gram gramo ⓜ *gra*·mo
grandchild nieto/a ⓜ/ⓕ *nye*·to/a

grandfather abuelo ⓜ *a·bwe·lo*
grandmother abuela ⓕ *a·bwe·la*
grapefruit pomelo ⓜ *po·me·lo*
grapes uvas ⓕ pl *oo·vas*
graphic art arte ⓜ gráfico *ar·te gra·fee·ko*
grass hierba ⓕ *yer·ba*
grave tumba ⓕ *toom·ba*
gray gris *grees*
great fantástico/a ⓜ/ⓕ *fan·tas·tee·ko/a*
green verde *ver·de*
greengrocery (shop) frutería ⓕ *froo·te·ree·a*
grocer (shopkeeper) frutero/a ⓜ/ⓕ *froo·te·ro/a*
grey gris *grees*
grocery tienda ⓕ de alimentación *tyen·da de a·lee·men·ta·thyon*
grow crecer *kre·ther*
guess adivinar *a·dee·vee·nar*
guesthouse pensión ⓕ *pen·syon*
guide (audio) guía ⓕ audio *gee·a ow·dyo*
guide (person) guía ⓜ&ⓕ *gee·a*
guide dog perro lazarillo ⓜ *pe·ro la·tha·ree·lyo*
guidebook guía ⓕ *gee·a*
guided tour recorrido ⓜ guiado *re·ko·ree·do gee·a·do*
guilty culpable *kool·pa·ble*
guitar guitarra ⓕ *gee·ta·ra*
gum chicle ⓜ *chee·kle*
gym gimnasio ⓜ *kheem·na·see·o*
gymnastics gimnasia ⓕ *kheem·na·sya*
gynaecologist ginecólogo/a ⓜ/ⓕ *khee·ne·ko·lo·go/a*

H

hair pelo ⓜ *pe·lo*
hairbrush cepillo ⓜ *the·pee·lyo*
hairdresser peluquero/a ⓜ/ⓕ *pe·loo·ke·ro/a*
halal halal *a·lal*
half medio/a ⓜ/ⓕ *me·dyo/a*
half a litre medio litro ⓜ *me·dyo lee·tro*
hall of residence residencia ⓕ de estudiantes *re·see·den·thya de es·too·dyan·tes*
hallucinate alucinar *a·loo·thee·nar*
ham jamón ⓜ *kha·mon*
hammer martillo ⓜ *mar·tee·lyo*
hammock hamaca ⓕ *a·ma·ka*
hand mano ⓕ *ma·no*
handbag bolso ⓜ *bol·so*
handicrafts artesanía ⓕ *ar·te·sa·nee·a*
handlebar manillar ⓜ *ma·nee·lyar*
handmade hecho a mano *e·cho a ma·no*
handsome hermoso ⓜ *er·mo·so*
happy feliz *fe·leeth*
harassment acoso ⓜ *a·ko·so*
harbour puerto ⓜ *pwer·to*
hard duro/a ⓜ/ⓕ *doo·ro/a*
hardware store ferretería ⓕ *fe·re·te·ree·a*
hash hachís ⓜ *a·chees*
hat sombrero ⓜ *som·bre·ro*
have tener *te·ner*
have a cold estar constipado/a ⓜ/ⓕ *es·tar kons·tee·pa·do/a*
have fun divertirse *dee·ver·teer·se*
hay fever alergia ⓕ al polen *a·ler·khya al po·len*
he él *el*
head cabeza ⓕ *ka·be·tha*
headache dolor ⓜ de cabeza *do·lor de ka·be·tha*
headlights faros ⓜ pl *fa·ros*
health salud ⓕ *sa·lood*
hear oír *o·eer*
hearing aid audífono ⓜ *ow·dee·fo·no*
heart corazón ⓜ *ko·ra·thon*
heart condition condición ⓕ cardíaca *kon·dee·thyon kar·dee·a·ka*
heat calor ⓜ *ka·lor*
heater estufa ⓕ *es·too·fa*
heavy pesado/a ⓜ/ⓕ *pe·sa·do/a*
helmet casco ⓜ *kas·ko*

help ayudar a·yoo·*dar*
hepatitis hepatitis ⓕ e·pa·*tee*·tees
her su soo
herbalist herbolario/a ⓜ/ⓕ er·bo·*la*·ree·o/a
herbs hierbas ⓕ pl *yer*·bas
here aquí a·*kee*
heroin heroína ⓕ e·ro·*ee*·na
herring arenque ⓜ a·*ren*·ke
high alto/a ⓜ/ⓕ *al*·to/a
high school instituto ⓜ eens·tee·*too*·to
hike ir de excursión eer de eks·koor·*syon*
hiking excursionismo ⓜ eks·koor·syo·*nees*·mo
hiking boots botas ⓕ pl de montaña *bo*·tas de mon·*ta*·nya
hiking routes caminos ⓜ pl rurales ka·*mee*·nos roo·*ra*·les
hill colina ⓕ ko·*lee*·na
Hindu hindú ⓜ&ⓕ een·*doo*
hire alquilar al·kee·*lar*
his su soo
historical histórico/a ⓜ/ⓕ ees·*to*·ree·ko/a
hitchhike hacer dedo a·*ther de*·do
HIV positive seropositivo/a ⓜ/ⓕ se·ro·po·see·*tee*·vo/a
hockey hockey ⓜ *kho*·kee
holiday (public) día festivo ⓜ *dee*·a fes·*tee*·vo
holidays vacaciones ⓕ pl va·ka·*thyo*·nes
homeless sin hogar seen o·*gar*
homosexual homosexual ⓜ&ⓕ o·mo·sek·*swal*
honey miel ⓕ myel
honeymoon luna ⓕ de miel *loo*·na de myel
horoscope horóscopo ⓜ o·*ros*·ko·po
horse caballo ⓜ ka·*ba*·lyo
horse riding equitación ⓕ e·kee·ta·*thyon*
horseradish rábano ⓜ picante *ra*·ba·no pee·*kan*·te
hospital hospital ⓜ os·pee·*tal*
hospitality (industry) hostelería ⓕ os·te·le·*ree*·a
hot caliente ka·*lyen*·te
hot water agua caliente ⓕ *a*·gwa ka·*lyen*·te
hotel hotel ⓜ o·*tel*
house casa ⓕ *ka*·sa
housework trabajo ⓜ de casa tra·*ba*·kho de *ka*·sa
how cómo *ko*·mo
how much cuánto *kwan*·to
hug abrazo ⓜ a·*bra*·tho
huge enorme e·*nor*·me
human rights derechos ⓜ pl humanos de·*re*·chos oo·*ma*·nos
humanities humanidades ⓕ pl oo·ma·nee·*da*·des
hungry tener hambre te·*ner am*·bre
hunting caza ⓕ *ka*·tha
hurt (damage) dañar da·*nyar*
hurt (pain) doler do·*ler*
husband marido ⓜ ma·*ree*·do

I

I yo yo
ice hielo ⓜ *ye*·lo
ice axe piolet ⓜ pyo·*le*
ice cream helado ⓜ e·*la*·do
ice cream parlour heladería ⓕ e·la·de·*ree*·a
ice hockey hockey ⓜ sobre hielo *kho*·kee *so*·bre *ye*·lo
identification identificación ⓕ ee·den·tee·fee·ka·*thyon*
identity card carnet ⓜ de identidad kar·*net* de ee·den·tee·*dad*
idiot idiota ⓜ&ⓕ ee·*dyo*·ta
if si see
ill enfermo/a ⓜ/ⓕ en·*fer*·mo/a
immigration inmigración ⓕ een·mee·gra·*thyon*
important importante eem·por·*tan*·te
in a hurry de prisa de *pree*·sa
in front of enfrente de en·*fren*·te de
included incluido een·kloo·*ee*·do

income tax impuesto ⓜ sobre la renta eem·pwes·to so·bre la ren·ta
India India ⓕ een·dya
Indian (food) hindú ⓜ&ⓕ een·doo
indicator indicador ⓜ een·dee·ka·dor
indigestion indigestión ⓕ een·dee·khes·tyon
industry industria ⓕ een·doos·trya
infection infección ⓕ een·fek·thyon
inflammation inflamación ⓕ een·fla·ma·thyon
influenza gripe ⓕ gree·pe
ingredient ingrediente ⓜ een·gre·dyen·te
inject inyectarse een·yek·tar·se
injection inyección ⓕ een·yek·thyon
injury herida ⓕ e·ree·da
innocent inocente ee·no·then·te
inside adentro a·den·tro
instructor instructor/a ⓜ/ⓕ een·strook·tor/a
insurance seguro ⓜ se·goo·ro
interesting interesante een·te·re·san·te
intermission intermedio ⓜ een·ter·me·dyo
international internacional een·ter·na·thyo·nal
internet internet een·ter·net
interpreter intérprete ⓜ&ⓕ een·ter·pre·te
intersection cruce ⓜ croo·the
interview entrevista ⓕ en·tre·vees·ta
invite invitar een·vee·tar
Ireland Irlanda ⓕ eer·lan·da
iron plancha ⓕ plan·cha
island isla ⓕ ees·la
IT informática ⓕ een·for·ma·tee·ka
Italy Italia ⓕ ee·ta·lya
itch picor ⓜ pee·kor
itemised desglosado/a ⓜ/ⓕ des·glo·sa·do/a
itinerary itinerario ⓜ ee·tee·ne·ra·ryo
IUD DIU ⓜ de·ee·oo

J

jacket chaqueta ⓕ cha·ke·ta
jail cárcel ⓕ kar·thel
jam mermelada ⓕ mer·me·la·da
Japan Japón ⓜ kha·pon
jar tarro ⓜ ta·rro
jaw mandíbula ⓕ man·dee·boo·la
jealous celoso/a ⓜ/ⓕ the·lo·so/a
jeans vaqueros ⓜ pl va·ke·ros
jeep jeep ⓜ jeep
jet lag jet lag ⓜ dyet lag
jewellery shop joyería ⓕ kho·ye·ree·a
Jewish judío/a ⓜ/ⓕ khoo·dee·o/a
job trabajo ⓜ tra·ba·kho
jockey jockey ⓜ yo·kee
jogging correr ko·rrer
joke broma ⓕ bro·ma
joke bromear bro·me·ar
journalist periodista ⓜ&ⓕ pe·ryo·dees·ta
judge juez/jueza ⓜ/ⓕ khweth/khwe·tha
jug jarra ⓕ kha·ra
juice zumo ⓜ thoo·mo
jump saltar sal·tar
jumper (sweater) jersey ⓜ kher·say
jump leads cables ⓜ pl de arranque ka·bles de a·ran·ke

K

ketchup salsa ⓕ de tomate sal·sa de to·ma·te
key llave ⓕ lya·ve
keyboard teclado ⓜ te·kla·do
kick dar una patada dar oo·na pa·ta·da
kill matar ma·tar
kilo(gram) kilo ⓜ kee·lo
kilometre kilómetro ⓜ kee·lo·me·tro
kind amable a·ma·ble
kindergarten guardería ⓕ gwar·de·ree·a
king rey ⓜ rey
kiss beso ⓜ be·so
kiss besar be·sar
kitchen cocina ⓕ ko·thee·na

kitten gatito/a ⓜ/ⓕ ga·tee·to/a
kiwifruit kiwi ⓜ kee·wee
knee rodilla ⓕ ro·dee·lya
knife cuchillo ⓜ koo·chee·lyo
know (someone) conocer ko·no·ther
know (something) saber sa·ber
kosher kosher ko·sher

L

lace (material) encaje ⓜ en·ka·khe
lager cerveza ⓕ rubia ther·ve·tha roo·bya
lake lago ⓜ la·go
lamb cordero ⓜ kor·de·ro
land tierra ⓕ tye·ra
landlady propietaria ⓕ pro·pye·ta·rya
landlord propietario ⓜ pro·pye·ta·ryo
language idioma ⓜ ee·dyo·ma
laptop ordenador ⓜ portátil or·de·na·dor por·ta·teel
lard manteca ⓕ man·te·ka
large grande gran·de
late tarde tar·de
laugh reírse re·eer·se
laundrette lavandería ⓕ la·van·de·ree·a
law ley ⓕ ley
lawyer abogado/a ⓜ/ⓕ a·bo·ga·do/a
leader líder ⓜ&ⓕ lee·der
leaf hoja ⓕ o·kha
leaflet folleto ⓜ fo·lye·to
learn aprender a·pren·der
leather cuero ⓜ kwe·ro
leave dejar de·khar
leave (behind/over) quedar ke·dar
lecturer profesor/profesora ⓜ/ⓕ pro·fe·sor/pro·fe·so·ra
ledge saliente ⓜ sa·lyen·te
leek puerro ⓜ pwe·ro
left izquierda ⓕ eeth·kyer·da
left luggage consigna ⓕ kon·seeg·na
left-wing de izquierdas de eeth·kyer·das
leg pierna ⓕ pyer·na
legal legal le·gal
legislation legislación ⓕ le·khees·la·thyon
lemon limón ⓜ lee·mon
lemonade limonada ⓕ lee·mo·na·da
lens objetivo ⓜ ob·khe·tee·vo
Lent Cuaresma ⓕ kwa·res·ma
lentils lentejas ⓕ pl len·te·khas
lesbian lesbiana ⓕ les·bee·a·na
less menos me·nos
letter carta ⓕ kar·ta
lettuce lechuga ⓕ le·choo·ga
liar mentiroso/a ⓜ/ⓕ men·tee·ro·so/a
library biblioteca ⓕ bee·blyo·te·ka
lice piojos ⓜ pl pyo·khos
license plate number matrícula ⓕ ma·tree·koo·la
lie (not stand) tumbarse toom·bar·se
life vida ⓕ vee·da
lifejacket chaleco ⓜ salvavidas cha·le·ko sal·va·vee·das
lift ascensor ⓜ as·then·sor
light (weight) leve le·ve
light luz ⓕ looth
light bulb bombilla ⓕ bom·bee·lya
light meter fotómetro ⓜ fo·to·me·tro
lighter encendedor ⓜ en·then·de·dor
like gustar(le) goos·tar(le)
lime lima ⓕ lee·ma
line línea ⓕ lee·ne·a
lip balm bálsamo ⓜ de labios bal·sa·mo de la·byos
lips labios ⓜ pl la·byos
lipstick pintalabios ⓜ peen·ta·la·byos
listen escuchar es·koo·char
live (life) vivir vee·veer
liver hígado ⓜ ee·ga·do
lizard lagartija ⓕ la·gar·tee·kha
local (nearby) local lo·kal
local train tren ⓜ de cercanías tren de ther·ka·nee·as
lock cerradura ⓕ the·ra·doo·ra
lock cerrar the·rar
locked cerrado/a ⓜ/ⓕ con llave the·ra·do/a kon lya·ve
lollies piruletas ⓕ pl pee·roo·le·tas
long largo/a ⓜ/ⓕ lar·go/a
long-distance a larga distancia a

lar·ga dees·tan·thya
look mirar mee·rar
look after cuidar kwee·dar
look for buscar boos·kar
lookout mirador ⓜ mee·ra·dor
lose perder per·der
lost perdido/a ⓜ/ⓕ per·dee·do/a
lost property office oficina ⓕ de objetos perdidos o·fee·thee·na de ob·khe·tos per·dee·dos
loud ruidoso/a ⓜ/ⓕ rwee·do·so/a
love querer ke·rer
lover amante ⓜ&ⓕ a·man·te
low bajo/a ⓜ/ⓕ ba·kho/a
lubricant lubricante ⓜ loo·bree·kan·te
luck suerte ⓕ swer·te
lucky afortunado/a ⓜ/ⓕ a·for·too·na·do/a
luggage equipaje ⓜ e·kee·pa·khe
luggage lockers consigna ⓕ automática kon·seeg·na ow·to·ma·tee·ka
luggage tag etiqueta ⓕ de equipaje e·tee·ke·ta de e·kee·pa·khe
lump bulto ⓜ bool·to
lunch almuerzo ⓜ al·mwer·tho
lungs pulmones ⓜ pl pool·mo·nes
luxury lujo ⓜ loo·kho

M

machine máquina ⓕ ma·kee·na
made of (cotton) hecho de (algodón) e·cho de (al·go·don)
magazine revista ⓕ re·vees·ta
magician mago/a ⓜ/ⓕ ma·go/a
mail correo ⓜ ko·re·o
mailbox buzón ⓜ boo·thon
main principal preen·thee·pal
make hacer a·ther
make fun of burlarse de boor·lar·se de
make-up maquillaje ⓜ ma·kee·lya·khe
mammogram mamografía ⓕ ma·mo·gra·fee·a
man hombre ⓜ om·bre
manager gerente ⓜ&ⓕ khe·ren·te
mandarin mandarina ⓕ man·da·ree·na
mango mango ⓜ man·go
many muchos/as ⓜ/ⓕ pl moo·chos/as
map mapa ⓜ ma·pa
margarine margarina ⓕ mar·ga·ree·na
marijuana marihuana ⓕ ma·ree·wa·na
marital status estado ⓜ civil es·ta·do thee·veel
market mercado ⓜ mer·ka·do
marriage matrimonio ⓜ ma·tree·mo·nyo
marry casarse ka·sar·se
martial arts artes ⓜ pl marciales ar·tes mar·thya·les
Mass misa ⓕ mee·sa
massage masaje ⓜ ma·sa·khe
masseur/masseuse masajista ⓜ&ⓕ ma·sa·khees·ta
mat esterilla ⓕ es·te·ree·lya
match partido ⓜ par·tee·do
matches cerillas ⓕ pl the·ree·lyas
mattress colchón ⓜ kol·chon
maybe quizás kee·thas
mayonnaise mayonesa ⓕ ma·yo·ne·sa
mayor alcalde/alcaldesa ⓜ/ⓕ al·kal·de/al·kal·de·sa
measles sarampión ⓜ sa·ram·pyon
meat carne ⓕ kar·ne
mechanic mecánico/a ⓜ/ⓕ me·ka·nee·ko
media medios ⓜ pl de comunicación me·dyos de ko·moo·nee·ka·thyon
medicine medicina ⓕ me·dee·thee·na
meditation meditación ⓕ me·dee·ta·thyon
meet encontrar en·kon·trar
melon melón ⓜ me·lon
member miembro ⓜ myem·bro
menstruation menstruación ⓕ mens·trwa·thyon
menu menú ⓜ me·noo
message mensaje ⓜ men·sa·khe
metal metal ⓜ me·tal
metre (measurement) metro ⓜ me·tro
metro metro ⓜ me·tro

metro station estación ⓕ de metro es·ta·*thyon* de *me*·tro
microwave microondas ⓜ mee·kro·*on*·das
midnight medianoche ⓕ me·dya·*no*·che
migraine migraña ⓕ mee·*gra*·nya
military service servicio ⓜ militar ser·*vee*·thyo mee·lee·*tar*
milk leche ⓕ *le*·che
millimetre milímetro ⓜ mee·*lee*·me·tro
million millón ⓜ mee·*lyon*
mince (meat) carne ⓜ picada *kar*·ne pee·*ka*·da
mind (look after) cuidar kwee·*dar*
mineral water agua ⓕ mineral *a*·gwa mee·ne·*ral*
minute minuto ⓜ mee·*noo*·to
mirror espejo ⓜ es·*pe*·kho
miscarriage aborto ⓜ natural a·*bor*·to na·too·*ral*
miss (feel sad) echar de menos e·*char* de *me*·nos
miss (someone) extrañar eks·tra·*nyar*
mistake error ⓜ e·*ror*
mix mezclar meth·*klar*
mobile phone teléfono ⓜ móvil te·*le*·fo·no *mo*·veel
modem módem ⓜ *mo*·dem
moisturiser crema ⓕ hidratante *kre*·ma ee·dra·*tan*·te
molar (tooth) muela ⓕ *mwe*·la
monastery monasterio ⓜ mo·nas·*te*·ryo
money dinero ⓜ dee·*ne*·ro
month mes ⓜ mes
monument monumento ⓜ mo·noo·*men*·to
(full) moon luna ⓕ (llena) *loo*·na (*lye*·na)
morning (6am–1pm) mañana ⓕ ma·*nya*·na
morning sickness náuseas ⓕ pl del embarazo *now*·se·as del em·ba·*ra*·tho
mosque mezquita ⓕ meth·*kee*·ta
mosquito mosquito ⓜ mos·*kee*·to
mosquito net mosquitera ⓕ mos·kee·*te*·ra
mother madre ⓕ *ma*·dre
mother-in-law suegra ⓕ *swe*·gra
motorboat motora ⓕ mo·*to*·ra
motorcycle motocicleta ⓕ mo·to·thee·*kle*·ta
motorway autovía ⓕ ow·to·*vee*·a
mountain montaña ⓕ mon·*ta*·nya
mountain bike bicicleta ⓕ de montaña bee·thee·*kle*·ta de mon·*ta*·nya
mountain path sendero ⓜ sen·*de*·ro
mountain range cordillera ⓕ kor·dee·*lye*·ra
mountaineering alpinismo ⓜ al·pee·*nees*·mo
mouse ratón ⓜ ra·*ton*
mouth boca ⓕ *bo*·ka
movie película ⓕ pe·*lee*·koo·la
mud lodo ⓜ *lo*·do
muesli muesli ⓜ *mwes*·lee
mum mamá ⓕ ma·*ma*
muscle músculo ⓜ *moos*·koo·lo
museum museo ⓜ moo·*se*·o
mushroom ⓜ champiñón cham·pee·*nyon*
music música ⓕ *moo*·see·ka
musician músico/a ⓜ/ⓕ *moo*·see·ko/a
Muslim musulmán/musulmana ⓜ/ⓕ moo·sool·*man*/moo·sool·*ma*·na
mussels mejillones ⓜ pl me·khee·*lyo*·nes
must deber de·*ber*
mustard mostaza ⓕ mos·*ta*·tha
mute mudo/a ⓜ/ⓕ *moo*·do/a
my mi mee

N

nail clippers cortauñas ⓜ pl kor·ta·*oo*·nyas
name nombre ⓜ *nom*·bre
napkin servilleta ⓕ ser·vee·*lye*·ta
nappy pañal ⓜ pa·*nyal*

nappy rash irritación Ⓕ de pañal ee·ree·ta·*thyon* de pa·*nyal*
national park parque Ⓜ nacional *par*·ke na·thyo·*nal*
nationality nacionalidad Ⓕ na·thyo·na·lee·*dad*
nature naturaleza Ⓕ na·too·ra·*le*·tha
nausea náuseas Ⓕ *now*·se·as
near cerca *ther*·ka
nearby cerca *ther*·ka
nearest más cercano/a Ⓜ/Ⓕ mas ther·*ka*·no/a
necessary necesario/a Ⓜ/Ⓕ ne·the·*sa*·ryo/a
neck cuello Ⓜ *kwe*·lyo
necklace collar Ⓜ ko·*lyar*
need necesitar ne·the·see·*tar*
needle (sewing) aguja Ⓕ a·*goo*·kha
needle (syringe) jeringa Ⓕ khe·*reen*·ga
neither ninguno/a Ⓜ/Ⓕ ning·*goo*·no/a
net red Ⓕ red
Netherlands Holanda Ⓕ o·*lan*·da
never nunca *noon*·ka
new nuevo/a Ⓜ/Ⓕ *nwe*·vo/a
New Year Año Nuevo Ⓜ a·nyo *nwe*·vo
New Year's Eve Nochevieja Ⓕ no·che·*vye*·kha
New Zealand Nueva Zelanda Ⓕ *nwe*·va the·*lan*·da
news noticias Ⓕ pl no·*tee*·thyas
news stand quiosco Ⓜ *kyos*·ko
newsagency quiosco Ⓜ *kyos*·ko
newspaper periódico Ⓜ pe·*ryo*·dee·ko
next (month) el proximo (mes) el *prok*·see·mo (mes)
next to al lado de al *la*·do de
nice simpático/a Ⓜ/Ⓕ seem·*pa*·tee·ko/a
nickname apodo Ⓜ a·*po*·do
night noche Ⓕ *no*·che
no no no
noisy ruidoso/a Ⓜ/Ⓕ rwee·*do*·so/a
none nada *na*·da
nonsmoking no fumadores no foo·ma·*do*·res
noodles fideos Ⓜ pl fee·*de*·os
noon mediodía Ⓜ me·dyo·*dee*·a
north norte Ⓜ *nor*·te
nose nariz Ⓕ na·*reeth*
note down apuntar a·poon·*tar*
notebook cuaderno Ⓜ kwa·*der*·no
nothing nada *na*·da
now ahora a·o·ra
nuclear energy energía Ⓕ nuclear e·ner·*khee*·a noo·kle·*ar*
nuclear testing pruebas Ⓕ pl nucleares *prwe*·bas noo·kle·a·res
number número Ⓜ *noo*·me·ro
nun monja Ⓕ *mon*·kha
nurse enfermero/a Ⓜ/Ⓕ en·fer·*me*·ro/a
nuts frutos secos Ⓜpl froo·tos se·kos

O

oats avenas Ⓕ pl a·*ve*·nas
ocean océano Ⓜ o·*the*·a·no
off (food) estropeado/a Ⓜ/Ⓕ es·tro·pe·a·do/a
office oficina Ⓕ o·fee·*thee*·na
office worker empleado/a Ⓜ/Ⓕ de oficina em·ple·a·do/a de o·fee·*thee*·na
offside fuera de juego *fwe*·ra de *khwe*·go
often a menudo a me·*noo*·do
oil aceite Ⓜ a·*they*·te
old viejo/a Ⓜ/Ⓕ *vye*·kho/a
olive oil aceite Ⓜ de oliva a·*they*·te de o·*lee*·va
Olympic Games Juegos Ⓜ pl Olímpicos *khwe*·gos o·*leem*·pee·kos
on en en
once una vez Ⓕ *oo*·na veth
one-way ticket billete Ⓜ sencillo bee·*lye*·te sen·*thee*·lyo
onion Ⓕ cebolla the·*bo*·lya
only solo *so*·lo
open abierto/a Ⓜ/Ⓕ a·*byer*·to/a
open abrir a·*breer*
opening hours horario Ⓜ de apertura

o·*ra*·ryo de a·per·*tu*·ra

opera ópera ⓕ *o*·pe·ra

opera house teatro ⓜ de la ópera te·*a*·tro de la *o*·pe·ra

operation operación ⓕ o·pe·ra·*thyon*

operator operador/operadora ⓜ/ⓕ o·pe·ra·*dor*/o·pe·ra·*do*·ra

opinion opinión ⓕ o·pee·*nyon*

opposite frente a *fren*·te a

or o o

orange (fruit) naranja ⓕ na·*ran*·kha

orange (colour) naranja na·*ran*·kha

orange jam mermelada de naranja ⓕ mer·me·*la*·da de na·*ran*·kha

orange juice zumo ⓜ de naranja *thoo*·mo de na·*ran*·kha

orchestra orquesta ⓕ or·*kes*·ta

order orden ⓜ *or*·den

order (arrange) ordenar or·de·*nar*

ordinary corriente ko·*ryen*·te

orgasm orgasmo ⓜ or·*gas*·mo

original original o·ree·khee·*nal*

other otro/a ⓜ/ⓕ *o*·tro/a

our nuestro/a ⓜ/ⓕ *nwes*·tro/a

outside fuera ⓜ *fwe*·ra

oven horno ⓜ *or*·no

overcoat abrigo ⓜ a·*bree*·go

overdose sobredosis ⓕ so·bre·*do*·sees

owe deber de·*ber*

owner dueño/a ⓜ/ⓕ *dwe*·nyo/a

oxygen oxígeno ⓜ ok·*see*·khe·no

oyster ⓕ ostra *os*·tra

ozone layer capa ⓕ de ozono *ka*·pa de o·*tho*·no

P

pacemaker marcapasos ⓜ mar·ka·*pa*·sos

package paquete ⓜ pa·*ke*·te

packet paquete ⓜ pa·*ke*·te

padlock candado ⓜ kan·*da*·do

page página ⓕ *pa*·khee·na

pain dolor ⓜ do·*lor*

painful doloroso/a ⓜ/ⓕ do·lo·*ro*·so/a

painkillers analgésicos ⓜ pl a·nal·*khe*·see·kos

paint pintar peen·*tar*

painter pintor/pintora ⓜ/ⓕ peen·*tor*/peen·*to*·ra

painting pintura ⓕ peen·*too*·ra

pair (couple) pareja ⓕ pa·*re*·kha

palace palacio ⓜ pa·*la*·thyo

pan cazuela ⓕ ka·*thwe*·la

pancetta tocino ⓜ to·*thee*·no

pants pantalones ⓜ pl pan·ta·*lo*·nes

panty liners salvaslips ⓜ pl sal·va·*sleeps*

paper papel ⓜ pa·*pel*

paperwork trabajo ⓜ administrativo tra·*ba*·kho ad·mee·nees·tra·*tee*·vo

paraplegic parapléjico/a ⓜ/ⓕ pa·ra·*ple*·khee·ko/a

parasailing esqui ⓜ acuático con paracaídas es·*kee* a·*kwa*·tee·ko kon pa·ra·ka·*ee*·das

parasol parasol ⓜ pa·ra·*sol*

parcel paquete ⓜ pa·*ke*·te

parents padres ⓜ pl *pa*·dres

park parque ⓜ *par*·ke

park (car) estacionar es·ta·thyo·*nar*

parliament parlamento ⓜ par·la·*men*·to

parsley perejil ⓜ pe·re·*kheel*

part parte ⓕ *par*·te

part-time a tiempo parcial a *tyem*·po par·*thyal*

party fiesta ⓕ *fyes*·ta

party (political) partido ⓜ par·*tee*·do

pass pase ⓜ *pa*·se

passenger pasajero/a ⓜ/ⓕ pa·sa·*khe*·ro

passport pasaporte ⓜ pa·sa·*por*·te

passport number número ⓜ de pasaporte *noo*·me·ro de pa·sa·*por*·te

past pasado ⓜ pa·*sa*·do

pasta pasta ⓕ *pas*·ta

pate (food) paté ⓜ pa·*te*

path sendero ⓜ sen·*de*·ro

pavement acera ⓕ a·*the*·ra

pay pagar pa·*gar*

payment pago ⓜ pa·go
peace paz ⓕ path
peach melocotón ⓜ me·lo·ko·ton
peak cumbre ⓕ koom·bre
peanuts cacahuetes ⓜ pl ka·ka·we·tes
pear pera ⓕ pe·ra
peas guisantes ⓜ pl gee·san·tes
pedal pedal ⓜ pe·dal
pedestrian peatón ⓜ&ⓕ pe·a·ton
pedestrian crossing paso ⓜ de cebra pa·so de the·bra
pen bolígrafo ⓜ bo·lee·gra·fo
pencil lápiz ⓜ la·peeth
penis pene ⓜ pe·ne
penknife navaja ⓕ na·va·kha
pensioner pensionista ⓜ&ⓕ pen·syo·nees·ta
people gente ⓕ khen·te
pepper (vegetable) pimiento ⓜ pee·myen·to
pepper (spice) pimienta ⓕ pee·myen·ta
per (day) por (día) por (dee·a)
percent por ciento por thyen·to
performance actuación ⓕ ak·twa·thyon
perfume perfume ⓜ per·foo·me
period pain dolor ⓜ menstrual do·lor mens·trwal
permission permiso ⓜ per·mee·so
permit permiso ⓜ per·mee·so
permit permitir per·mee·teer
person persona ⓕ per·so·na
perspire sudar soo·dar
petition petición ⓕ pe·tee·thyon
petrol gasolina ⓕ ga·so·lee·na
petrol station gasolinera ⓕ ga·so·lee·ne·ra
pharmacy farmacia ⓕ far·ma·thya
photo foto ⓕ fo·to
photographer fotógrafo/a ⓜ/ⓕ fo·to·gra·fo/a
photography fotografía ⓕ fo·to·gra·fee·a
phrasebook libro ⓜ de frases lee·bro de fra·ses
pick up (collect) recoger re·ko·kher
pickaxe piqueta ⓕ pee·ke·ta
pickles encurtidos ⓜ pl en·koor·tee·dos
picnic comida ⓕ en el campo ko·mee·da en el kam·po
pie pastel ⓜ pas·tel
piece trozo ⓜ tro·tho
pier muelle ⓜ mwe·lye
pig cerdo ⓜ ther·do
pill pastilla ⓕ pas·tee·lya
Pill, the (contraceptive) píldora ⓕ peel·do·ra
pillow almohada ⓕ al·mwa·da
pillowcase funda ⓕ de almohada foon·da de al·mwa·da
pineapple piña ⓕ pee·nya
pink rosa ro·sa
pistachio pistacho ⓜ pees·ta·cho
place lugar ⓜ loo·gar
place of birth lugar ⓜ de nacimiento loo·gar de na·thee·myen·to
plane avión ⓜ a·vyon
planet planeta ⓜ pla·ne·ta
plant planta ⓕ plan·ta
plant sembrar sem·brar
plasters (Band-Aids) tiritas ⓕ pl tee·ree·tas
plastic plástico ⓜ plas·tee·ko
plate plato ⓜ pla·to
plateau meseta ⓕ me·se·ta
platform plataforma ⓕ pla·ta·for·ma
play (theatre) obra ⓕ o·bra
play (musical instrument) tocar to·kar
play (sport/games) jugar khoo·gar
plug (electrical) enchufe en·choo·fe
plum ⓕ ciruela thee·rwe·la
pocket bolsillo ⓜ bol·see·lyo
poetry poesía ⓕ po·e·see·a
point apuntar a·poon·tar
point (tip) punto ⓜ poon·to
poisonous venenoso/a ⓜ/ⓕ ve·ne·no·so/a
poker póquer ⓜ po·ker
police policía ⓕ po·lee·thee·a
police station comisaría ⓕ

ko·mee·sa·ree·a
policy política ⓕ po·lee·tee·ka
policy (insurance) póliza ⓕ po·lee·tha
politician político/política ⓜ/ⓕ po·lee·tee·ko/a
politics política ⓕ po·lee·tee·ka
pollen polen ⓜ po·len
polls sondeos ⓜ pl son·de·os
pollution contaminación ⓕ kon·ta·mee·na·thyon
pool (swimming) piscina ⓕ pees·thee·na
poor pobre po·bre
popular popular po·poo·lar
pork cerdo ⓜ ther·do
port puerto ⓜ pwer·to
port (wine) oporto ⓜ o·por·to
possible posible po·see·ble
post code código postal ⓜ ko·dee·go pos·tal
post office correos ⓜ ko·re·os
postage franqueo ⓜ fran·ke·o
postbox buzón ⓜ boo·thon
postcard postal ⓕ pos·tal
poster póster ⓜ pos·ter
pot (casserole) cazuela ⓕ ka·thwe·la
pot (plant) tiesto ⓜ tyes·to
potato patata ⓕ pa·ta·ta
pottery (activity) alfarería ⓕ al·fa·re·ree·a
pottery (ceramics) cerámica ⓕ the·ra·mee·ka
pound (money) libra ⓕ lee·bra
poverty pobreza ⓕ po·bre·tha
power poder ⓜ po·der
prawns gambas ⓕ pl gam·bas
prayer oración ⓕ o·ra·thyon
prayer book devocionario ⓜ de·vo·thyo·na·ryo
prefer preferir pre·fe·reer
pregnancy test prueba ⓕ del embarazo prwe·ba del em·ba·ra·tho
pregnant embarazada ⓕ em·ba·ra·tha·da
premenstrual tension síndrome premenstrual ⓜ seen·dro·me pre·mens·trwal
prepare preparar pre·pa·rar
president presidente/a ⓜ/ⓕ pre·see·den·te/a
pressure presión ⓕ pre·syon
pretty bonito/a ⓜ/ⓕ bo·nee·to/a
prevent prevenir pre·ve·neer
price precio ⓜ pre·thyo
priest sacerdote ⓜ sa·ther·do·te
prime minister primer ministro/primera ministra ⓜ/ⓕ pree·mer mee·nees·tro/pree·me·ra mee·nees·tra
prison cárcel ⓕ kar·thel
prisoner prisionero/a ⓜ/ⓕ pree·syon·ne·ro/a
private privado/a ⓜ/ⓕ pree·va·do/a
private hospital clínica ⓕ klee·nee·ka
produce producir pro·doo·theer
profit beneficio ⓜ be·ne·fee·thyo
programme programa ⓜ pro·gra·ma
projector proyector ⓜ pro·yek·tor
promise promesa ⓕ pro·me·sa
protect proteger pro·te·kher
protected (species) protegido/a ⓜ/ⓕ pro·te·khee·do/a
protest protesta ⓕ pro·tes·ta
protest protestar pro·tes·tar
provisions provisiones ⓕ pl pro·vee·syo·nes
prune ciruela ⓕ pasa thee·rwe·la pa·sa
pub pub ⓜ poob
public holiday día festivo ⓜ dee·a fes·tee·vo
public toilet servicios ⓜ pl ser·vee·thyos
pull tirar tee·rar
pump bomba ⓕ bom·ba
pumpkin calabaza ⓕ ka·la·ba·tha
puncture pinchar peen·char
punish castigar kas·tee·gar
puppy cachorro ⓜ ka·cho·ro
pure puro/a ⓜ/ⓕ poo·ro/a
purple lila lee·la
push empujar em·poo·khar

put poner po·ner

Q

qualifications cualificaciones ⓕ pl kwa·lee·fee·ka·thyo·nes
quality calidad ⓕ ka·lee·dad
quarantine cuarentena ⓕ kwa·ren·te·na
quarrel pelea ⓕ pe·le·a
quarter cuarto ⓜ kwar·to
quay muelle ⓜ mwe·lye
queen reina ⓕ rey·na
question pregunta ⓕ pre·goon·ta
question cuestionar kwes·tyo·nar
queue cola ⓕ ko·la
quick rápido/a ⓜ/ⓕ ra·pee·do/a
quiet tranquilo/a ⓜ/ⓕ tran·kee·lo/a
quiet tranquilidad ⓕ tran·kee·lee·dad
quit dejar de·khar

R

rabbit conejo ⓜ ko·ne·kho
race (people) raza ⓕ ra·tha
race (sport) carrera ⓕ ka·re·ra
racetrack (bicycles) velódromo ⓜ ve·lo·dro·mo
racetrack (cars) circuito ⓜ de carreras theer·kwee·to de ka·re·ras
racetrack (horses) hipódromo ⓜ ee·po·dro·mo
racetrack (runners) pista ⓕ pees·ta
racing bike bicicleta ⓕ de carreras bee·thee·kle·ta de ka·re·ras
racquet raqueta ⓕ ra·ke·ta
radiator radiador ⓜ ra·dya·dor
radish rábano ⓜ ra·ba·no
railway station estación ⓕ de tren es·ta·thyon de tren
rain lluvia ⓕ lyoo·vya
raincoat impermeable ⓜ eem·per·me·a·ble
raisin uva ⓕ pasa oo·va pa·sa
rally concentración ⓕ kon·then·tra·thyon
rape violar vyo·lar
rare raro/a ⓜ/ⓕ ra·ro/a
rash sarpullido ⓜ sar·poo·yee·do
raspberry frambuesa ⓕ fram·bwe·sa
rat rata ⓕ ra·ta
rate of pay sueldo ⓜ swel·do
raw crudo/a ⓜ/ⓕ kroo·do/a
razor afeitadora ⓕ a·fey·ta·do·ra
razor blades cuchillas ⓕ pl de afeitar koo·chee·lyas de a·fey·tar
read leer le·er
ready listo/a ⓜ/ⓕ lees·to/a
realise darse cuenta de dar·se kwen·ta de
realistic realista re·a·lees·ta
reason razón ⓕ ra·thon
receipt recibo ⓜ re·thee·bo
receive recibir re·thee·beer
recently recientemente re·thyen·te·men·te
recognise reconocer re·ko·no·ther
recommend recomendar re·ko·men·dar
recording grabación ⓕ gra·ba·thyon
recyclable reciclable re·thee·kla·ble
recycle reciclar re·thee·klar
red rojo/a ⓜ/ⓕ ro·kho/a
referee árbitro ⓜ ar·bee·tro
reference referencias ⓕ pl re·fe·ren·thyas
refrigerator nevera ⓕ ne·ve·ra • frigorífico ⓜ free·go·ree·fee·ko
refugee refugiado/a ⓜ/ⓕ re·foo·khya·do/a
refund reembolso ⓜ re·em·bol·so
refund reembolsar re·em·bol·sar
refuse rechazar re·cha·thar
registered mail correo ⓜ certificado ko·re·o ther·tee·fee·ka·do
regret lamentar la·men·tar
relationship relación ⓕ re·la·thyon
relax relajarse re·la·khar·se
relic reliquia ⓕ re·lee·kya
religion religión ⓕ re·lee·khyon
religious religioso/a ⓜ/ⓕ re·lee·khyo·so/a

remember recordar re·kor·*dar*
remote remoto/a ⓜ/ⓕ re·*mo*·to/a
remote control mando ⓜ a distancia *man*·do a dees·*tan*·thya
rent alquiler ⓜ al·kee·*ler*
rent alquilar al·kee·*lar*
repair reparar re·pa·*rar*
repeat repetir re·pe·*teer*
republic república ⓕ re·*poo*·blee·ka
reservation reserva ⓕ re·*ser*·va
reserve reservar re·ser·*var*
rest descansar des·kan·*sar*
rest descanso ⓜ des·*kan*·so
restaurant restaurante ⓜ res·tow·*ran*·te
resumé currículum ⓜ koo·*ree*·koo·loom
retired jubilado/a ⓜ/ⓕ khoo·bee·*la*·do/a
return volver vol·*ver*
return ticket billete ⓜ de ida y vuelta bee·*lye*·te de *ee*·da ee *vwel*·ta
review crítica ⓕ *kree*·tee·ka
rhythm ritmo ⓜ *reet*·mo
rice arroz ⓜ a·*roth*
rich rico/a ⓜ/ⓕ *ree*·ko/a
ride paseo ⓜ pa·*se*·o
ride montar mon·*tar*
right (correct) correcto/a ⓜ/ⓕ ko·*rek*·to/a
right (not left) derecha de·*re*·cha
right-wing derechista de·re·*chees*·ta
ring (phone) llamada ⓕ lya·*ma*·da
ring llamar por teléfono lya·*mar* por te·*le*·fo·no
rip-off estafa ⓕ es·*ta*·fa
risk riesgo ⓜ *ryes*·go
river río ⓜ *ree*·o
road carretera ⓕ ka·re·*te*·ra
rob robar ro·*bar*
rock (stone) roca ⓕ *ro*·ka
rock (music) rock ⓜ rok
rock climbing escalada ⓕ es·ka·*la*·da
rock group grupo ⓜ de rock *groo*·po de rok
rollerblading patinar pa·*tee*·nar
romantic romántico/a ⓜ/ⓕ ro·*man*·tee·ko/a
room habitación ⓕ a·bee·ta·*thyon*
room number número ⓜ de la habitación *noo*·me·ro de la a·bee·ta·*thyon*
rope cuerda ⓕ *kwer*·da
round redondo/a ⓜ/ⓕ re·*don*·do/a
roundabout rotonda ⓕ ro·*ton*·da
route ruta ⓕ *roo*·ta
rowing remo ⓜ *re*·mo
rubber goma ⓕ *go*·ma
rubbish basura ⓕ ba·*soo*·ra
rucksack mochila ⓕ mo·*chee*·la
rug alfombra ⓕ al·*fom*·bra
rugby rugby ⓜ *roog*·bee
ruins ruinas ⓕ pl *rwee*·nas
rules reglas ⓕ pl *re*·glas
rum ron ron
run correr ko·*rer*
run out of quedarse sin ke·*dar*·se seen

S

sad triste *trees*·te
saddle sillín ⓜ see·*lyeen*
safe seguro/a ⓜ/ⓕ se·*goo*·ro/a
safe caja ⓕ fuerte *ka*·kha *fwer*·te
safe sex sexo ⓜ seguro *sek*·so se·*goo*·ro
saint santo/a ⓜ/ⓕ *san*·to/a
salad ensalada ⓕ en·sa·*la*·da
salary salario ⓜ sa·*la*·ryo
salmon salmón ⓜ sal·*mon*
salt sal ⓕ sal
same igual ee·*gwal*
sand arena ⓕ a·*re*·na
sandals sandalias ⓕ pl san·*da*·lyas
sanitary towels compresas ⓕ pl kom·*pre*·sas
sauna sauna ⓕ *sow*·na
sausage salchicha ⓕ sal·*chee*·cha
save salvar sal·*var*
save (money) ahorrar a·o·*rar*
say decir de·*theer*
scale/climb trepar tre·*par*

scarf bufanda ⓕ boo·fan·da
school escuela ⓕ es·kwe·la
science ciencia ⓕ thyen·thya
scientist científico/a ⓜ/ⓕ thyen·tee·fee·ko/a
scissors tijeras ⓕ pl tee·khe·ras
score marcar mar·kar
score (a goal) meter (un gol) me·ter (oon gol)
scoreboard marcador ⓜ mar·ka·dor
Scotland Escocia ⓕ es·ko·thya
screen pantalla ⓕ pan·ta·lya
script guión ⓜ gee·on
sculpture escultura ⓕ es·kool·too·ra
sea mar ⓜ mar
seasick mareado/a ⓜ/ⓕ ma·re·a·do/a
seaside costa ⓕ kos·ta
season estación ⓕ es·ta·thyon
season (in sport) temporada ⓕ tem·po·ra·da
seat asiento ⓜ a·syen·to
seatbelt cinturón ⓜ de seguridad theen·too·ron de se·goo·ree·dad
second (place) segundo/a ⓜ/ⓕ se·goon·do/a
second (time) segundo ⓜ se·goon·do
secondary school instituto ⓜ eens·tee·too·to
secondhand de segunda mano de se·goon·da ma·no
secretary secretario/a ⓜ/ⓕ se·kre·ta·ryo/a
see ver ver
selfish egoísta e·go·ees·ta
self service autoservicio ⓜ ow·to·ser·vee·thyo
sell vender ven·der
send enviar en·vee·ar
sensual sensual sen·swal
separate separado/a ⓜ/ⓕ se·pa·ra·do/a
separate separar se·pa·rar
series serie ⓕ se·rye
serious serio/a ⓜ/ⓕ se·ryo/a
service charge cargo por servicio ⓜ kar·go por ser·vee·thyo
several varios/as ⓜ/ⓕ va·ryos/as
sew coser ko·ser
sex sexo ⓜ sek·so
sexism machismo ⓜ ma·chees·mo
sexy sexy sek·see
shadow sombra ⓕ som·bra
shampoo champú ⓜ cham·poo
shape forma ⓕ for·ma
share (a dorm) compartir (un dormitorio) kom·par·teer (oon dor·mee·to·ryo)
share (with) compartir kom·par·teer
shave afeitarse a·fey·tar·se
shaving cream espuma ⓕ de afeitar es·poo·ma de a·fey·tar
she ella ⓕ e·lya
sheep oveja ⓕ o·ve·kha
sheet (bed) sábana ⓕ sa·ba·na
sheet (of paper) hoja ⓕ o·kha
shelf estante ⓜ es·tan·te
ship barco ⓜ bar·ko
ship enviar en·vee·ar
shirt camisa ⓕ ka·mee·sa
shoe shop zapatería ⓕ tha·pa·te·ree·a
shoelace cordón ⓜ kor·don
shoes zapatos ⓜ pl tha·pa·tos
shoot disparar dees·pa·rar
shop tienda ⓕ tyon·da
shopping centre centro ⓜ comercial then·tro ko·mer·thyal
short (height) bajo/a ⓜ/ⓕ ba·kho/a
short (length) corto/a ⓜ/ⓕ kor·to/a
shortage escasez ⓕ es·ka·seth
shorts pantalones ⓜ pl cortos kor·tos pan·ta·lo·nes
shoulders hombros ⓜ pl om·bros
shout gritar gree·tar
show espectáculo ⓜ es·pek·ta·koo·lo
show mostrar mos·trar
show enseñar en·se·nyar
shower ducha ⓕ doo·cha
shut cerrado/a ⓜ/ⓕ the·ra·do/a
shut cerrar the·rar
shy tímido/a ⓜ/ⓕ tee·mee·do/a
sick enfermo/a ⓜ/ⓕ en·fer·mo/a
side lado ⓜ la·do

sign señal ⓕ se·*nyal*
sign firmar feer·*mar*
signature firma ⓕ *feer*·ma
silk seda ⓕ *se*·da
silver plateado/a ⓜ/ⓕ pla·te·a·do/a
silver plata ⓕ *pla*·ta
similar similar see·mee·*lar*
simple sencillo/a ⓜ/ⓕ sen·*thee*·lyo/a
since (May) desde (mayo) *des*·de (*ma*·yo)
sing cantar kan·*tar*
Singapore Singapur ⓜ seen·ga·*poor*
singer cantante ⓜ&ⓕ kan·*tan*·te
single soltero/a ⓜ/ⓕ sol·*te*·ro/a
single room habitación ⓕ individual a·bee·ta·*thyon* een·dee·vee·*dwal*
sister hermana ⓕ er·*ma*·na
sit sentarse sen·*tar*·se
size (clothes) talla ⓕ *ta*·lya
skateboarding monopatinaje ⓜ mo·no·pa·tee·*na*·khe
ski esquiar es·kee·*ar*
skiing esquí ⓜ es·*kee*
skimmed milk leche ⓕ desnatada *le*·che des·na·*ta*·da
skin piel ⓕ pyel
skirt falda ⓕ *fal*·da
sky cielo ⓜ *thye*·lo
skydiving paracaidismo ⓜ pa·ra·kai·*dees*·mo
sleep dormir dor·*meer*
sleeping bag saco ⓜ de dormir *sa*·ko de dor·*meer*
sleeping car coche cama ⓜ *ko*·che *ka*·ma
sleeping pills pastillas ⓕ pl para dormir pas·*tee*·lyas *pa*·ra dor·*meer*
(to be) sleepy tener sueño te·*ner* *swe*·nyo
slow lento/a ⓜ/ⓕ *len*·to/a
slowly despacio des·*pa*·thyo
small pequeño/a ⓜ/ⓕ pe·*ke*·nyo/a
smell olor ⓜ o·*lor*
smell oler o·*ler*
smile sonreír son·re·*eer*
smoke fumar foo·*mar*
snack tentempié ⓜ ten·tem·*pye*
snail caracol ⓜ ka·ra·*kol*
snake serpiente ⓕ ser·*pyen*·te
snorkel tubo ⓜ de snorkel *too*·bo de *snor*·kel
snorkel hacer snorkel a·*ther* *snor*·kel
snow nieve ⓕ *nye*·ve
snowboarding surf ⓜ sobre la nieve soorf *so*·bre la *nye*·ve
soap jabón ⓜ kha·*bon*
soap opera telenovela ⓕ te·le·no·*ve*·la
soccer fútbol ⓜ *foot*·bol
socialist socialista ⓜ&ⓕ so·thya·*lees*·ta
socks calcetines ⓜ pl kal·the·*tee*·nes
soft drink refresco ⓜ re·*fres*·ko
soldier soldado ⓜ sol·*da*·do
some unos/as ⓜ/ⓕ *oo*·nos/as
some (any) alguno/a ⓜ/ⓕ al·*goon*/ al·*goo*·na
someone alguien *al*·gyen
something algo *al*·go
sometimes de vez en cuando de veth en *kwan*·do
son hijo ⓜ *ee*·kho
song canción ⓕ kan·*thyon*
soon pronto *pron*·to
sore dolorido/a ⓜ/ⓕ do·lo·*ree*·do/a
soup sopa ⓕ *so*·pa
sour cream nata ⓕ agria *na*·ta *a*·grya
south sur ⓜ soor
souvenir recuerdo ⓜ re·*kwer*·do
souvenir shop tienda ⓕ de recuerdos *tyen*·da de re·*kwer*·dos
sow sembrar sem·*brar*
soy milk leche ⓕ de soja *le*·che de *so*·kha
soy sauce salsa ⓕ de soja *sal*·sa de *so*·kha
space espacio ⓜ es·*pa*·thyo
Spain España ⓕ es·*pa*·nya
sparkling espumoso/a ⓜ/ⓕ es·poo·*mo*·so
speak hablar a·*blar*
special especial es·pe·*thyal*
specialist especialista ⓜ&ⓕ

es·pe·thya·lees·ta

speed velocidad ⓕ ve·lo·thee·dad

speeding exceso ⓜ de velocidad eks·the·so de ve·lo·thee·dad

speedometer velocímetro ⓜ ve·lo·thee·me·tro

spider araña ⓕ a·ra·nya

spinach espinacas ⓕ pl es·pee·na·kas

spoon cuchara ⓕ koo·cha·ra

sport deporte ⓜ de·por·te

sports store tienda ⓕ deportiva tyen·da de·por·tee·va

sportsperson deportista ⓜ&ⓕ de·por·tees·ta

sprain torcedura ⓕ tor·the·doo·ra

spring (wire) muelle ⓜ mwe·lye

spring (season) primavera ⓕ pree·ma·ve·ra

square (shape) cuadrado ⓜ kwa·dra·do

(main) square plaza ⓕ (mayor) pla·tha (ma·yor)

stadium estadio ⓜ es·ta·dyo

stage escenario ⓜ es·the·na·ryo

stairway escalera ⓕ es·ka·le·ra

stamp sello ⓜ se·lyo

standby ticket billete ⓜ de lista de espera bee·lye·te de lees·ta de es·pe·ra

stars estrellas ⓕ pl es·tre·lyas

start comenzar ko·men·thar

station estación ⓕ es·ta·thyon

statue estatua ⓕ es·ta·twa

stay (remain) quedarse ke·dar·se

stay (somewhere) alojarse a·lo·khar·se

STD enfermedad ⓕ de transmisión sexual en·fer·me·dad de trans·mi·syon se·kso·al

steak (beef) bistec ⓜ bees·tek

steal robar ro·bar

steep escarpado/a ⓜ/ⓕ es·kar·pa·do/a

step paso ⓜ pa·so

stereo equipo ⓜ de música e·kee·po de moo·see·ka

stingy tacaño/a ⓜ/ⓕ ta·ka·nyo/a

stock (broth) caldo ⓜ kal·do

stockings medias ⓕ pl me·dyas

stomach estómago ⓜ es·to·ma·go

stomachache dolor ⓜ de estómago do·lor de es·to·ma·go

stone piedra ⓕ pye·dra

stoned colocado/a ⓜ/ⓕ ko·lo·ka·do/a

stop parada ⓕ pa·ra·da

stop parar pa·rar

storm tormenta ⓕ tor·men·ta

story cuento ⓜ kwen·to

straight recto/a ⓜ/ⓕ rek·to/a

strange extraño/a ⓜ/ⓕ ek·stra·nyo/a

stranger desconocido/a ⓜ/ⓕ des·ko·no·thee·do/a

strawberry fresa ⓕ fre·sa

stream arroyo ⓜ a·ro·yo

street calle ⓕ ka·lye

string cuerda ⓕ kwer·da

strong fuerte fwer·te

stubborn testarudo/a ⓜ/ⓕ tes·ta·roo·do/a

student estudiante ⓜ&ⓕ es·too·dyan·te

studio estudio ⓜ es·too·dyo

stupid estúpido/a ⓜ/ⓕ es·too·pee·do/a

style estilo ⓜ es·tee·lo

subtitles subtítulos ⓜ pl soob·tee·too·los

suburb barrio ⓜ ba·ryo

subway metro ⓜ me·tro

suffer sufrir soo·freer

sugar azúcar ⓜ a·thoo·kar

suitcase maleta ⓕ ma·le·ta

summer verano ⓜ ve·ra·no

sun sol ⓜ sol

sunblock crema ⓕ solar kre·ma so·lar

sunburn quemadura ⓕ de sol ke·ma·doo·ra de sol

sun-dried tomato tomate ⓜ secado al sol to·ma·te se·ka·do al sol

sunflower oil aceite ⓜ de girasol a·they·te de khee·ra·sol

sunglasses gafas ⓕ pl de sol *ga*·fas de sol
(to be) sunny hace sol a·the sol
sunrise amanecer ⓜ a·ma·ne·*ther*
sunset puesta ⓕ del sol *pwes*·ta del sol
supermarket supermercado ⓜ soo·per·mer·*ka*·do
superstition superstición ⓕ soo·pers·tee·*thyon*
supporters (sports) hinchas ⓜ&ⓕ pl *een*·chas
surf hacer surf a·*ther* soorf
surface mail por vía terrestre por *vee*·a te·*res*·tre
surfboard tabla de surf ⓕ *ta*·bla de soorf
surname apellido ⓜ a·pe·*lyee*·do
surprise sorpresa ⓕ sor·*pre*·sa
survive sobrevivir so·bre·vee·*veer*
sweater jersey ⓜ kher·*sey*
Sweden Suecia ⓕ *swe*·thya
sweet dulce *dool*·the
sweets (candy) dulces ⓜ pl *dool*·thes
(boiled) sweets caramelos ⓜ pl ka·ra·*me*·los
swim nadar na·*dar*
swimming pool piscina ⓕ pees·*thee*·na
swimsuit bañador ⓜ ba·nya·*dor*
Switzerland Suiza ⓕ *swee*·tha
synagogue sinagoga ⓕ see·na·*go*·ga
synthetic sintético/a ⓜ/ⓕ seen·*te*·tee·ko/a
syringe jeringa ⓕ khe·*reen*·ga

T

table mesa ⓕ *me*·sa
table tennis ping pong ⓜ peeng pong
tablecloth mantel ⓜ man·*tel*
tail rabo ⓜ *ra*·bo
tailor sastre ⓜ *sas*·tre
take (away) llevar lye·*var*
take (the train) tomar to·*mar*
take (photo) sacar sa·*kar*
take photographs sacar fotos sa·*kar* *fo*·tos
talk hablar a·*blar*
tall alto/a ⓜ/ⓕ *al*·to/a
tampons tampones ⓜ pl tam·*po*·nes
tank (petrol) depósito ⓜ de·*po*·see·to
tanning lotion bronceador ⓜ bron·the·a·*dor*
tap grifo ⓜ *gree*·fo
tasty sabroso/a ⓜ/ⓕ sa·*bro*·so/a
taxes impuestos ⓜ pl eem·*pwes*·tos
taxi taxi ⓜ *tak*·see
taxi stand parada ⓕ de taxis pa·*ra*·da de *tak*·sees
tea té ⓜ te
teacher profesor/profesora ⓜ/ⓕ pro·fe·*sor*/pro·fe·*so*·ra
team equipo ⓜ e·*kee*·po
teaspoon cucharita ⓕ koo·cha·*ree*·ta
technique técnica ⓕ *tek*·nee·ka
teeth dientes ⓜ pl *dyen*·tes
telegram telegrama ⓜ te·le·*gra*·ma
telephone teléfono ⓜ te·*le*·fo·no
telephone llamar (por teléfono) lya·*mar* (por te·*le*·fo·no)
telescope telescopio ⓜ te·les·*ko*·pyo
television televisión ⓕ te·le·vee·*syon*
tell decir de·*theer*
temperature (fever) fiebre ⓕ *fye*·bre
temperature (weather) temperatura ⓕ tem·pe·ra·*too*·ra
temple templo ⓜ *tem*·plo
tennis tenis ⓜ *te*·nees
tennis court pista ⓕ de tenis *pees*·ta de *te*·nees
tent tienda ⓕ (de campaña) *tyen*·da (de kam·*pa*·nya)
tent pegs piquetas ⓕ pl pee·*ke*·tas
terrible terrible te·*ree*·ble
test prueba ⓕ *prwe*·ba
thank dar gracias dar *gra*·thyas
theatre teatro ⓜ te·*a*·tro
their su soo
they ellos/ellas ⓜ/ⓕ e·lyos/e·lyas
thief ladrón/ladrona ⓜ/ⓕ la·*dron*/la·*dro*·na

thin delgado/a ⓜ/ⓕ del·ga·do/a
think pensar pen·sar
third tercio ⓜ ter·thyo
thirst sed ⓕ seth
this este/a ⓜ/ⓕ es·te/a
this month este mes es·te mes
thread hilo ⓜ ee·lo
throat garganta ⓕ gar·gan·ta
ticket billete ⓜ bee·lye·te
ticket collector revisor/revisora ⓜ/ⓕ re·vee·sor/re·vee·so·ra
ticket machine máquina ⓕ de billetes ma·kee·na de bee·lye·tes
ticket office taquilla ⓕ ta·kee·lya
tide marea ⓕ ma·re·a
tight apretado/a ⓜ/ⓕ a·pre·ta·do/a
tights medias ⓕ pl me·dyas
till caja ⓕ ka·kha
time (watch) hora ⓕ o·ra
time (passing) tiempo ⓜ tyem·po
time difference diferencia ⓕ de horas dee·fe·ren·thya de o·ras
timetable horario ⓜ o·ra·ryo
tin (can) lata ⓕ la·ta
tin (metal) hojalata ⓕ o·kha·la·ta
tin opener abrelatas ⓜ a·bre·la·tas
tiny pequeñito/a ⓜ/ⓕ pe·ke·nyee·to/a
tip (restaurant) propina ⓕ pro·pee·na
tired cansado/a ⓜ/ⓕ kan·sa·do/a
tissues pañuelos ⓜ pl de papel pa·nywe·los de pa·pel
toast tostada ⓕ tos·ta·da
toaster tostadora ⓕ tos·ta·do·ra
tobacco tabaco ⓜ ta·ba·ko
tobacconist estanquero ⓜ es·tan·ke·ro
tobogganing ir en tobogán eer en to·bo·gan
today hoy oy
toe dedo ⓜ del pie de·do del pye
tofu tofú ⓜ to·foo
together juntos/as ⓜ/ⓕ khoon·tos/as
toilet servicio ⓜ ser·vee·thyo
toilet paper papel ⓜ higiénico pa·pel ee·khye·nee·ko

tomato tomate ⓜ to·ma·te
tomato sauce salsa ⓕ de tomate sal·sa de to·ma·te
tomorrow mañana ma·nya·na
tomorrow afternoon mañana por la tarde ma·nya·na por la tar·de
tomorrow evening mañana por la noche ma·nya·na por la no·che
tomorrow morning mañana por la mañana ma·nya·na por la ma·nya·na
tone tono ⓜ to·no
tonight esta noche es·ta no·che
too (expensive) demasiado (caro/a) ⓜ/ⓕ de·ma·sya·do (ka·ro/a)
tooth diente ⓜ dyen·te
toothache dolor ⓜ de muelas do·lor de mwe·las
toothbrush cepillo ⓜ de dientes the·pee·lyo de dyen·tes
toothpaste pasta ⓕ dentífrica pas·ta den·tee·free·ka
toothpick palillo ⓜ pa·lee·lyo
torch linterna ⓕ leen·ter·na
touch tocar to·kar
tour visita ⓕ vee·see·ta
tourist turista ⓜ&ⓕ too·rees·ta
tourist office oficina ⓕ de turismo o·fee·thee·na de too·rees·mo
towards hacia a·thya
towel toalla ⓕ to·a·lya
tower torre ⓕ to·re
toxic waste residuos ⓜ pl tóxicos re·see·dwos tok·see·kos
toyshop juguetería ⓕ khoo·ge·te·ree·a
track (car racing) circuito ⓜ theer·koo·to
track (footprints) rastro ⓜ ras·tro
trade comercio ⓜ ko·mer·thyo
traffic tráfico ⓜ tra·fee·ko
traffic lights semáforos ⓜ pl se·ma·fo·ros
trail camino ⓜ ka·mee·no
train tren ⓜ tren
train station estación ⓕ de tren es·ta·thyon de tren

tram tranvía ⓜ tran·vee·a
transit lounge sala ⓕ de embarque sa·la de em·bar·ke
translate traducir tra·doo·theer
transport medios ⓜ pl de transporte me·dyos de trans·por·te
travel viajar vya·khar
travel agency agencia ⓕ de viajes a·khen·thya de vya·khes
travel books guías ⓕ pl de viaje gee·as de vya·khe
travel sickness mareo ⓜ ma·re·o
tree árbol ⓜ ar·bol
trip viaje ⓜ vya·khe
trousers pantalones ⓜ pl pan·ta·lo·nes
truck camión ⓜ ka·myon
trust confianza ⓕ kon·fee·an·tha
trust confiar kon·fee·ar
try probar pro·bar
try (to do something) intentar (hacer algo) een·ten·tar (a·ther al·go)
t-shirt camiseta ⓕ ka·mee·se·ta
tube (inner) cámara ⓕ de aire ka·ma·ra de ai·re
tuna atún ⓜ a·toon
tune melodía ⓕ me·lo·dee·a
turkey pavo ⓜ pa·vo
turn doblar do·blar
TV tele ⓕ te·le
TV series serie ⓕ se·rye
tweezers pinzas ⓕ pl peen·thas
twice dos veces dos ve·thes
twin beds dos camas ⓕ pl dos ka·mas
twins gemelos ⓜ pl khe·me·los
type tipo ⓜ tee·po
type teclear te·kle·ar
typical típico/a ⓜ/ⓕ tee·pee·ko/a
tyre neumático ⓜ ne·oo·ma·tee·ko

U

ultrasound ecografía ⓕ e·ko·gra·fee·a
umbrella (rain) paraguas ⓜ pa·ra·gwas
umpire árbitro ⓜ ar·bee·tro
uncomfortable incómodo/a ⓜ/ⓕ een·ko·mo·do/a
underpants (men) calzoncillos ⓜ pl kal·thon·thee·lyos
underpants (women) bragas ⓕ pl bra·gas
understand entender en·ten·der
underwear ropa interior ⓕ ro·pa een·te·ryor
unemployed en el paro en el pa·ro
unfair injusto een·khoos·to
uniform uniforme ⓜ oo·nee·for·me
universe universo ⓜ oo·nee·ver·so
university universidad ⓕ oo·nee·ver·see·dad
unleaded sin plomo seen plo·mo
unsafe inseguro/a ⓜ/ⓕ een·se·goo·ro/a
until (June) hasta (junio) as·ta (khoo·nyo)
unusual extraño/a ⓜ/ⓕ eks·tra·nyo/a
up arriba a·ree·ba
uphill cuesta arriba kwes·ta a·ree·ba
urgent urgente oor·khen·te
USA Estados ⓜ pl Unidos es·ta·dos oo·nee·dos
useful útil oo·teel

V

vacant vacante va·kan·te
vacation vacaciones ⓕ pl va·ka·thyo·nes
vaccine vacuna ⓕ va·koo·na
vagina vagina ⓕ va·khee·na
validate validar va·lee·dar
valley valle ⓜ va·lye
valuable valioso/a ⓜ/ⓕ va·lyo·so/a
value valor ⓜ va·lor
van caravana ⓕ ka·ra·va·na
VAT IVA ⓜ ee·va
veal ternera ⓕ ter·ne·ra
vegetable verdura ⓕ ver·doo·ra
vegetables verduras ⓕ pl ver·doo·ras
vegetarian vegetariano/a ⓜ/ⓕ

ve·khe·ta·*rya*·no/a
vein vena ⓕ *ve*·na
venue local ⓜ lo·*kal*
very muy mooy
video games videojuegos ⓜ pl vee·*de*·o·*khwe*·gos
view vista ⓕ *vees*·ta
village pueblo ⓜ *pwe*·blo
vine parra ⓕ *pa*·ra
vinegar vinagre ⓜ vee·*na*·gre
vineyard viñedo ⓜ vee·*nye*·do
virus virus ⓜ *vee*·roos
visa visado ⓜ vee·*sa*·do
visit visitar vee·see·*tar*
vitamins vitaminas ⓕ pl vee·ta·*mee*·nas
vodka vodka ⓜ *vod*·ka
voice voz ⓕ voth
volume volumen ⓜ vo·*loo*·men
vote votar vo·*tar*

W

wage sueldo ⓜ *swel*·do
wait esperar es·pe·*rar*
waiter camarero/a ⓜ/ⓕ ka·ma·*re*·ro/a
waiting room sala ⓕ de espera *sa*·la de es·*pe*·ra
walk caminar ka·mee·*nar*
wall pared ⓕ pa·*red*
wallet cartera ⓕ kar·*te*·ra
walnuts nueces ⓕ pl *nwe*·thes
want querer ke·*rer*
war guerra ⓕ *ge*·rra
wardrobe armario ⓜ ar·*ma*·ryo
warm templado/a ⓜ/ⓕ tem·*pla*·do/a
warn advertir ad·ver·*teer*
wash (oneself) lavarse la·*var*·se
wash (something) lavar la·*var*
washing machine lavadora ⓕ la·va·*do*·ra
watch reloj ⓜ de pulsera re·*lokh* de pool·*se*·ra
watch mirar mee·*rar*
water agua ⓕ *a*·gwa
— tap del grifo del *gree*·fo
— bottle cantimplora ⓕ kan·teem·*plo*·ra
waterfall cascada ⓕ kas·*ka*·da
watermelon sandía ⓕ san·*dee*·a
waterproof impermeable eem·per·me·*a*·ble
waterskiing esquí ⓜ acuático es·*kee* a·*kwa*·tee·ko
wave ola ⓕ *o*·la
way camino ⓜ ka·*mee*·no
we nosotros/nosotras ⓜ/ⓕ no·*so*·tros/no·*so*·tras
weak débil ⓜ&ⓕ *de*·beel
wealthy rico/a ⓜ/ⓕ *ree*·ko/a
wear llevar lye·*var*
weather tiempo ⓜ *tyem*·po
wedding boda ⓕ *bo*·da
wedding cake tarta ⓕ nupcial *tar*·ta noop·*thyal*
wedding present regalo ⓜ de bodas re·*ga*·lo de *bo*·das
weekend fin de semana ⓜ feen de se·*ma*·na
weigh pesar pe·*sar*
weight peso ⓜ *pe*·so
weights pesas ⓕ pl *pe*·sas
welcome bienvenida ⓕ byen·ve·*nee*·da
welcome dar la bienvenida dar la byen·ve·*nee*·da
welfare bienestar ⓜ byen·es·*tar*
welfare state estado ⓜ del bienestar es·*ta*·do del byen·es·*tar*
well bien byen
well pozo ⓜ *po*·tho
west oeste ⓜ o·*es*·te
wet mojado/a ⓜ/ⓕ mo·*kha*·do/a
what que ke
wheel rueda ⓕ *rwe*·da
wheelchair silla ⓕ de ruedas *see*·lya de *rwe*·das
when cuando *kwan*·do
where donde *don*·de
whisky güisqui ⓜ *gwees*·kee
white blanco/a ⓜ/ⓕ *blan*·ko/a

white-water rafting rafting ⓜ *rahf*·teen
who quien kyen
why por qué por ke
wide ancho/a ⓜ/ⓕ *an*·cho/a
wife esposa ⓕ es·*po*·sa
win ganar ga·*nar*
wind viento ⓜ *vyen*·to
window ventana ⓕ ven·*ta*·na
window-shopping mirar los escaparates mee·*rar* los es·ka·pa·*ra*·tes
windscreen parabrisas ⓜ pa·ra·*bree*·sas
windsurfing hacer windsurf a·*ther* *ween*·soorf
wine vino ⓜ *vee*·no
wine shop bodega ⓕ bo·*de*·ga
wineglass copa ⓕ de vino *ko*·pa de *vee*·no
winery bodega ⓕ bo·*de*·ga
wings alas ⓕ pl *a*·las
winner ganador/ganadora ⓜ/ⓕ ga·na·*dor*/ga·na·*do*·ra
winter invierno ⓜ een·*vyer*·no
wire alambre ⓜ a·*lam*·bre
wish desear de·se·*ar*
with con kon
within (an hour) dentro de (una hora) *den*·tro de (*oo*·na *o*·ra)
without sin seen
woman mujer ⓕ moo·*kher*
wonderful maravilloso/a ⓜ/ⓕ ma·ra·vee·*lyo*·so/a
wood madera ⓕ ma·*de*·ra
wool lana ⓕ *la*·na
word palabra ⓕ pa·*la*·bra
work trabajo ⓜ tra·*ba*·kho
work trabajar tra·ba·*khar*
work experience experiencia ⓕ laboral eks·pe·*ryen*·thya la·bo·*ral*
work permit permiso ⓜ de trabajo per·*mee*·so de tra·*ba*·kho
workout entreno ⓜ en·*tre*·no
workshop taller ⓜ ta·*lyer*
world mundo ⓜ *moon*·do
World Cup Copa ⓕ Mundial *ko*·pa moon·*dyal*
worms lombrices ⓕ pl lom·*bree*·thes
worried preocupado/a ⓜ/ⓕ pre·o·koo·*pa*·do/a
worship adoración ⓕ a·do·ra·*thyon*
wrist muñeca ⓕ moo·*nye*·ka
write escribir es·kree·*beer*
writer escritor/escritora ⓜ/ⓕ es·kree·*tor*/es·kree·*to*·ra
wrong equivocado/a ⓜ/ⓕ e·kee·vo·*ka*·do/a

Y

yellow amarillo/a ⓜ/ⓕ a·ma·*ree*·lyo/a
yes sí see
(not) yet todavía (no) to·da·*vee*·a (no)
yesterday ayer a·*yer*
yoga yoga ⓜ *yo*·ga
yoghurt yogur ⓜ yo·*goor*
you inf sg tú too
you ⓜ/ⓕ inf pl vosotros/as vo·*so*·tros/as
you pol pl ustedes oo·*ste*·des
you pol sg usted oo·*sted*
young joven *kho*·ven
your pol sg su soo
your inf sg tu too
youth hostel albergue ⓜ juvenil al·*ber*·ge khoo·ve·*neel*

Z

zodiac zodíaco ⓜ tho·*dee*·a·ko
zoo zoológico ⓜ zo·o·*lo*·khee·ko
zucchini calabacín ⓜ ka·la·ba·*theen*

DICTIONARY

Spanish to English

ESPAÑOL–INGLÉS

SPANISH – ENGLISH A

Nouns in the dictionary have their gender indicated by ⓜ or ⓕ. If it's a plural noun, you'll also see pl. Where a word that could be either a noun or a verb has no gender indicated, it's a verb.

A

abajo a·*ba*·kho below
abanico ⓜ a·ba·*nee*·ko fan (hand held)
abarrotado a·ba·ro·*ta*·do crowded
abeja ⓕ a·*be*·kha bee
abierto/a ⓜ/ⓕ a·*byer*·to/a open
abogado/a ⓜ/ⓕ a·bo·*ga*·do/a lawyer
aborto ⓜ a·*bor*·to abortion • miscarriage
abrazo ⓜ a·*bra*·tho hug
abrebotellas ⓜ a·bre·bo·*te*·lyas bottle opener
abrelatas ⓜ a·bre·*la*·tas can opener • tin opener
abrigo ⓜ a·*bree*·go overcoat
abrir a·*breer* open
abuela ⓕ a·*bwe*·la grandmother
abuelo ⓜ a·*bwe*·lo grandfather
aburrido/a ⓜ/ⓕ a·boo·*ree*·do/a bored • boring
acabar a·ka·*bar* end
acampar a·kam·*par* camp
acantilado ⓜ a·kan·tee·*la*·do cliff
accidente ⓜ ak·thee·*den*·te accident
aceite ⓜ a·*they*·te oil
aceptar a·thep·*tar* accept
acera ⓕ a·*the*·ra pavement
acondicionador ⓜ a·kon·dee·thyo·na·*dor* conditioner
acoso ⓜ a·*ko*·so harassment
activista ⓜ&ⓕ ak·tee·*vees*·ta activist
actuación ⓕ ak·twa·*thyon* performance
acupuntura ⓕ a·koo·poon·*too*·ra acupuncture
adaptador ⓜ a·dap·ta·*dor* adaptor
adentro a·*den*·tro inside
adivinar a·dee·vee·*nar* guess
administración ⓕ ad·mee·nees·tra·*thyon* administration
admitir ad·mee·*teer* admit
adoración ⓕ a·do·ra·*thyon* worship
aduana ⓕ a·*dwa*·na customs
adulto/a ⓜ/ⓕ a·*dool*·to/a adult
aeróbics ⓜ ai·*ro*·beeks aerobics
aerolínea ⓕ ai·ro·*lee*·nya airline
aeropuerto ⓜ ai·ro·*pwer*·to airport
afeitadora ⓕ a·fey·ta·*do*·ra razor
afeitarse a·fey·*tar*·se shave
aficionado/a ⓜ/ⓕ a·fee·thyo·*na*·do/a amateur
afortunado/a ⓜ/ⓕ a·for·too·*na*·do/a lucky

África ⓕ a·free·ka Africa
aftershave ⓜ af·ter·sha·eev aftershave
agencia ⓕ **de viajes** a·khen·thya de vya·khes travel agency
agenda ⓕ a·khen·da diary
agente ⓜ **inmobiliario** a·khen·te een·mo·bee·lya·ryo estate agent
agresivo/a ⓜ/ⓕ a·gre·see·vo/a aggressive
agricultor(a) ⓜ/ⓕ a·gree·kool·tor/ a·gree·kool·to·ra farmer
agricultura ⓕ a·gree·kool·too·ra agriculture
agua ⓕ a·gwa water
— caliente ka·lyen·te hot water
— mineral mee·ne·ral mineral water
aguacate ⓜ a·gwa·ka·te avocado
aguja ⓕ a·goo·kha needle (sewing)
ahora a·o·ra now
ahorrar a·o·rar save (money)
aire ⓜ ai·re air
— acondicionado a·kon·dee·thyo·na·do air-conditioning
ajedrez ⓜ a·khe·dreth chess
al lado de al la·do de next to
alambre ⓜ a·lam·bre wire
alba ⓕ al·ba dawn
albaricoque ⓜ al·ba·ree·ko·ke apricot
albergue ⓜ **juvenil** al·ber·ge khoo·ve·neel youth hostel
alcachofa ⓕ al·ka·cho·fa artichoke
alcalde/alcaldesa ⓜ/ⓕ al·kal·de/ al·kal·de·sa mayor
alcohol ⓜ al·kol alcohol
Alemania ⓕ a·le·ma·nya Germany
alergia ⓕ a·ler·khya allergy
— al polen al po·len hay fever
alfarería ⓕ al·fa·re·ree·a pottery (activity)
alfombra ⓕ al·fom·bra rug
algo al·go something
algodón ⓜ al·go·don cotton
alguien al·gyen someone
algún al·goon some
alguno/a ⓜ/ⓕ al·goo·no/a any • some
almendras ⓕ pl al·men·dras almonds
almohada ⓕ al·mwa·da pillow
almuerzo ⓜ al·mwer·tho lunch
alojamiento ⓜ a·lo·kha·myen·to accommodation
alojarse a·lo·khar·se stay (somewhere)
alpinismo ⓜ al·pee·nees·mo mountaineering
alquilar al·kee·lar hire • rent
alquiler ⓜ al·kee·ler rent
— de coche de ko·che car hire
altar ⓜ al·tar altar
alto/a ⓜ/ⓕ al·to/a high • tall
altura ⓕ al·too·ra altitude
amable a·ma·ble kind
amanecer ⓜ a·ma·ne·ther sunrise
amante ⓜ&ⓕ a·man·te lover
amarillo/a ⓜ/ⓕ a·ma·ree·lyo/a yellow
amigo/a ⓜ/ⓕ a·mee·go/a friend
ampolla ⓕ am·po·lya blister
anacardo ⓜ a·na·kar·do cashew nut
analgésicos ⓜ pl a·nal·khe·see·kos painkillers
análisis de sangre ⓜ a·na·lee·sees de san·gre blood test
anarquista ⓜ/ⓕ a·nar·kees·ta anarchist
ancho/a ⓜ/ⓕ an·cho/a wide
andar an·dar walk
animal ⓜ a·nee·mal animal
Año ⓜ **Nuevo** a·nyo nwe·vo New Year
antes an·tes before
antibióticos ⓜ pl an·tee·byo·tee·kos antibiotics
anticonceptivos ⓜ pl an·tee·kon·thep·tee·vos contraceptives
antigüedad ⓕ an·tee·gwe·dad antique
antiguo/a ⓜ/ⓕ an·tee·gwo/a ancient
antiséptico ⓜ an·tee·sep·tee·ko antiseptic
antología ⓕ an·to·lo·khee·a anthology
anuncio ⓜ a·noon·thyo advertisement

aparcamiento ⓜ a·par·ka·*myen*·to car park
apellido ⓜ a·pe·*lyee*·do surname
apéndice ⓜ a·*pen*·dee·the appendix
apodo ⓜ a·*po*·do nickname
aprender a·pren·*der* learn
apretado/a ⓜ/ⓕ a·pre·*ta*·do/a tight
apuesta ⓕ a·*pwes*·ta bet
apuntar a·poon·*tar* note down • record
aquí a·*kee* here
araña ⓕ a·*ra*·nya spider
árbitro ⓜ *ar*·bee·tro referee
árbol ⓜ *ar*·bol tree
arena ⓕ a·*re*·na sand
armario ⓜ ar·*ma*·ryo cupboard • wardrobe
arqueológico/a ⓜ/ⓕ ar·ke·o·*lo*·khee·ko/a archaeological
arquitecto/a ⓜ/ⓕ ar·kee·*tek*·to/a architect
arquitectura ⓕ ar·kee·tek·*too*·ra architecture
arriba a·*ree*·ba above • up
arroyo ⓜ a·*ro*·yo stream
arroz ⓜ a·*roth* rice
arte ⓜ *ar*·te art
— gráfico *gra*·fee·ko graphic art
artes ⓜ pl **marciales** *ar*·tes mar·*thya*·les martial arts
artesanía ⓕ ar·te·sa·*nee*·a crafts
artista ⓜ&ⓕ ar·*tees*·ta artist
ascensor ⓜ as·then·*sor* lift • elevator
Asia ⓕ *a*·sya Asia
asiento ⓜ a·*syen*·to seat
— de seguridad para bebes de se·goo·ree·*dad* *pa*·ra *be*·bes child seat
asma ⓜ *as*·ma asthma
aspirina ⓕ as·pee·*ree*·na aspirin
atascado/a ⓜ/ⓕ a·tas·*ka*·do/a blocked
atletismo ⓜ at·le·*tees*·mo athletics
atmósfera ⓕ at·*mos*·fe·ra atmosphere
atún ⓜ a·*toon* tuna
audífono ⓜ ow·*dee*·fo·no hearing aid
Australia ⓕ ow·*stra*·lya Australia
autobús ⓜ ow·to·*boos* bus
autocar ⓜ ow·to·*kar* bus (intercity)
autoservicio ⓜ ow·to·ser·*vee*·thyo self-service
autovía ⓕ ow·to·*vee*·a motorway
avenas ⓕ pl a·*ve*·nas oats
avenida ⓕ a·ve·*nee*·da avenue
avergonzado/a ⓜ/ⓕ a·ver·gon·*tha*·do/a embarrassed
avión ⓜ a·*vyon* plane
ayer a·*yer* yesterday
ayudar a·yoo·*dar* help
azúcar ⓜ a·*thoo*·kar sugar
azul a·*thool* blue

B

bailar bai·*lar* dance
bajo/a ⓜ/ⓕ *ba*·kho/a low • short (height)
balcón ⓜ bal·*kon* balcony
ballet ⓜ ba·*le* ballet
baloncesto ⓜ ba·lon·*thes*·to basketball
bálsamo ⓜ **de labios** *bal*·sa·mo de *la*·byos lip balm
bañador ⓜ ba·nya·*dor* bathing suit
banco ⓜ *ban*·ko bank
bandera ⓕ ban·*de*·ra flag
bañera ⓕ ba·*nye*·ra bath
baño ⓜ *ba*·nyo bathroom
bar ⓜ bar bar
barato/a ⓜ/ⓕ ba·*ra*·to/a cheap
barco ⓜ *bar*·ko boat
barrio ⓜ *ba*·ryo suburb
basura ⓕ ba·*soo*·ra rubbish • trash
batería ⓕ ba·te·*ree*·a battery (car) • drums
bebé ⓜ be·*be* baby
beicón ⓜ bay·*kon* bacon
béisbol ⓜ *beys*·bol baseball
beneficio ⓜ be·ne·*fee*·thyo profit
berenjenas ⓕ pl be·ren·*khe*·nas aubergine • eggplant
besar be·*sar* kiss
beso ⓜ *be*·so kiss
biblia ⓕ *bee*·blya bible

biblioteca ⓕ bee·blyo·te·ka library
bicho ⓜ bee·cho bug
bici ⓕ bee·thee bike
bicicleta ⓕ bee·thee·kle·ta bicycle
— de carreras de ka·re·ras racing bike
— de montaña de mon·ta·nya mountain bike
bien byen well
bienestar ⓜ byen·es·tar welfare
bienvenida ⓕ byen·ve·nee·da welcome
billete ⓜ bee·lye·te ticket • banknote
— de ida y vuelta de ee·da ee vwel·ta return ticket
— de lista de espera de lees·ta de es·pe·ra standby ticket
biografía ⓕ bee·o·gra·fee·a biography
bistec ⓜ bees·tek steak (beef)
blanco y negro blan·ko ee ne·gro B&W (film)
blanco/a ⓜ/ⓕ blan·ko/a white
boca ⓕ bo·ka mouth
bocado ⓜ bo·ka·do bite (food)
boda ⓕ bo·da wedding
bodega ⓕ bo·de·ga winery • wine shop
bol ⓜ bol bowl
bolas ⓕ pl **de algodón** bo·las de al·go·don cotton balls
bolígrafo ⓜ bo·lee·gra·fo pen
bollos ⓜ pl bo·lyos rolls (bread)
bolo ⓜ bo·lo gig
bolsillo ⓜ bol·see·lyo pocket
bolso ⓜ bol·so bag • handbag
bomba ⓕ bom·ba bomb • pump
bombilla ⓕ bom·bee·lya light bulb
bondadoso/a ⓜ/ⓕ bon·da·do·so/a caring
bonito/a ⓜ/ⓕ bo·nee·to/a pretty
bordo ⓜ bor·do edge
a bordo a bor·do aboard
borracho/a ⓜ/ⓕ bo·ra·cho/a drunk
bosque ⓜ bos·ke forest
botas ⓕ pl bo·tas boots
— de montaña de mon·ta·nya hiking boots
botella ⓕ bo·te·lya bottle
botiquín ⓜ **de primeros auxilios** bo·tee·keen de pree·me·ros ow·ksee·lyos first-aid kit
botones ⓜ pl bo·to·nes buttons
boxeo ⓜ bo·kse·o boxing
bragas ⓕ pl bra·gas underpants (women)
brazo ⓜ bra·tho arm
broma ⓕ bro·ma joke
bronceador ⓜ bron·the·a·dor tanning lotion
bronquitis ⓕ bron·kee·tees bronchitis
brotes ⓜ pl **de soja** bro·tes de so·kha bean sprouts
brújula ⓕ broo·khoo·la compass
brumoso broo·mo·so foggy
buceo ⓜ boo·the·o diving
budista ⓜ&ⓕ boo·dees·ta Buddhist
bueno/a ⓜ/ⓕ bwe·no/a good
bufanda ⓕ boo·fan·da scarf
bufé ⓜ boo·fe buffet
bulto ⓜ bool·to lump
burlarse de boor·lar·se de make fun of
burro ⓜ boo·ro donkey
buscar boos·kar look for
buzón ⓜ boo·thon mailbox • postbox

C

caballo ⓜ ka·ba·lyo horse
cabeza ⓕ ka·be·tha head
cable ⓜ ka·ble cable
cables ⓜ pl **de arranque** ka·bles de a·ran·ke jump leads
cabra ⓕ ka·bra goat
cacahuetes ⓜ pl ka·ka·we·tes peanuts
cacao ⓜ ka·kow cocoa
cachorro ⓜ ka·cho·ro puppy
cada ka·da each
cadena ⓕ **de bici** ka·de·na de bee·thee bike chain
café ⓜ ka·fe coffee • cafe
caída ⓕ ka·ee·da fall

caja ⓕ *ka*·kha box • till • cash register
— fuerte *fwer*·te safe
cajero ⓜ **automático** ka·*khe*·ro ow·to·*ma*·tee·ko cashpoint
calabacín ⓜ ka·la·ba·*theen* courgette • zucchini
calabaza ⓕ ka·la·*ba*·tha pumpkin
calcetines ⓜ pl kal·the·*tee*·nes socks
calculadora ⓕ kal·koo·la·*do*·ra calculator
caldo ⓜ *kal*·do stock • broth
calefacción ⓕ ka·le·fak·*thyon* central heating
calendario ⓜ ka·len·*da*·ryo calendar
calidad ⓕ ka·lee·*dad* quality
caliente ka·*lyen*·te hot
calle ⓕ *ka*·lye street
calor ⓜ ka·*lor* heat
calzoncillos ⓜ pl kal·thon·*thee*·lyos underpants (men)
calzones ⓜ pl kal·*tho*·nes boxer shorts
cama ⓕ *ka*·ma bed
— de matrimonio de ma·tree·*mo*·nyo double bed
cámara ⓕ **(fotográfica)** *ka*·ma·ra (fo·to·*gra*·fee·ka) camera
cámara ⓕ **de aire** *ka*·ma·ra de *ai*·re inner tube
camarero/a ⓜ/ⓕ ka·ma·*re*·ro/a waiter
cambiar kam·*byar* change • exchange (money)
cambio *kam*·byo ⓜ loose change • exchange
— de dinero de dee·*ne*·ro currency exchange
caminar ka·mee·*nar* walk
camino ⓜ ka·*mee*·no trail • way
caminos ⓜ pl **rurales** ka·*mee*·nos roo·*ra*·les hiking routes
camión ⓜ ka·*myon* truck
camisa ⓕ ka·*mee*·sa shirt
camiseta ⓕ ka·mee·*se*·ta t-shirt
camping ⓜ *kam*·peen campsite
campo ⓜ *kam*·po countryside • field
Canadá ⓕ ka·na·*da* Canada
canasta ⓕ ka·*nas*·ta basket
cancelar kan·the·*lar* cancel
cáncer ⓜ *kan*·ther cancer
canción ⓕ kan·*thyon* song
candado ⓜ kan·*da*·do padlock
cangrejo ⓜ kan·*gre*·kho crab
canguro ⓜ kan·*goo*·ro babysitter
cansado/a ⓜ/ⓕ kan·*sa*·do/a tired
cantalupo ⓜ kan·ta·*loo*·po cantaloupe
cantante ⓜ&ⓕ kan·*tan*·te singer
cantar kan·*tar* sing
cantimplora ⓕ kan·teem·*plo*·ra water bottle
capa ⓕ ka·*po*·te cloak
capa ⓕ **de ozono** *ka*·pa de o·*tho*·no ozone layer
capilla ⓕ ka·*pee*·lya chapel
cara ⓕ *ka*·ra face
caracol ⓜ ka·ra·*kol* snail
caramelos ⓜ pl ka·ra·*me*·los boiled sweets • candies
caravana ⓕ ka·ra·*va*·na caravan • van • traffic jam
cárcel ⓕ *kar*·thel prison
cargo por servicio ⓜ *kar*·go por ser·*vee*·thyo service charge
carne ⓕ *kar*·ne meat
— de vaca de *va*·ka beef
— picada pee·*ka*·da mince meat
carnet ⓜ kar·*ne* licence
— de conducir de kon·doo·*theer* driving licence
— de identidad de ee·den·tee·*dad* identity card
carnicería ⓕ kar·nee·the·*ree*·a butcher's shop
caro/a ⓜ/ⓕ *ka*·ro/a expensive
carpintero ⓜ kar·peen·*te*·ro carpenter
carrera ⓕ ka·*re*·ra race (sport)
carta ⓕ *kar*·ta letter
cartas ⓕ pl *kar*·tas cards
cartón ⓜ kar·*ton* carton • cardboard
casa ⓕ *ka*·sa house

(en) casa (en) *ka*·sa (at) home
casarse ka·*sar*·se marry
cascada ⓕ kas·*ka*·da waterfall
casco ⓜ *kas*·ko helmet
casete ⓜ ka·*se*·te cassette
casi *ka*·see almost
casino ⓜ ka·*see*·no casino
castigar kas·tee·*gar* punish
castillo ⓜ kas·*tee*·lyo castle
catedral ⓕ ka·te·*dral* cathedral
católico/a ⓜ/ⓕ ka·*to*·lee·ko/a Catholic
caza ⓕ *ka*·tha hunting
cazuela ⓕ ka·*thwe*·la casserole pot
cebolla ⓕ the·*bo*·lya onion
celebración ⓕ the·le·bra·*thyon* celebration
celebrar the·le·*brar* celebrate (an event)
celoso/a ⓜ/ⓕ the·*lo*·so/a jealous
cementerio ⓜ the·men·*te*·ryo cemetery
cena ⓕ *the*·na dinner
cenicero ⓜ the·nee·*the*·ro ashtray
centímetro ⓜ then·*tee*·me·tro centimetre
céntimo ⓜ *then*·tee·mo cent
centro ⓜ *then*·tro centre
— comercial ko·mer·*thyal* shopping centre
— de la ciudad de la thyu·*dad* city centre
cepillo ⓜ the·*pee*·lyo hairbrush
— de dientes de *dyen*·tes toothbrush
cerámica ⓕ the·*ra*·mee·ka ceramic
cerca ⓕ *ther*·ka fence
cerca *ther*·ka near • nearby
cerdo ⓜ *ther*·do pork • pig
cereales ⓜ pl the·re·a·les cereal
cerillas ⓕ pl las the·*ree*·lyas matches
cerrado/a ⓜ/ⓕ the·*ra*·do/a closed
— con llave kon *lya*·ve locked
cerradura ⓕ the·ra·*doo*·ra lock
cerrar the·*rar* close • lock • shut
certificado ⓜ ther·tee·fee·*ka*·do certificate
cerveza ⓕ ther·*ve*·tha beer
— rubia *roo*·bya lager
chaleco ⓜ **salvavidas** cha·*le*·ko sal·va·*vee*·das lifejacket
champán ⓜ cham·*pan* Champagne
champiñón ⓜ cham·pee·*nyon* mushroom
champú ⓜ cham·*poo* shampoo
chaqueta ⓕ cha·*ke*·ta jacket
cheque ⓜ *che*·ke cheque (bank)
chica ⓕ *chee*·ka teenage girl
chicle ⓜ *chee*·kle chewing gum
chico ⓜ *chee*·ko teenage boy
chocolate ⓜ cho·ko·*la*·te chocolate
choque ⓜ *cho*·ke crash
ciclismo ⓜ thee·*klees*·mo cycling
ciclista ⓜ&ⓕ thee·*klees*·ta cyclist
ciego/a ⓜ/ⓕ *thye*·go/a blind
cielo ⓜ *thye*·lo heaven • sky
ciencia ⓕ *thyen*·thya science
científico/a ⓜ/ⓕ thyen·*tee*·fee·ko/a scientist
cigarrillo ⓜ thee·ga·*ree*·lyo cigarette
cigarro ⓜ thee·*ga*·ro cigarette
cine ⓜ *thee*·ne cinema
cinturón ⓜ **de seguridad** theen·too·*ron* de se·goo·ree·*dad* seatbelt
circuito ⓜ **de carreras** theer·*koo*·to de ka·*re*·ras racetrack (cars)
ciruela ⓕ thee·*rwe*·la plum
— pasa *pa*·sa prune
cistitis ⓕ thees·*tee*·tees cystitis
cita ⓕ *thee*·ta appointment
citarse thee·*tar*·se date
ciudad ⓕ thyu·*dad* city
ciudadanía ⓕ thyu·da·da·*nee*·a citizenship
clase ⓕ **preferente** *kla*·se pre·fe·*ren*·te business class
clase ⓕ **turística** *kla*·se too·*rees*·tee·ka economy class
clásico/a ⓜ/ⓕ *kla*·see·ko/a classical
clienta/e ⓜ/ⓕ klee·*en*·ta/e client
clínica ⓕ *klee*·nee·ka private hospital • clinic

cobrar (un cheque) ko·*brar* (oon *che*·ke) cash (a cheque)
coca ⓕ *ko*·ka cocaine
cocaína ⓕ ko·ka·*ee*·na cocaine
coche ⓜ *ko*·che car
— cama *ka*·ma sleeping car
cocina ⓕ ko·*thee*·na kitchen
cocinar ko·thee·*nar* cook
cocinero ⓜ ko·thee·*ne*·ro chef • cook
coco ⓜ *ko*·ko coconut
codeína ⓕ ko·de·*ee*·na codeine
código ⓜ **postal** *ko*·dee·go pos·*tal* post code
col ⓜ kol cabbage
cola ⓕ *ko*·la queue
colchón ⓜ kol·*chon* mattress
colega ⓜ&ⓕ ko·*le*·ga colleague • friend
coles ⓜ pl **de Bruselas** *ko*·les de broo·*se*·las Brussels sprouts
coliflor ⓕ ko·lee·*flor* cauliflower
colina ⓕ ko·*lee*·na hill
collar ⓜ ko·*lyar* necklace
color ⓜ ko·*lor* colour
comedia ⓕ ko·*me*·dya comedy
comenzar ko·men·*thar* begin • start
comer ko·*mer* eat
comercio ⓜ ko·*mer*·thyo trade
comida ⓕ ko·*mee*·da food
— de bebé de be·*be* baby food
— en el campo en el *kam*·po picnic
comisaría ⓕ ko·mee·sa·*ree*·a police station
cómo *ko*·mo how
cómodo/a ⓜ/ⓕ *ko*·mo·do/a comfortable
compact ⓜ kom·*pakt* CD
compañero/a ⓜ/ⓕ kom·pa·*nye*·ro/a companion
compañía ⓕ kom·pa·*nyee*·a company
compartir kom·par·*teer* share (with)
comprar kom·*prar* buy
compresas ⓕ pl kom·*pre*·sas sanitary towels
compromiso ⓜ kom·pro·*mee*·so engagement
comunión ⓕ ko·moo·*nyon* communion
comunista ⓜ&ⓕ ko·moo·*nees*·ta communist
con kon with
coñac ⓜ ko·*nyak* brandy
concentración ⓕ kon·then·tra·*thyon* rally
concierto ⓜ kon·*thyer*·to concert
condición ⓕ **cardíaca** kon·dee·*thyon* kar·*dee*·a·ka heart condition
condones ⓜ pl kon·*do*·nes condoms
conducir kon·doo·*theer* drive
conejo ⓜ ko·*ne*·kho rabbit
conexión ⓕ ko·ne·*ksyon* connection
confesión ⓕ kon·fe·*syon* confession
confianza ⓕ kon·fee·*an*·tha trust
confiar kon·fee·*ar* trust
confirmar kon·feer·*mar* confirm
congelar kon·khe·*lar* freeze
conocer ko·no·*ther* know (someone)
conocido/a ⓜ/ⓕ ko·no·*thee*·do/a famous
consejo ⓜ kon·*se*·kho advice
conservador(a) ⓜ/ⓕ kon·ser·va·*dor*/ kon·ser·va·*do*·ra conservative
consigna ⓕ kon·*seeg*·na left luggage
— automática ow·to·*ma*·tee·ka luggage lockers
construir kons·troo·*eer* build
consulado ⓜ kon·soo·*la*·do consulate
contaminación ⓕ kon·ta·mee·na·*thyon* pollution
contar kon·*tar* count
contrato ⓜ kon·*tra*·to contract
control ⓜ kon·*trol* checkpoint
convento ⓜ kon·*ven*·to convent • monastery
copa ⓕ *ko*·pa drink
— de vino de *vee*·no wineglass
Copa ⓕ **Mundial** *ko*·pa moon·*dyal* World Cup
copos de maíz *ko*·pos de ma·*eeth* corn flakes
corazón ⓜ ko·ra·*thon* heart

cordero ⓜ *kor·de·ro* lamb
cordillera ⓕ *kor·dee·lye·ra* mountain range
cordón ⓜ *kor·don* shoelace
correcto/a ⓜ/ⓕ *ko·rek·to/a* right (correct)
correo ⓜ *ko·re·o* mail
— urgente *oor·khen·te* express mail
correos *ko·re·os* post office
correr *ko·rer* run • jogging
corrida ⓕ **de toros** *ko·ree·da de to·ros* bullfight
corriente ⓕ *ko·ryen·te* current (electricity)
corriente *ko·ryen·te* ordinary
corrupto/a ⓜ/ⓕ *ko·roop·to/a* corrupt
cortar *kor·tar* cut
cortauñas ⓜ pl *kor·ta·oo·nyas* nail clippers
corto/a ⓜ/ⓕ *kor·to/a* short (length)
cosecha ⓕ *ko·se·cha* crop
coser *ko·ser* sew
costa ⓕ *kos·ta* coast • seaside
costar *kos·tar* cost
crecer *kre·ther* grow
crema ⓕ *kre·ma* cream
— hidratante *ee·dra·tan·te* moisturising cream
— solar *so·lar* sunblock
críquet ⓜ *kree·ket* cricket
cristiano/a ⓜ/ⓕ *krees·tya·no/a* Christian
crítica ⓕ *kree·tee·ka* review
cruce ⓜ *kroo·the* intersection
crudo/a ⓜ/ⓕ *kroo·do/a* raw
cuaderno ⓜ *kwa·der·no* notebook • square
cualificaciones ⓕ pl *kwa·lee·fee·ka·thyo·nes* qualifications
cualquier ⓜ&ⓕ *kwal·kyer* any
cuando *kwan·do* when
cuánto *kwan·to* how much
cuarentena ⓕ *kwa·ren·te·na* quarantine
Cuaresma ⓕ *kwa·res·ma* Lent
cuarto ⓜ *kwar·to* quarter
cubiertos ⓜ pl *koo·byer·tos* cutlery
cubo ⓜ *koo·bo* bucket
cucaracha ⓕ *koo·ka·ra·cha* cockroach
cuchara ⓕ *koo·cha·ra* spoon
cucharita ⓕ *koo·cha·ree·ta* teaspoon
cuchillas ⓕ pl **de afeitar** *koo·chee·lyas de a·fey·tar* razor blades
cuchillo ⓜ *koo·chee·lyo* knife
cuenta ⓕ *kwen·ta* bill
— bancaria *ban·ka·rya* bank account
cuento ⓜ *kwen·to* story
cuerda ⓕ *kwer·da* rope • string
— para tender la ropa *pa·ra ten·der la ro·pa* clothes line
cuero ⓜ *kwe·ro* leather
cuerpo ⓜ *kwer·po* body
cuesta abajo *kwes·ta a·ba·kho* downhill
cuesta arriba *kwes·ta a·ree·ba* uphill
cuestionar *kwes·tyo·nar* question
cuevas ⓕ pl *kwe·vas* caves
cuidar *kwee·dar* care for • mind (look after)
cuidar de *kwee·dar de* care (for someone)
culo ⓜ *koo·lo* bum (of body)
culpable *kool·pa·ble* guilty
cumbre ⓕ *koom·bre* peak
cumpleaños ⓜ *koom·ple·a·nyos* birthday
currículum ⓜ *koo·ree·koo·loom* resumé • CV
curry ⓜ *koo·ree* curry
cuscus ⓜ *koos·koos* couscous

D

dados ⓜ pl *da·dos* dice (die)
dañar *da·nyar* hurt (damage)
dar *dar* give
— de comer *de ko·mer* feed
— gracias *gra·thyas* thank
— la bienvenida *la byen·ve·nee·da* welcome
— una patada *oo·na pa·ta·da* kick

darse cuenta de dar·se kwen·ta de realise
de de from
— (cuatro) estrellas de (kwa·tro) es·tre·lyas (four-)star
— izquierdas de eeth·kyer·das left-wing
— pena de pe·na terrible
— primera clase de pree·me·ra kla·se first-class
— segunda mano de se·goon·da ma·no secondhand
— vez en cuando de veth en kwan·do sometimes
deber de·ver owe • must • should
débil de·beel weak
decidir de·thee·deer decide
decir de·theer say • tell
dedo ⓜ de·do finger
— del pie del pye toe
defectuoso/a ⓜ/ⓕ de·fek·two·so/a faulty
deforestación ⓕ de·fo·res·ta·thyon deforestation
dejar de·khar leave • quit
delgado/a ⓜ/ⓕ del·ga·do/a thin
delirante de·lee·ran·te delirious
demasiado caro/a ⓜ/ⓕ de·ma·sya·do ka·ro/a too (expensive)
democracia ⓕ de·mo·kra·thya democracy
demora ⓕ de·mo·ra delay
dentista ⓜ&ⓕ den·tees·ta dentist
dentro de (una hora) den·tro de (oo·na o·ra) within (an hour)
deporte ⓜ de·por·te sport
deportista ⓜ&ⓕ de·por·tees·ta sportsperson
depósito ⓜ de·po·see·to deposit • (petrol) tank
derecha ⓕ de·re·cha right (not left)
derechista de·re·chees·ta right-wing
derechos ⓜ pl **civiles** de·re·chos thee·vee·les civil rights
derechos ⓜ pl **humanos** de·re·chos oo·ma·nos human rights
desayuno ⓜ des·a·yoo·no breakfast
descansar des·kan·sar rest
descanso ⓜ des·kan·so rest • pause
descendiente ⓜ des·then·dyen·te descendant
descomponerse des·kom·po·ner·se decompose
descubrir des·koo·breer discover
descuento ⓜ des·kwen·to discount
desde (mayo) des·de (ma·yo) since (May)
desear de·se·ar wish
desfase horario ⓜ des·fa·se o·ra·ryo jet lag
desglosado/a ⓜ/ⓕ des·glo·sa·do/a itemised
desierto ⓜ de·syer·to desert
desodorante ⓜ de·so·do·ran·te deodorant
despacio des·pa·thyo slowly
despertador ⓜ des·per·ta·dor alarm clock
después de des·pwes de after
destino ⓜ des·tee·no destination
destruir des·troo·eer destroy
detalle ⓜ de·ta·lye detail
detener de·te·ner arrest
detrás de de·tras de behind
devocionario ⓜ de·vo·thyo·na·ryo prayer book
día ⓜ dee·a day
— festivo fes·tee·vo public holiday
diabetes ⓕ dee·a·be·tes diabetes
diafragma ⓜ dee·a·frag·ma diaphragm
diariamente dya·rya·men·te daily
diarrea ⓕ dee·a·re·a diarrhoea
dieta ⓕ dee·e·ta diet
dibujar dee·boo·khar draw
diccionario ⓜ deek·thyo·na·ryo dictionary
diente (de ajo) dyen·te (de a·kho) clove (garlic)
dientes ⓜ pl dyen·tes teeth
diferencia ⓕ **de horas** dee·fe·ren·thya de o·ras time difference
diferente dee·fe·ren·te different
difícil dee·fee·theel difficult

dinero ⓜ dee·ne·ro money
— en efectivo en e·fek·tee·vo cash
Dios dyos god
dirección ⓕ dee·rek·thyon address
directo/a ⓜ/ⓕ dee·rek·to/a direct
director(a) ⓜ/ⓕ dee·rek·tor/dee·rek·to·ra director
discapacitado/a ⓜ/ⓕ dees·ka·pa·thee·ta·do/a disabled
disco ⓜ dees·ko disk
discoteca ⓕ dees·ko·te·ka club
discriminación ⓕ dees·kree·mee·na·thyon discrimination
discutir dees·koo·teer argue
diseño ⓜ dee·se·nyo design
disparar dees·pa·rar shoot
DIU ⓜ de·ee·oo IUD
diversión ⓕ dee·ver·syon fun
divertirse dee·ver·teer·se enjoy (oneself)
doblar do·blar turn • bend
doble do·ble double
docena ⓕ do·the·na dozen
doctor(a) ⓜ/ⓕ dok·tor/dok·to·ra doctor
dólar ⓜ do·lar dollar
doler do·ler hurt (pain)
dolor ⓜ do·lor pain
— de cabeza de ka·be·tha headache
— de estómago de es·to·ma·go stomachache
— de muelas de mwe·las toothache
— menstrual mens·trwal period pain
dolorido/a ⓜ/ⓕ do·lo·ree·do/a sore
doloroso/a ⓜ/ⓕ do·lo·ro·so/a painful
donde don·de where
dormir dor·meer sleep
dos ⓜ/ⓕ pl dos two
— camas ka·mas twin beds
— veces ve·thes twice
drama ⓜ dra·ma drama
droga ⓕ dro·ga drug
drogadicción ⓕ dro·ga·deek·thyon drug addiction
drogas ⓕ pl dro·gas drugs
ducha ⓕ doo·cha shower
dueño/a ⓜ/ⓕ dwe·nyo/a owner
dulce dool·the sweet
dulces ⓜ pl dool·thes sweets • candy
duro/a ⓜ/ⓕ doo·ro/a hard

E

echar de menos e·char de me·nos miss (feel sad)
eczema ⓕ ek·the·ma eczema
edad ⓕ e·dad age
edificio ⓜ e·dee·fee·thyo building
editor(a) ⓜ/ⓕ e·dee·tor/e·dee·to·ra editor
educación ⓕ e·doo·ka·thyon education
egoísta e·go·ees·ta selfish
ejemplo ⓜ e·khem·plo example
ejército ⓜ e·kher·thee·to army
el ⓜ el the
él ⓜ el he
elecciones ⓕ pl e·lek·thyo·nes elections
electricidad ⓕ e·lek·tree·thee·dad electricity
elegir e·le·kheer pick • choose
ella ⓕ e·lya she
ellos/ellas ⓜ/ⓕ e·lyos/e·lyas they
embajada ⓕ em·ba·kha·da embassy
embajador(a) ⓜ/ⓕ em·ba·kha·dor/em·ba·kha·do·ra ambassador
embarazada em·ba·ra·tha·da pregnant
embarcarse em·bar·kar·se board (ship etc)
embrague ⓜ em·bra·ge clutch
emergencia ⓕ e·mer·khen·thya emergency
emocional e·mo·thyo·nal emotional
empleado/a ⓜ/ⓕ em·ple·a·do/a employee
empleado/a ⓜ/ⓕ **de oficina** em·ple·a·do/a de o·fee·thee·na office worker
empujar em·poo·khar push
empresario/a ⓜ/ⓕ em·pre·sa·ryo/a business person

en en on
— el extranjero el eks·tran·khe·ro abroad
— el paro el pa·ro unemployed
encaje ⓜ en·ka·khe lace (material)
encantador(a) ⓜ/ⓕ en·kan·ta·dor/en·kan·ta·do·ra charming
encendedor ⓜ en·then·de·dor lighter
enchufe ⓜ en·choo·fe electrical plug
encontrar en·kon·trar find • meet
encurtidos ⓜ pl en·koor·tee·dos pickles
energía ⓕ **nuclear** e·ner·khee·a noo·kle·ar nuclear energy
enfadado/a ⓜ/ⓕ en·fa·da·do/a angry
enfermedad ⓕ en·fer·me·dad disease
— de transmisión sexual de trans·mi·syon se·kso·al STD
enfermero/a ⓜ/ⓕ en·fer·me·ro/a nurse
enfermo/a ⓜ/ⓕ en·fer·mo/a sick
enfrente de en·fren·te de in front of
enorme e·nor·me huge
ensalada en·sa·la·da salad
enseñar en·se·nyar show • teach
entender en·tren·der understand
entrar en·trar enter
entre en·tre among • between
entregar en·tre·gar deliver
entrenador(a) ⓜ/ⓕ en·tre·na·dor/en·tre·na·do·ra coach
entreno ⓜ en·tre·no workout
entrevista ⓕ en·tre·vees·ta interview
enviar en·vee·ar send • ship off
epilepsia ⓕ e·pee·lep·sya epilepsy
equipaje ⓜ e·kee·pa·khe luggage
equipo ⓜ e·kee·po equipment • team
— de inmersión ⓕ de een·mer·syon diving equipment
— de música ⓜ de moo·see·ka stereo
equitación ⓕ e·kee·ta·thyon horse riding
equivocado/a ⓜ/ⓕ e·kee·vo·ka·do/a wrong
error ⓜ e·ror mistake
escalada ⓕ es·ka·la·da rock climbing
escalera ⓕ es·ka·le·ra stairway
escalera ⓕ **mecánica** es·ka·le·ra me·kan·ica escalator
escarcha ⓕ es·kar·cha frost
escarpado/a ⓜ/ⓕ es·kar·pa·do/a steep
escasez ⓕ es·ka·seth shortage
escenario ⓜ es·the·na·ryo stage
Escocia ⓕ es·ko·thya Scotland
escoger es·ko·kher choose
escribir es·kree·beer write
escritor(a) ⓜ/ⓕ es·kree·tor/es·kree·to·ra writer
escuchar es·koo·char listen
escuela ⓕ es·kwe·la school
escultura ⓕ es·kool·too·ra sculpture
espacio ⓜ es·pa·thyo space
espalda ⓕ es·pal·da back (body)
España ⓕ es·pa·nya Spain
especial es·pe·thyal special
especialista ⓜ&ⓕ es·pe·thya·lees·ta specialist
especies ⓕ pl **en peligro de extinción** es·pe·thyes en pe·lee·gro de eks·teen·thyon endangered species
espectáculo ⓜ es·pek·ta·koo·lo show
espejo ⓜ es·pe·kho mirror
esperar es·pe·rar wait
espinacas ⓕ es·pee·na·kas spinach
esposa ⓕ es·po·sa wife
espuma ⓕ **de afeitar** es·poo·ma de a·fey·tar shaving cream
espumoso/a ⓜ/ⓕ es·poo·mo·so/a sparkling • foamy
esquí ⓜ es·kee skiing
— acuático a·kwa·tee·ko waterskiing
esquiar es·kee·ar ski
esquina ⓕ es·kee·na corner
esta noche es·ta no·che tonight
este/a ⓜ/ⓕ es·te/a this
estación ⓕ es·ta·thyon season • station
— de autobuses de ow·to·boo·ses bus station
— de metro de me·tro metro station
— de tren de tren railway station

E – F SPANISH – ENGLISH

estacionar es·ta·thyo·*nar* park (car)
estadio Ⓜ es·*ta*·dyo stadium
estado Ⓜ **civil** es·*ta*·do thee·*veel* marital status
estado Ⓜ **del bienestar** es·*ta*·do del byen·es·*tar* welfare state • wellbeing
Estados Ⓜ pl **Unidos** es·*ta*·dos oo·*nee*·dos USA
estafa ⓕ es·*ta*·fa rip-off
estanquero Ⓜ es·tan·*ke*·ro tobacconist
estante Ⓜ es·*tan*·te shelf
estar es·*tar* to be
— constipado/a Ⓜ/ⓕ kons·tee·*pa*·do/a have a cold
— de acuerdo de a·*kwer*·do agree
estatua ⓕ es·*ta*·twa statue
este *es*·te east
esterilla ⓕ es·te·*ree*·lya mat
estilo Ⓜ es·*tee*·lo style
estómago Ⓜ es·*to*·ma·go stomach
estrellas ⓕ pl es·*tre*·lyas stars
estreñimiento Ⓜ es·tre·nyee·*myen*·to constipation
estropeado/a Ⓜ/ⓕ es·tro·pe·a·do/a off (food)
estudiante Ⓜ&ⓕ es·too·*dyan*·te student
estudio Ⓜ es·*too*·dyo studio
estufa ⓕ es·*too*·fa heater
estupendo/a Ⓜ/ⓕ es·too·pen·do/a great • brilliant
estúpido/a Ⓜ/ⓕ es·*too*·pee·do/a stupid
etiqueta ⓕ **de equipaje** e·tee·*ke*·ta de e·kee·*pa*·khe luggage tag
euro Ⓜ e·oo·ro euro
Europa ⓕ e·oo·*ro*·pa Europe
eutanasia ⓕ e·oo·ta·*na*·sya euthanasia
excelente eks·the·*len*·te excellent
excursionismo Ⓜ eks·koor·syo·*nees*·mo hiking
experiencia ⓕ eks·pe·*ryen*·thya experience
— laboral ⓕ la·bo·*ral* work experience
exponer eks·po·*ner* exhibit
exposición ⓕ eks·po·see·*thyon* exhibition
expreso eks·*pre*·so express
extrañar eks·tra·*nyar* miss (someone)
extranjero/a Ⓜ/ⓕ eks·tran·*khe*·ro/a foreign

F

fábrica ⓕ *fa*·bree·ka factory
fácil *fa*·theel easy
facturación ⓕ **de equipajes** fak·too·ra·*thyon* de e·kee·*pa*·khes check-in
falda ⓕ *fal*·da skirt
falta ⓕ *fal*·ta fault (mechanical)
familia ⓕ fa·*mee*·lya family
fantástico/a Ⓜ/ⓕ fan·*tas*·tee·ko/a fantastic • great
farmacia ⓕ far·*ma*·thya chemist (shop) • pharmacy
farmacéutico Ⓜ far·ma·thee·*oo*·tee·ko chemist (person)
faros Ⓜ pl *fa*·ros headlights
fecha ⓕ *fe*·cha date (time)
— de nacimiento de na·thee·*myen*·to date of birth
feliz fe·*leeth* happy
ferretería ⓕ fe·re·te·*ree*·a hardware store
festival Ⓜ fes·tee·*val* festival
ficción ⓕ feek·*thyon* fiction
fideos Ⓜ pl fee·*de*·os noodles
fiebre ⓕ *fye*·bre fever
— glandular glan·doo·*lar* glandular fever
fiesta ⓕ *fyes*·ta party
filete Ⓜ fee·*le*·te fillet
film Ⓜ feelm film
fin Ⓜ feen end
— de semana de se·*ma*·na weekend
final Ⓜ fee·*nal* end
firma ⓕ *feer*·ma signature
firmar feer·*mar* sign
flor ⓕ flor flower

florista ⓜ&ⓕ flo·rees·ta florist
folleto ⓜ fo·lye·to brochure • leaflet
forma ⓕ for·ma shape
fotografía ⓕ fo·to·gra·fee·a photograph
fotógrafo/a ⓜ/ⓕ fo·to·gra·fo/a photographer
fotómetro ⓜ fo·to·me·tro light meter
frágil fra·kheel fragile
frambuesa ⓕ fram·bwe·sa raspberry
franqueo ⓜ fran·ke·o postage
freír fre·eer fry
frenos ⓜ pl fre·nos brakes
frente a fren·te a opposite
fresa ⓕ fre·sa strawberry
frigerífico ⓜ free·go·ree·fee·ko refrigerator
frío/a ⓜ/ⓕ free·o/a cold
frontera ⓕ fron·te·ra border
fruta ⓕ froo·ta fruit
fruta ⓕ **seca** froo·ta se·ka dried fruit
frutería ⓕ froo·te·ree·a greengrocery (shop)
frutero/a ⓜ/ⓕ froo·te·ro/a grocer (shopkeeper)
frutos secos ⓜpl froo·tos se·kos nuts
fuego ⓜ fwe·go fire
fuera ⓜ fwe·ra outside
fuera de juego fwe·ra de khwe·go offside
fuerte fwer·te strong
fumar foo·mar smoke
funda ⓕ **de almohada** foon·da de al·mwa·da pillowcase
funeral ⓜ foo·ne·ral funeral
fútbol ⓜ foot·bol football • soccer
futuro ⓜ foo·too·ro future

G

gafas ⓕ pl ga·fas glasses
— de sol de sol sunglasses
— de submarinismo de soob·ma·ree·nees·mo goggles
galleta ⓕ ga·lye·ta biscuit
galletas ⓕ pl **saladas** ga·lye·tas sa·la·das crackers
gambas ⓕ pl gam·bas prawns
ganador(a) ⓜ/ⓕ ga·na·dor/ga·na·do·ra winner
ganar ga·nar earn • win
garbanzos ⓜ pl gar·ban·thos chickpeas
garganta ⓕ gar·gan·ta throat
gasolina ⓕ ga·so·lee·na petrol
gasolinera ⓕ ga·so·lee·ne·ra petrol station
gatito/a ⓜ/ⓕ ga·tee·to/a kitten
gato/a ⓜ/ⓕ ga·to/a cat
gay gay gay
gemelos ⓜ pl khe·me·los twins
general khe·ne·ral general
gente ⓕ khen·te people
gimnasia ⓕ kheem·na·sya gymnastics
gimnasio ⓜ kheem·na·see·o gym
ginebra ⓕ khee·ne·bra gin
ginecólogo/a ⓜ/ⓕ khee·ne·ko·lo·go/a gynaecologist
gobierno ⓜ go·byer·no government
gol ⓜ gol goal
goma ⓕ go·ma rubber
gordo/a ⓜ/ⓕ gor·do/a fat
grabación ⓕ gra·ba·thyon recording
gracioso/a ⓜ/ⓕ gra·thyo·so/a funny
gramo ⓜ gra·mo gram
grande gran·de big • large
grandes ⓜpl **almacenes** gran·des al·ma·the·nes department store
granja ⓕ gran·kha farm
gratis gra·tees free (of charge)
grifo ⓜ gree·fo tap
gripe ⓕ gree·pe influenza
gris grees grey
gritar gree·tar shout
grupo ⓜ groo·po group
  de rock de rok rock band
— sanguíneo san·gee·ne·o blood group
guantes ⓜ pl gwan·tes gloves
guardarropa ⓜ gwar·da·ro·pa cloakroom

guardería ⓕ gwar·de·*ree*·a childminding service • nursery school • kindergarten
guerra ⓕ *ge*·ra war
guía ⓜ&ⓕ *gee*·a guide (person)
guía ⓕ *gee*·a guidebook
— audio *ow*·dyo audioguide
— de ocio de *o*·thyo entertainment guide
guías ⓕ pl **de viaje** *gee*·as de *vya*·khe travel books
guindilla ⓕ geen·*dee*·lya chili
guión ⓜ gee·*on* script
guiri ⓜ *gee*·ree foreign tourist (slang)
guisantes ⓜ pl gee·*san*·tes peas
güisqui *gwees*·kee whisky
guitarra ⓕ gee·*ta*·ra guitar
gustar(le) goos·*tar*(·le) like

H

habitación ⓕ a·bee·ta·*thyon* bedroom • room
— doble *do*·ble double room
— individual een·dee·vee·*dwal* single room
hablar a·*blar* speak • talk
hace sol a·the sol it is sunny
hacer a·*ther* do • make
— dedo *de*·do hitchhike
— snorkel *snor*·kel snorkelling
— surf soorf surf
— windsurf *ween*·soorf windsurfing
hachís ⓜ a·*chees* hash
hacia a·thya towards
— abajo a·*ba*·kho down
halal a·*lal* halal
hamaca ⓕ a·*ma*·ka hammock
harina ⓕ a·*ree*·na flour
hasta (junio) *as*·ta (*khoo*·nyo) until (June)
hecho/a ⓜ/ⓕ *e*·cho/a made
— a mano a *ma*·no handmade
— de (algodón) de (al·go·*don*) made of (cotton)
heladería ⓕ e·la·de·*ree*·a ice cream parlour
helado ⓜ e·*la*·do ice cream
hepatitis ⓕ e·pa·*tee*·tees hepatitis
herbolario ⓜ er·bo·*la*·ryo herbalist (shop)
herida ⓕ e·*ree*·da injury
hermana ⓕ er·*ma*·na sister
hermano ⓜ er·*ma*·no brother
hermoso/a ⓜ/ⓕ er·*mo*·so/a beautiful
heroína ⓕ e·ro·*ee*·na heroin
hielo ⓜ *ye*·lo ice
hierba ⓕ *yer*·ba grass
hierbas ⓕ pl *yer*·bas herbs
hígado ⓜ *ee*·ga·do liver
higos ⓜ pl *ee*·gos figs
hija ⓕ *ee*·kha daughter
hijo ⓜ *ee*·kho son
hijos ⓜ pl *ee*·khos children
hilo ⓜ *ee*·lo thread
— dental den·*tal* dental floss
hinchas ⓜ&ⓕ pl *een*·chas supporters (sports)
hindú ⓜ&ⓕ een·*doo* Hindu • Indian
hipódromo ⓜ ee·*po*·dro·mo racetrack (horses)
histórico/a ⓜ/ⓕ ees·*to*·ree·ko/a historical
hockey ⓜ *kho*·kee hockey
— sobre hielo *so*·bre *ye*·lo ice hockey
hoja ⓕ *o*·kha leaf • sheet (of paper)
hojalata ⓕ o·kha·*la*·ta tin (metal)
Holanda ⓕ o·*lan*·da Netherlands
hombre ⓜ *om*·bre man
hombros ⓜ pl *om*·bros shoulders
homosexual ⓜ&ⓕ o·mo·se·*kswal* homosexual
hora ⓕ *o*·ra time
horario ⓜ o·*ra*·ryo timetable
horario ⓜ **de apertura** o·*ra*·ryo de a·per·*tu*·ra opening hours
hormiga ⓕ or·*mee*·ga ant
horno ⓜ *or*·no oven
horóscopo ⓜ o·*ros*·ko·po horoscope
hospital ⓜ os·pee·*tal* hospital
hostelería ⓕ os·te·le·*ree*·a hospitality (industry)

hotel (m) o·*tel* hotel
hoy oy today
hueso (m) *we*·so bone
huevo (m) *we*·vo egg
humanidades (f) pl oo·ma·nee·*da*·des humanities

I

identificación (f) ee·den·tee·fee·ka·*thyon* identification
idioma (m) ee·*dyo*·ma language
idiota (m)/(f) ee·*dyo*·ta idiot
iglesia (f) ee·*gle*·sya church
igual ee·*gwal* same
igualdad (f) ee·gwal·*dad* equality
impermeable (m) eem·per·me·a·ble raincoat
impermeable eem·per·me·a·ble waterproof
importante eem·por·*tan*·te important
impuesto (m) eem·*pwes*·to tax
— sobre la renta so·bre la *ren*·ta income tax
incluido een·kloo·*ee*·do included
incómodo/a (m)/(f) een·*ko*·mo·do/a uncomfortable
India (f) *een*·dya India
indicador (m) een·dee·ka·*dor* indicator
indicar een·dee·*kar* indicate • point
indigestión (f) een·dee·khes·*tyon* indigestion
industria (f) een·*doos*·trya industry
infección (f) een·fek·*thyon* infection
inflamación (f) een·fla·ma·*thyon* inflammation
informática (f) een·for·*ma*·tee·ka IT
ingeniería (f) een·khe·nye·*ree*·a engineering
ingeniero/a (m)/(f) een·khe·*nye*·ro/a engineer
Inglaterra (f) een·gla·*te*·ra England
inglés (m) een·*gles* English • English language
ingrediente (m) een·gre·*dyen*·te ingredient
injusto/a (m)/(f) een·*khoos*·to/a unfair
inmigración (f) een·mee·gra·*thyon* immigration
inocente ee·no·*then*·te innocent
inseguro/a (m)/(f) een·se·*goo*·ro/a unsafe
instituto (m) eens·tee·*too*·to high school • secondary school
instructor/a (m)/(f) een·strook·*tor*/a instructor
intentar (hacer algo) een·ten·*tar* (a·*ther al*·go) try (to do something)
interesante een·te·re·*san*·te interesting
intermedio (m) een·ter·*me*·dyo intermission
internacional een·ter·na·thyo·*nal* international
Internet (m) *een*·ter·net Internet
intérprete (m)&(f) een·*ter*·pre·te interpreter
inundación (f) ee·noon·da·*thyon* flooding
invierno (m) een·*vyer*·no winter
invitar een·vee·*tar* invite
inyección (f) een·yek·*thyon* injection
inyectar(se) een·yek·*tar(*·se) inject (oneself)
ir eer go
— de compras de *kom*·pras go shopping
— de excursión de eks·koor·*syon* hiking
— en tobogán en to·bo·*gan* go tobogganing
Irlanda (f) eer·*lan*·da Ireland
irritación (f) **de pañal** ee·ree·ta·*thyon* de pa·*nyal* nappy rash
isla (f) *ees*·la island
itinerario (m) ee·tee·ne·*ra*·ryo itinerary
IVA (m) *ee*·va VAT • sales tax
izquierda (f) eeth·*kyer*·da left

J

jabón ⓜ kha·*bon* soap
jamón ⓜ kha·*mon* ham
Japón ⓜ kha·*pon* Japan
jarabe ⓜ kha·*ra*·be cough medicine
jardín ⓜ **botánico** khar·*deen* bo·*ta*·nee·ko botanic garden
jarra ⓕ *kha*·ra jug
jeep ⓜ *jeep* jeep
jefe/a ⓜ/ⓕ *khe*·fe/a boss • leader
— de sección de sek·*thyon* manager
jengibre ⓜ khen·*khee*·bre ginger
jeringa ⓕ khe·*reen*·ga syringe
jersey ⓜ kher·*sey* jumper • sweater
jet lag ⓜ dyet lag jet lag
jockey ⓜ *yo*·kee jockey
joven *kho*·ven young
joyería ⓕ kho·ye·*ree*·a jeweller (shop)
jubilado/a ⓜ/ⓕ khoo·bee·*la*·do/a retired
judías ⓕ pl khoo·*dee*·as beans
judío/a ⓜ/ⓕ khoo·*dee*·o/a Jewish
juegos ⓜ pl **olímpicos** *khwe*·gos o·*leem*·pee·kos Olympic Games
juez ⓜ khweth judge
jueza ⓕ *khwe*·tha judge
jugar khoo·*gar* play (sport/games)
juguetería ⓕ khoo·ge·te·*ree*·a toyshop
juntos/as ⓜ/ⓕ pl *khoon*·tos/as together

K

kilo ⓜ *kee*·lo kilo
kilómetro ⓜ kee·*lo*·me·tro kilometre
kiwi ⓜ *kee*·wee kiwifruit
kosher *ko*·sher Kosher

L

labios ⓜ pl *la*·byos lips
lado ⓜ *la*·do side
ladrón ⓜ la·*dron* thief
lagartija ⓕ la·gar·*tee*·kha lizard
lago ⓜ *la*·go lake
lamentar la·men·*tar* regret
lana ⓕ *la*·na wool
lápiz ⓜ *la*·peeth pencil
— de labios de *la*·byos lipstick
largo/a ⓜ/ⓕ *lar*·go/a long
lata ⓕ *la*·ta can • tin
lavadora ⓕ la·va·*do*·ra washing machine
lavandería ⓕ la·van·de·*ree*·a laundrette
lavar la·*var* wash (something)
lavarse la·*var*·se wash (oneself)
leche ⓕ *le*·che milk
— de soja de *so*·kha soy milk
— desnatada des·na·*ta*·da skimmed milk
lechuga ⓕ le·*choo*·ga lettuce
leer le·*er* read
legal le·*gal* legal
legislación ⓕ le·khees·la·*thyon* legislation
legumbre ⓕ le·*goom*·bre legume
lejos *le*·khos far
leña ⓕ *le*·nya firewood
lentejas ⓕ pl len·*te*·khas lentils
lentes ⓜ pl **de contacto** *len*·tes de kon·*tak*·to contact lenses
lento/a ⓜ/ⓕ *len*·to/a slow
lesbiana ⓕ les·bee·*a*·na lesbian
leve *le*·ve light
ley ⓕ ley law
libra ⓕ *lee*·bra pound (money)
libre *lee*·bre free (not bound)
librería ⓕ lee·bre·*ree*·a bookshop
libro ⓜ *lee*·bro book
— de frases de *fra*·ses phrasebook
líder ⓜ *lee*·der leader
ligar lee·*gar* chat up (a person)
lila *lee*·la purple
lima *lee*·ma lime
límite ⓜ **de equipaje** *lee*·mee·te de e·kee·*pa*·khe baggage allowance
limón ⓜ lee·*mon* lemon
limonada ⓕ lee·mo·*na*·da lemonade
limpio/a ⓜ/ⓕ *leem*·pyo/a clean

línea ⓕ *lee*·ne·a line
linterna ⓕ leen·*ter*·na flashlight • torch
listo/a ⓜ/ⓕ *lees*·to/a ready
llamada ⓕ lya·*ma*·da phone call
llamar por teléfono lya·*mar* por te·*le*·fo·no to make a phone call
llano/a ⓜ/ⓕ *lya*·no/a flat • level
llave ⓕ *lya*·ve key
llegadas ⓕ pl lye·*ga*·das arrivals
llegar lye·*gar* arrive
llenar lye·*nar* fill
lleno/a ⓜ/ⓕ *lye*·no/a full
llevar lye·*var* carry • wear
lluvia ⓕ *lyoo*·vya rain
lo que lo ke what
local ⓜ lo·*kal* venue
local lo·*kal* local (nearby)
loco/a ⓜ/ⓕ *lo*·ko/a crazy
lodo ⓜ *lo*·do mud
lombrices ⓕ pl lom·*bree*·thes worms
los dos los dos both
lubricante ⓜ loo·bree·*kan*·te lubricant
luces ⓕ pl *loo*·thes lights
luchar contra loo·*char kon*·tra fight against
lugar ⓜ loo·*gar* place
— de nacimiento de na·thee·*myen*·to place of birth
lujo ⓜ *loo*·kho luxury
luna ⓕ *loo*·na moon
— llena *lye*·na full moon
— de miel de myel honeymoon
luz ⓕ looth light • electricity

M

machismo ⓜ ma·*chees*·mo sexism
madera ⓕ ma·*de*·ra wood
madre ⓕ *ma*·dre mother
madrugada ⓕ ma·droo·*ga*·da early morning
mago/a ⓜ/ⓕ *ma*·go/a magician
maíz ⓜ ma·*eeth* corn
maleta ⓕ ma·*le*·ta suitcase
maletín ⓜ ma·le·*teen* briefcase
malo/a ⓜ/ⓕ *ma*·lo/a bad
mamá ⓕ ma·*ma* mum
mamografía ⓕ ma·mo·gra·*fee*·a mammogram
mañana ⓕ ma·*nya*·na tomorrow • morning (6am–1pm)
— por la mañana por la ma·*nya*·na tomorrow morning
— por la noche por la *no*·che tomorrow evening
— por la tarde por la *tar*·de tomorrow afternoon
mandarina ⓕ man·da·*ree*·na mandarin
mandíbula ⓕ man·*dee*·boo·la jaw
mando ⓜ **a distancia** *man*·do a dees·*tan*·thya remote control
mango ⓜ *man*·go mango
manifestación ⓕ ma·nee·fes·ta·*thyon* demonstration
manillar ⓜ ma·nee·*lyar* handlebar
mano ⓕ *ma*·no hand
manta ⓕ *man*·ta blanket
manteca ⓕ man·*te*·ka lard
mantel ⓜ man·*tel* tablecloth
mantequilla ⓕ man·te·*kee*·lya butter
manzana ⓕ man·*tha*·na apple
mapa ⓜ *ma*·pa map
maquillaje ⓜ ma·kee·*lya*·khe make-up
máquina ⓕ *ma*·kee·na machine
— de billetes de bee·*lye*·tes ticket machine
— de tabaco de ta·*ba*·ko cigarette machine
mar ⓜ mar sea
marido ⓜ ma·*ree*·do husband
maravilloso/a ⓜ/ⓕ ma·ra·vee·*lyo*·so/a wonderful
marcador ⓜ mar·ka·*dor* scoreboard
marcapasos ⓜ mar·ka·*pa*·sos pacemaker
marcar mar·*kar* score
marea ⓕ ma·*re*·a tide
mareado/a ⓜ/ⓕ ma·re·a·do/a dizzy • seasick
mareo ⓜ ma·*re*·o travel sickness

SPANISH – ENGLISH L – M

margarina ⓕ mar·ga·*ree*·na margarine
marihuana ⓕ ma·ree·*wa*·na marijuana
mariposa ⓕ ma·ree·*po*·sa butterfly
marrón ma·*ron* brown
martillo ⓜ mar·*tee*·lyo hammer
más cercano/a ⓜ/ⓕ mas ther·*ka*·no/a nearest
masaje ⓜ ma·*sa*·khe massage
masajista ⓜ&ⓕ ma·sa·*khees*·ta masseur
matar ma·*tar* kill
matrícula ⓕ ma·*tree*·koo·la licence plate number
matrimonio ⓜ ma·tree·*mo*·nyo marriage
mayonesa ⓕ ma·yo·*ne*·sa mayonnaise
mecánico ⓜ me·*ka*·nee·ko mechanic
mechero ⓜ me·*che*·ro lighter
medianoche ⓕ me·dya·*no*·che midnight
medias ⓕ pl *me*·dyas stockings • tights
medicina ⓕ me·dee·*thee*·na medicine
médico/a ⓜ/ⓕ *me*·dee·co/a doctor
medio ⓜ **ambiente** *me*·dyo am·*byen*·te environment
medio/a ⓜ/ⓕ *me*·dyo/a half
mediodía ⓜ me·dyo·*dee*·a noon
medios ⓜ pl **de comunicación** *me*·dyos de ko·moo·nee·ka·*thyon* media
medios ⓜ pl **de transporte** *me*·dyos de trans·*por*·te means of transport
meditación ⓕ me·dee·ta·*thyon* meditation
mejillones ⓜ pl me·khee·*lyo*·nes mussels
mejor me·*khor* better • best
melocotón ⓜ me·lo·ko·*ton* peach
melodía ⓕ me·lo·*dee*·a tune
melón ⓜ me·*lon* melon
mendigo/a ⓜ/ⓕ men·*dee*·go/a beggar
menos *me*·nos less
mensaje ⓜ men·*sa*·khe message
menstruación ⓕ mens·trwa·*thyon* menstruation
mentiroso/a ⓜ/ⓕ men·tee·*ro*·so/a liar
menú ⓜ me·*noo* menu
menudo/a ⓜ/ⓕ me·*noo*·do/a what a (exclamation)
a menudo a me·*noo*·do often
mercado ⓜ mer·*ka*·do market
mermelada ⓕ mer·me·*la*·da jam
— de naranja de na·*ran*·kha orange jam
mes ⓜ mes month
mesa ⓕ *me*·sa table
meseta ⓕ me·*se*·ta plateau
metal ⓜ me·*tal* metal
meter (un gol) me·*ter* (oon gol) score (a goal)
metro ⓜ *me*·tro metre
metro ⓜ *me*·tro metro • subway
mezclar meth·*klar* mix
mezquita ⓕ meth·*kee*·ta mosque
mi mee my
microondas ⓜ mee·kro·*on*·das microwave
miel ⓕ myel honey
miembro ⓜ *myem*·bro member
migraña ⓕ mee·*gra*·nya migraine
milímetro ⓜ mee·*lee*·me·tro millimetre
millón ⓜ mee·*lyon* million
minuto ⓜ mee·*noo*·to minute
mirador ⓜ mee·ra·*dor* lookout
mirar mee·*rar* look • watch
— los escaparates los es·ka·pa·*ra*·tes window-shopping
misa ⓕ *mee*·sa Mass
mochila ⓕ mo·*chee*·la backpack • rucksack
módem ⓜ *mo*·dem modem
(carne) molida (*kar*·ne) mo·*lee*·da mince (meat)
mojado/a ⓜ/ⓕ mo·*kha*·do/a wet
monasterio ⓜ mo·nas·*te*·ryo monastery
monedas ⓕ pl mo·*ne*·das coins
monja ⓕ *mon*·kha nun

monopatinaje ⓜ mo·no·pa·tee·*na*·khe skateboarding
montaña ⓕ mon·*ta*·nya mountain
montar mon·*tar* ride
— en bicicleta en bee·thee·*kle*·ta cycle
monumento ⓜ mo·noo·*men*·to monument
moratón ⓜ mor·a·*ton* bruise
mordedura ⓕ mor·de·*doo*·ra bite (dog)
morir mo·*reer* die
mosquitera ⓕ mos·kee·*te*·ra mosquito net
mosquito ⓜ mos·*kee*·to mosquito
mostaza ⓕ mos·*ta*·tha mustard
mostrador ⓜ mos·tra·*dor* counter
mostrar mos·*trar* show
motocicleta ⓕ mo·to·thee·*kle*·ta motorcycle
motor ⓜ mo·*tor* engine
motora ⓕ mo·*to*·ra motorboat
muchas/os ⓜ/ⓕ pl *moo*·chas/os many
mudo/a ⓜ/ⓕ *moo*·do/a mute
muebles ⓜ pl *mwe*·bles furniture
muela ⓕ *mwe*·la molar (tooth)
muelle ⓜ *mwe*·lye spring (wire) • pier • quay
muerto/a ⓜ/ⓕ *mwer*·to/a dead
muesli ⓜ *mwes*·lee muesli
mujer ⓕ moo·*kher* woman
multa ⓕ *mool*·ta fine (penalty)
mundo ⓜ *moon*·do world
muñeca ⓕ moo·*nye*·ka doll • wrist
murallas ⓕ pl moo·*ra*·lyas city walls
músculo ⓜ *moos*·koo·lo muscle
museo ⓜ moo·*se*·o museum
— de arte de *ar*·te art gallery
música ⓕ *moo*·see·ka music
músico/a ⓜ/ⓕ *moo*·see·ko/a musician
— ambulante am·boo·*lan*·te busker
muslo ⓜ *moos*·lo drumstick (chicken) • thigh
musulmán(a) ⓜ/ⓕ moo·sool·*man*/moo·sool·*ma*·na Muslim
muy *mooy* very

N

nacionalidad ⓕ na·thyo·na·lee·*dad* nationality
nada *na*·da none • nothing
nadar na·*dar* swim
naranja ⓕ na·*ran*·kha orange
nariz ⓕ na·*reeth* nose
nata ⓕ agria *na*·ta *a*·grya sour cream
naturaleza ⓕ na·too·ra·*le*·tha nature
náuseas ⓕ *now*·se·as nausea
náuseas ⓕ pl del embarazo *now*·se·as del em·ba·*ra*·tho morning sickness
navaja ⓕ na·*va*·kha penknife
Navidad ⓕ na·vee·*dad* Christmas
necesario/a ⓜ/ⓕ ne·the·*sa*·ryo/a necessary
necesitar ne·the·see·*tar* need
negar ne·*gar* deny
negocio ⓜ ne·*go*·thyo business
negro/a ⓜ/ⓕ *ne*·gro/a black
neumático ⓜ ne·oo·*ma*·tee·ko tyre
nevera ⓕ ne·*ve*·ra refrigerator
nieto/a ⓜ/ⓕ *nye*·to/a grandchild
nieve ⓕ *nye*·ve snow
ninguno/a ⓜ/ⓕ ning·*goo*·no/a neither
niño/a ⓜ/ⓕ *nee*·nyo/a child
no no no
— fumadores foo·ma·*do*·res non-smoking
— incluido een·kloo·*ee*·do excluded
noche ⓕ *no*·che night
Nochebuena ⓕ no·che·*bwe*·na Christmas Eve
Nochevieja ⓕ no·che·*vye*·kha New Year's Eve
nombre ⓜ *nom*·bre name
— de pila de *pee*·la first name
norte ⓜ *nor*·te north
nosotros/as ⓜ/ⓕ pl no·*so*·tros/no·*so*·tras we
noticias ⓕ pl no·*tee*·thyas news
— de actualidad de ak·twal·ee·*dad* current affairs

novia ⓕ *no*·vya girlfriend
novio ⓜ *no*·vyo boyfriend
nube ⓕ *noo*·be cloud
nublado noo·*bla*·do cloudy
nueces *nwe*·thes walnuts
nuestro/a ⓜ/ⓕ *nwes*·tro/a our
Nueva Zelanda ⓕ *nwe*·va the·*lan*·da New Zealand
nuevo/a ⓜ/ⓕ *nwe*·vo/a new
número ⓜ *noo*·me·ro number
— de la habitación de la a·bee·ta·*thyon* room number
— de pasaporte de pa·sa·*por*·te passport number
nunca *noon*·ka never

O

o o or
obra ⓕ *o*·bra play (theatre) • building site • building work
océano ⓜ o·*the*·a·no ocean
ocupado/a ⓜ/ⓕ o·koo·*pa*·do/a busy
ocupar o·koo·*par* occupy
oeste ⓜ o·*es*·te west
oficina ⓕ o·fee·*thee*·na office
— de objetos perdidos de ob·*khe*·tos per·*dee*·dos lost property office
— de turismo de too·*rees*·mo tourist office
oír o·*eer* hear
ojo ⓜ *o*·kho eye
ola ⓕ *o*·la wave
olor ⓜ o·*lor* smell
olvidar ol·vee·*dar* forget
ópera ⓕ *o*·pe·ra opera
operación ⓕ o·pe·ra·*thyon* operation
opinión ⓕ o·pee·*nyon* opinion
oporto ⓜ o·*por*·to port (wine)
oportunidad ⓕ o·por·too·nee·*dad* chance
oración ⓕ o·ra·*thyon* prayer
orden ⓜ *or*·den order
ordenador ⓜ or·de·na·*dor* computer
— portátil por·*ta*·teel laptop
ordenar or·de·*nar* order • arrange • tidy
oreja ⓕ o·*re*·kha ear
orgasmo ⓜ or·*gas*·mo orgasm
original o·ree·khee·*nal* original • unusual
orquesta ⓕ or·*kes*·ta orchestra
oscuro/a ⓜ/ⓕ os·*koo*·ro/a dark
ostra ⓕ *os*·tra oyster
otoño ⓜ o·*to*·nyo autumn
otra vez *o*·tra veth again
otro/a ⓜ/ⓕ *o*·tro/a other • another
oveja ⓕ o·*ve*·kha sheep
oxígeno ⓜ o·*ksee*·khe·no oxygen

P

padre ⓜ *pa*·dre father
padres ⓜ pl *pa*·dres parents
pagar pa·*gar* pay
página ⓕ *pa*·khee·na page
pago ⓜ *pa*·go payment
país ⓜ pa·*ees* country
pájaro ⓜ *pa*·kha·ro bird
palabra ⓕ pa·*la*·bra word
palacio ⓜ pa·*la*·thyo palace
palillo ⓜ pa·*lee*·lyo toothpick
pan ⓜ pan bread
— blanco blan·ko white bread
— integral in·te·*gral* wholemeal bread
panadería ⓕ pa·na·de·*ree*·a bakery
pañal ⓜ pa·*nyal* nappy • diaper
pantalla ⓕ pan·*ta*·lya screen
pantalones ⓜ pl pan·ta·*lo*·nes trousers • pants
— cortos *kor*·tos shorts
pañuelos ⓜ pl **de papel** pa·*nywe*·los de pa·*pel* tissues
papá ⓜ pa·*pa* dad
papel ⓜ pa·*pel* paper
— de fumar de foo·*mar* cigarette papers
— higiénico ee·*khye*·nee·ko toilet paper
paquete ⓜ pa·*ke*·te packet • package
para llevar pa·ra lye·*var* to take away
parabrisas ⓜ pa·ra·*bree*·sas windscreen
paracaidismo ⓜ pa·ra·kai·*dees*·mo skydiving

parada ⓕ *pa·ra·da* stop
— de autobús *de ow·to·boos* bus stop
— de taxis *de ta·ksees* taxi stand
paraguas ⓜ *pa·ra·gwas* umbrella
parapléjico/a ⓜ/ⓕ *pa·ra·ple·khee·ko/a* paraplegic
parar *pa·rar* stop
parasol ⓜ *pa·ra·sol* parasol
pared ⓕ *pa·red* wall
pareja ⓕ *pa·re·kha* pair (couple)
parlamento ⓜ *par·la·men·to* parliament
paro ⓜ *pa·ro* dole
parque ⓜ *par·ke* park
— nacional *na·thyo·nal* national park
parra ⓕ *pa·ra* vine
parte ⓕ *par·te* part
partida ⓕ **de nacimiento** *par·tee·da de na·thee·myen·to* birth certificate
partido ⓜ *par·tee·do* match (sport) • (political) party
pasado ⓜ *pa·sa·do* past
pasado mañana *pa·sa·do ma·nya·na* day after tomorrow
pasajero ⓜ *pa·sa·khe·ro* passenger
pasaporte ⓜ *pa·sa·por·te* passport
Pascua ⓕ *pas·kwa* Easter
pase ⓜ *pa·se* pass
paseo ⓜ *pa·se·o* street • stroll
paso ⓜ *pa·so* step
— de cebra *de the·bra* pedestrian crossing
pasta ⓕ *pas·ta* pasta
— dentífrica *den·tee·free·ka* toothpaste
pastel ⓜ *pas·tel* cake • pie
— de cumpleaños *de koom·ple·a·nyos* birthday cake
pastelería ⓕ *pas·te·le·ree·a* cake shop
pastilla ⓕ *pas·tee·lya* pill
pastillas ⓕ pl **para dormir** *pas·tee·lyas pa·ra dor·moor* sleeping pills
patata ⓕ *pa·ta·ta* potato
paté ⓜ *pa·te* pate (food)
patinar *pa·tee·nar* rollerblading • ice skating
pato ⓜ *pa·to* duck
pavo ⓜ *pa·vo* turkey
paz ⓕ *path* peace
peatón ⓜ&ⓕ *pe·a·ton* pedestrian
pecho ⓜ *pe·cho* chest
pechuga ⓕ *pe·choo·ga* breast (poultry)
pedal ⓜ *pe·dal* pedal
pedir *pe·deer* ask (for something)
peine ⓜ *pey·ne* comb
pelea ⓕ *pe·le·a* fight
película ⓕ *pe·lee·koo·la* movie • film (camera)
— en color *en ko·lor* colour film
peligroso/a ⓜ/ⓕ *pe·lee·gro·so/a* dangerous
pelo ⓜ *pe·lo* hair
pelota ⓕ *pe·lo·ta* ball
— de golf *de golf* golf ball
peluquero/a ⓜ/ⓕ *pe·loo·ke·ro/a* hairdresser
pendientes ⓜ pl *pen·dyen·tes* earrings
pene ⓜ *pe·ne* penis
pensar *pen·sar* think
pensión ⓕ *pen·syon* guesthouse
pensionista ⓜ&ⓕ *pen·syo·nees·ta* pensioner
pepino ⓜ *pe·pee·no* cucumber
pequeñito/a ⓜ/ⓕ *pe·ke·nyee·to/a* tiny
pequeño/a ⓜ/ⓕ *pe·ke·nyo/a* small
pera ⓕ *pe·ra* pear
perder *per·der* lose
perdido/a ⓜ/ⓕ *per·dee·do/a* lost
perdonar *per·do·nar* forgive
perejil ⓜ *pe·re·kheel* parsley
perfume ⓜ *per·foo·me* perfume
periódico ⓜ *pe·ryo·dee·ko* newspaper
periodista ⓜ&ⓕ *pe·ryo·dees·ta* journalist
permiso ⓜ *per·mee·so* permission • permit
— de trabajo ⓜ *de tra·ba·kho* work permit

permitir *per·mee·teer* allow • permit
pero *pe·ro* but
perro/a ⓜ/ⓕ *pe·ro/a* dog
perro ⓜ **lazarillo** *pe·ro la·tha·ree·lyo* guide dog
persona ⓕ *per·so·na* person
pesado/a ⓜ/ⓕ *pe·sa·do/a* heavy • annoying
pesar *pe·sar* weigh
pesas ⓕ pl *pe·sas* weights
pesca ⓕ *pes·ka* fishing
pescadería ⓕ *pes·ka·de·ree·a* fish shop
pescado ⓜ *pes·ka·do* fish (as food)
peso ⓜ *pe·so* weight
petición ⓕ *pe·tee·thyon* petition
pez ⓜ *peth* fish
picadura ⓕ *pee·ka·doo·ra* bite (insect)
picor ⓜ *pee·kor* itch
pie ⓜ *pye* foot
piedra ⓕ *pye·dra* stone
piel ⓕ *pyel* skin
pierna ⓕ *pyer·na* leg
pila ⓕ *pee·la* battery (small)
píldora ⓕ *peel·do·ra* the Pill
pimienta ⓕ *pee·myen·ta* pepper
pimiento ⓜ *pee·myen·to* bell pepper
— rojo *ro·kho* red pepper
— verde *ver·de* green pepper
piña ⓕ *pee·nya* pineapple
pinchar *peen·char* puncture
ping pong ⓜ *peeng pong* table tennis
pintar *peen·tar* paint
pintor(a) ⓜ/ⓕ *peen·tor/peen·to·ra* painter
pintura ⓕ *peen·too·ra* painting
pinzas ⓕ pl *peen·thas* tweezers
piojos ⓜ pl *pyo·khos* lice
piqueta ⓕ *pee·ke·ta* pickaxe
piquetas ⓕ pl *pee·ke·tas* tent pegs
piruletas ⓕ pl *pee·roo·le·tas* lollies
piscina ⓕ *pees·thee·na* swimming pool
pista ⓕ *pees·ta* court • racetrack • rink
— de tenis *de te·nees* tennis court
pistacho ⓜ *pees·ta·cho* pistachio
plancha ⓕ *plan·cha* iron
planeta ⓜ *pla·ne·ta* planet
planta ⓕ *plan·ta* plant
plástico ⓜ *plas·tee·ko* plastic
plata ⓕ *pla·ta* silver
plataforma ⓕ *pla·ta·for·ma* platform
plátano ⓜ *pla·ta·no* banana
plateado/a ⓜ/ⓕ *pla·te·a·do/a* silver
plato ⓜ *pla·to* plate
playa ⓕ *pla·ya* beach
plaza ⓕ *pla·tha* square
— de toros *de to·ros* bullring
pobre *po·bre* poor
pobreza ⓕ *po·bre·tha* poverty
pocos *po·kos* few
poder *po·der* can (be able)
poder ⓜ *po·der* power
poesía ⓕ *po·e·see·a* poetry
polen ⓜ *po·len* pollen
policía ⓕ *po·lee·thee·a* police
política ⓕ *po·lee·tee·ka* policy • politics
político/política ⓜ/f *po·lee·tee·ko/a* politician
póliza ⓕ *po·lee·tha* policy (insurance)
pollo ⓜ *po·lyo* chicken
pomelo ⓜ *po·me·lo* grapefruit
poner *po·ner* put
popular *po·poo·lar* popular
póquer ⓜ *po·ker* poker
por (día) *por (dee·a)* per (day)
por ciento *por thyen·to* percent
por qué *por ke* why
por vía aérea *por vee·a a·e·re·a* air mail
por vía terrestre *por vee·a te·res·tre* surface mail
porque *por·ke* because
portero/a ⓜ/ⓕ *por·te·ro/a* goalkeeper
posible *po·see·ble* possible
postal ⓕ *pos·tal* postcard
póster ⓜ *pos·ter* poster
potro ⓜ *po·tro* foal
pozo ⓜ *po·tho* well (with water)

precio ⓜ *pre*·thyo price
— de entrada de en·*tra*·da admission price
— del cubierto del koo·*byer*·to cover charge
preferir pre·fe·*reer* prefer
pregunta ⓕ pre·*goon*·ta question
preguntar pre·goon·*tar* ask (a question)
preocupado/a ⓜ/ⓕ pre·o·koo·*pa*·do/a worried
preocuparse por pre·o·koo·*par*·se por care (about something)
preparar pre·pa·*rar* prepare
presidente/a ⓜ/ⓕ pre·see·*den*·te/a president
presión ⓕ pre·*syon* pressure
— arterial ar·te·*ryal* blood pressure
prevenir pre·ve·*neer* prevent
primavera ⓕ pree·ma·*ve*·ra spring (season)
primer ministro ⓜ pree·*mer* mee·*nees*·tro prime minister
primera ministra ⓕ pree·*me*·ra mee·*nees*·tra prime minister
primero/a ⓜ/ⓕ pree·*me*·ro/a first
principal preen·thee·*pal* main
prisa ⓕ *pree*·sa hurry
prisionero/a ⓜ/ⓕ pree·syon·*ne*·ro/a prisoner
privado/a ⓜ/ⓕ pree·*va*·do/a private
probar pro·*bar* try
producir pro·doo·*theer* produce
productos ⓜ pl **congelados** pro·*dook*·tos kon·khe·*la*·dos frozen foods
profesor(a) ⓜ/ⓕ pro·fe·*sor*/ pro·fe·*so*·ra lecturer • teacher
profundo/a ⓜ/ⓕ pro·*foon*·do/a deep
programa ⓜ pro·*gra*·ma programme
prolongación ⓕ pro·lon·ga·*thyon* extension (visa)
promesa ⓕ pro·*me*·sa promise
prometida ⓕ pro·me·*tee*·da fiancée
prometido ⓜ pro·me·*tee*·do fiancé
pronto *pron*·to soon
propietaria ⓕ pro·pye·*ta*·rya landlady
propietario ⓜ pro·pye·*ta*·ryo landlord
propina ⓕ pro·*pee*·na tip (restaurant)
proteger pro·te·*kher* protect
protegido/a ⓜ/ⓕ pro·te·*khee*·do/a protected
protesta ⓕ pro·*tes*·ta protest
provisiones ⓕ pl pro·bee·*syo*·nes provisions
proyector ⓜ pro·yek·*tor* projector
prudente proo·*den*·te cautious
prueba ⓕ *prwe*·ba test
— del embarazo del em·ba·*ra*·tho pregnancy test kit
pruebas ⓕ pl **nucleares** *prwe*·bas noo·kle·*a*·res nuclear testing
pub ⓜ poob pub
pueblo ⓜ *pwe*·blo village
puente ⓜ *pwen*·te bridge
puerro ⓜ *pwe*·ro leek
puerta ⓕ *pwer*·ta door
puerto ⓜ *pwer*·to port • harbour
puesta ⓕ **del sol** *pwes*·ta del sol sunset
pulga ⓕ *pool*·ga flea
pulmones ⓜ pl pool·*mo*·nes lungs
punto ⓜ *poon*·to point (tip/score)
puro ⓜ *poo*·ro cigar
puro/a ⓜ/ⓕ *poo*·ro/a pure

Q

que ke what
(el mes) que viene (el mes) ke *vye*·ne next (month)
quedar ke·*dar* leave (behind)
quedarse ke·*dar*·se stay (remain)
quedarse sin ke·*dar*·se seen run out of
quejarse ke·*khar*·se complain
quemadura ⓕ ke·ma·*doo*·ra burn
— de sol de sol sunburn
querer ke·*rer* love • want
queso ⓜ *ke*·so cheese
— crema *kre*·ma cream cheese
— de cabra de *ka*·bra goat's cheese

quien kyen who
quincena ⓕ keen·the·na fortnight
quiosco ⓜ kyos·ko news stand • newsagency
quiste ⓜ **ovárico** kees·te o·va·ree·ko ovarian cyst
quizás kee·thas maybe

R

rábano ⓜ ra·ba·no radish
— picante pee·kan·te horseradish
rápido/a ⓜ/ⓕ ra·pee·do/a fast
raqueta ⓕ ra·ke·ta racquet
raro/a ⓜ/ⓕ ra·ro/a rare (item)
rastro ⓜ ras·tro track (footprints) • trace • trail
rata ⓕ ra·ta rat
ratón ⓜ ra·ton mouse
raza ⓕ ra·tha race (people)
razón ⓕ ra·thon reason
realista re·a·lees·ta realistic
rechazar re·cha·thar refuse
recibir re·thee·beer receive
recibo ⓜ re·thee·bo receipt
reciclable re·thee·kla·ble recyclable
reciclar re·thee·klar recycle
recientemente re·thyen·te·men·te recently
recoger re·ko·kher pick up • collect
recogida ⓕ **de equipajes** re·ko·khee·da de e·kee·pa·khes baggage claim
recolección ⓕ **de fruta** re·ko·lek·thyon de froo·ta fruit picking
recomendar re·ko·men·dar recommend
reconocer re·ko·no·ther recognise
recordar re·kor·dar remember
recorrido ⓜ **guiado** re·ko·ree·do gee·a·do guided tour
recto/a ⓜ/ⓕ rek·to/a straight
recuerdo ⓜ re·kwer·do souvenir
red ⓕ red net • network
redondo/a ⓜ/ⓕ re·don·do/a round
reembolsar re·em·bol·sar refund
reembolso ⓜ re·em·bol·so refund
referencias ⓕ pl re·fe·ren·thyas references
refresco ⓜ re·fres·ko soft drink
refugiado/a ⓜ/ⓕ re·foo·khya·do/a refugee
regalar re·ga·lar give as a gift
regalo ⓜ re·ga·lo gift
— de bodas de bo·das wedding present
régimen ⓜ re·khee·men diet
reglas ⓕ pl re·glas rules
reina ⓕ rey·na queen
reírse re·eer·se laugh
relación ⓕ re·la·thyon relationship
relajarse re·la·khar·se relax
religión ⓕ re·lee·khyon religion
religioso/a ⓜ/ⓕ re·lee·khyo·so/a religious
reliquia ⓕ re·lee·kya relic
reloj ⓜ re·lokh clock
— de pulsera de pool·se·ra watch
remo ⓜ re·mo rowing
remolacha ⓕ re·mo·la·cha beetroot • beet
remoto/a ⓜ/ⓕ re·mo·to/a remote
reparar re·pa·rar repair
repartir re·par·teer divide up (share)
repetir re·pe·teer repeat
república ⓕ re·poo·blee·ka republic
requesón ⓜ re·ke·son cottage cheese
reserva ⓕ re·ser·va reservation
reservar re·ser·var book (make a reservation)
resfriado ⓜ res·free·a·do cold
residencia ⓕ **de estudiantes** re·see·den·thya de es·too·dyan·tes hall of residence
residuos ⓜ pl **tóxicos** re·see·dwos to·ksee·kos toxic waste
respirar res·pee·rar breathe
respuesta ⓕ res·pwes·ta answer
restaurante ⓜ res·tow·ran·te restaurant
revisar re·vee·sar check
revisor(a) ⓜ/ⓕ re·vee·sor/re·vee·so·ra ticket collector

revista ⓕ re·*vees*·ta magazine
rey ⓜ rey king
rico/a ⓜ/ⓕ *ree*·ko/a rich
riesgo ⓜ *ryes*·go risk
río ⓜ *ree*·o river
ritmo ⓜ *reet*·mo rhythm
robar ro·*bar* rob • steal
roca ⓕ *ro*·ka rock
rock ⓜ rok rock (music)
rodilla ⓕ ro·*dee*·lya knee
rojo/a ⓜ/ⓕ *ro*·kho/a red
romántico/a ⓜ/ⓕ ro·*man*·tee·ko/a romantic
romper rom·*per* break
ron ⓜ ron rum
ropa ⓕ *ro*·pa clothing
— de cama de *ka*·ma bedding
— interior een·te·*ryor* underwear
rosa *ro*·sa pink
roto/a ⓜ/ⓕ *ro*·to/a broken
rotonda ⓕ ro·*ton*·da roundabout
rueda ⓕ *rwe*·da wheel
rugby ⓜ *roog*·bee rugby
ruidoso/a ⓜ/ⓕ rwee·*do*·so/a loud • noisy
ruinas ⓕ pl *rwee*·nas ruins
ruta ⓕ *roo*·ta route

S

sábado ⓜ *sa*·ba·do Saturday
sábana ⓕ *sa*·ba·na sheet (bed)
saber sa·*ber* know (something)
sabroso/a ⓜ/ⓕ sa·*bro*·so/a tasty
sacar sa·*kar* take out • take (photo)
sacerdote ⓜ sa·ther·*do*·te priest
saco ⓜ **de dormir** sa·ko de dor·*meer* sleeping bag
sal ⓕ sal salt
sala ⓕ **de espera** *sa*·la de es·*pe*·ra waiting room
sala ⓕ **de embarque** *sa*·la de em·*bar*·ke transit lounge
salario ⓜ sa·*la*·ryo salary
salchicha ⓕ sal·*chee*·cha sausage
saldo ⓜ *sal*·do balance (account)
salida ⓕ sa·*lee*·da departure • exit
saliente ⓜ sa·*lyen*·te ledge
salir con sa·*leer* kon go out with
salir de sa·*leer* de depart
salmón ⓜ sal·*mon* salmon
salón de belleza ⓜ sa·*lon* de be·*lye*·tha beauty salon
salsa ⓕ *sal*·sa sauce
— de guindilla de geen·*dee*·lya chili sauce
— de soja de *so*·kha soy sauce
— de tomate de to·*ma*·te tomato sauce • ketchup
saltar sal·*tar* jump
salud ⓕ sa·*lood* health
salvar sal·*var* save
salvaslips ⓜ pl sal·va·*sleeps* panty liners
sandalias ⓕ pl san·*da*·lyas sandals
sandía ⓕ san·*dee*·a watermelon
sangrar san·*grar* bleed
sangre ⓕ *san*·gre blood
santo/a ⓜ/ⓕ *san*·to/a saint
sarampión ⓜ sa·ram·*pyon* measles
sarpullido ⓜ sar·poo·*yee*·do rash
sartén ⓕ sar·*ten* frying pan
sastre ⓜ *sas*·tre tailor
sauna ⓕ *sow*·na sauna
secar se·*kar* dry
secretario/a ⓜ/ⓕ se·kre·*ta*·ryo/a secretary
sed ⓕ seth thirst
seda ⓕ *se*·da silk
seguir se·*geer* follow
segundo/a ⓜ/ⓕ se·*goon*·do/a second
seguro ⓜ se·*goo*·ro insurance
seguro/a ⓜ/ⓕ se·*goo*·ro/a safe
sello ⓜ *se*·lyo stamp
semáforos ⓜ pl se·*ma*·fo·ros traffic lights
Semana ⓕ **Santa** se·*ma*·na *san*·ta Easter Week
sembrar sem·*brar* plant • sow
señal ⓕ se·*nyal* sign

sencillo/a ⓜ/ⓕ sen·*thee*·lyo/a simple
(un billete) sencillo ⓜ (oon bee·*lye*·te) sen·*thee*·lyo one-way (ticket)
sendero ⓜ sen·*de*·ro mountain path • path
senos ⓜ pl *se*·nos breasts
sensibilidad ⓕ sen·see·bee·lee·*dad* sensitivity
sensual sen·*swal* sensual
sentarse sen·*tar*·se sit
sentimientos ⓜ pl sen·tee·*myen*·tos feelings
sentir sen·*teer* feel
separado/a ⓜ/ⓕ se·pa·*ra*·do/a separate
separar se·pa·*rar* separate
ser ser be
serie ⓕ *se*·rye series
serio/a ⓜ/ⓕ *se*·ryo/a serious
seropositivo/a ⓜ/ⓕ se·ro·po·see·*tee*·vo/a HIV positive
serpiente ⓕ ser·*pyen*·te snake
servicio ⓜ ser·*vee*·thyo service • service charge
— militar mee·lee·*tar* military service
servicios ⓜ pl ser·*vee*·thyos toilets
servilleta ⓕ ser·vee·*lye*·ta napkin
sexo ⓜ *sek*·so sex
— seguro se·*goo*·ro safe sex
sexy *sek*·see sexy
si see if
sí see yes
SIDA ⓜ *see*·da AIDS
sidra ⓕ *see*·dra cider
siempre *syem*·pre always
silla ⓕ *see*·lya chair
— de ruedas de *rwe*·das wheelchair
sillín ⓜ see·*lyeen* saddle
similar see·mee·*lar* similar
simpático/a ⓜ/ⓕ seem·*pa*·tee·ko/a nice
sin seen without
— hogar o·*gar* homeless
— plomo *plo*·mo unleaded
sinagoga ⓕ see·na·*go*·ga synagogue
síndrome premenstrual ⓜ *seen*·dro·me pre·mens·*trwal* premenstrual tension
Singapur ⓜ seen·ga·*poor* Singapore
sintético/a ⓜ/ⓕ seen·*te*·tee·ko/a synthetic
soborno ⓜ so·*bor*·no bribe
sobre *so*·bre about • on top of
sobre ⓜ *so*·bre envelope
sobredosis ⓕ so·bre·*do*·sees overdose
sobrevivir so·bre·vee·*veer* survive
socialista ⓜ&ⓕ so·thya·*lees*·ta socialist
sol ⓜ sol sun
soldado ⓜ sol·*da*·do soldier
solo *so*·lo only
solo/a ⓜ/ⓕ *so*·lo/a alone
soltero/a ⓜ/ⓕ sol·*te*·ro/a single
sombra ⓕ *som*·bra shadow
sombrero ⓜ som·*bre*·ro hat
soñar so·*nyar* dream
sondeos ⓜ pl son·*de*·os polls
sonreír son·re·*eer* smile
sopa ⓕ *so*·pa soup
sordo/a ⓜ/ⓕ *sor*·do/a deaf
sorpresa ⓕ sor·*pre*·sa surprise
su soo her • his • their
subir soo·*beer* climb
submarinismo ⓜ soob·ma·ree·*nees*·mo diving
subtítulos ⓜ pl soob·*tee*·too·los subtitles
sucio/a ⓜ/ⓕ *soo*·thyo/a dirty • foul
sucursal ⓕ soo·koor·*sal* branch office
sudar soo·*dar* perspire
suegra ⓕ *swe*·gra mother-in-law
suegro ⓜ *swe*·gro father-in-law
sueldo ⓜ *swel*·do wage • rate of pay
suelo ⓜ *swe*·lo floor
suerte ⓕ *swer*·te luck
suficiente soo·fee·*thyen*·te enough
sufrir soo·*freer* suffer
sujetador ⓜ soo·khe·ta·*dor* bra

supermercado ⓜ soo·per·mer·*ka*·do supermarket
supermercado ⓜ **pequeño** soo·per·mer·*ka*·do pe·*ke*·nyo convenience store
superstición ⓕ soo·pers·tee·*thyon* superstition
sur ⓜ soor south
surf ⓜ **sobre la nieve** soorf *so*·bre la *nye*·ve snowboarding

T

tabaco ⓜ ta·*ba*·ko tobacco
tabla ⓕ **de surf** *ta*·bla de soorf surfboard
tablero ⓜ **de ajedrez** ta·*ble*·ro de a·khe·*dreth* chess board
tacaño/a ⓜ/ⓕ ta·*ka*·nyo/a stingy
talco ⓜ *tal*·ko baby powder
talla ⓕ *ta*·lya size (clothes)
taller ⓜ ta·*lyer* workshop
también tam·*byen* also
tampones ⓜ pl tam·*po*·nes tampons
tapones ⓜ pl **para los oídos** ta·*po*·nes *pa*·ra los o·*ee*·dos earplugs
taquilla ⓕ ta·*kee*·lya ticket office
tarde *tar*·de late
tarde ⓕ *tar*·de evening • afternoon
tarjeta tar·*khe*·ta card
— de crédito de *kre*·dee·to credit card
— de embarque de em·*bar*·ke boarding pass
tarro ⓜ *ta*·rro jar
tarta ⓕ **nupcial** *tar*·ta noop·*thyal* wedding cake
taxi ⓜ *ta*·ksee taxi
taza ⓕ *ta*·tha cup
té ⓜ te tea
teatro ⓜ te·*a*·tro theatre
teclado ⓜ te·*kla*·do keyboard
teclear te·kle·*ar* type
técnica ⓕ *tek*·nee·ka technique
tela ⓕ *te*·la fabric
tele ⓕ *te*·le TV

teleférico ⓜ te·le·*fe*·ree·ko cable car
teléfono ⓜ te·*le*·fo·no telephone
— móvil *mo*·veel mobile/cell phone
telegrama ⓜ te·le·*gra*·ma telegram
telenovela ⓕ te·le·no·*ve*·la soap opera
telescopio ⓜ te·les·*ko*·pyo telescope
televisión ⓕ te·le·vee·*syon* television
temperatura ⓕ tem·pe·ra·*too*·ra temperature (weather)
templado/a ⓜ/ⓕ tem·*pla*·do/a warm
templo ⓜ *tem*·plo temple
temporada ⓕ tem·po·*ra*·da season (in sport or TV shows)
temprano tem·*pra*·no early
tenedor ⓜ te·ne·*dor* fork
tener te·*ner* have
— hambre *am*·bre to be hungry
— prisa *pree*·sa to be in a hurry
— sed seth to be thirsty
— sueño *swe*·nyo to be sleepy
tenis ⓜ *te*·nees tennis
tentempié ⓜ ten·tem·*pye* snack
tercio ⓜ *ter*·thyo third
terminar ter·mee·*nar* finish
ternera ⓕ ter·*ne*·ra veal
ternero ⓜ ter·*ne*·ro calf
terremoto ⓜ te·re·*mo*·to earthquake
testarudo/a ⓜ/ⓕ tes·ta·*roo*·do/a stubborn
tía ⓕ *tee*·a aunt
tiempo ⓜ *tyem*·po time • weather
a— a *tyem*·po on time
a— completo/parcial a *tyem*·po kom·*ple*·to/par·*thyal* full-time/part-time
tienda ⓕ **(de campaña)** *tyen*·da (de kam·*pa*·nya) tent
tienda ⓕ *tyen*·da shop
— de alimentación de a·lee·men·ta·*thyon* grocery shop
— de fotografía de fo·to·gra·*fee*·a camera shop
— de eléctrodomésticos de e·*lek*·tro·do·*mes*·tee·kos electrical store

SPANISH – ENGLISH S – T

— de cámping de *kam*·peen camping store
— de recuerdos de re·*kwer*·dos souvenir shop
— de ropa de *ro*·pa clothing store
— deportiva de·por·*tee*·va sports store
tierra ⓕ *tye*·ra earth • land
tiesto ⓜ *tyes*·to pot (plant)
tijeras ⓕ pl tee·*khe*·ras scissors
tímido/a ⓜ/ⓕ *tee*·mee·do/a shy
típico/a ⓜ/ⓕ *tee*·pee·ko/a typical
tipo ⓜ *tee*·po type
— de cambio de *kam*·byo exchange rate
tirar tee·*rar* pull
tiritas ⓕ pl tee·*ree*·tas plasters • Band-Aids
título ⓜ *tee*·too·lo degree
toalla ⓕ to·*a*·lya towel
toallita ⓕ to·a·*lyee*·ta flannel • facecloth
tobillo ⓜ to·*bee*·lyo ankle
tocar to·*kar* touch
— la guitarra la gee·*ta*·ra play guitar
tocino ⓜ to·*thee*·no pancetta
todavía (no) to·da·*vee*·a (no) (not) yet
todo *to*·do all • everything
todoterreno ⓜ to·do·te·*rre*·no four-wheel drive vehicle
tofú ⓜ to·*foo* tofu
tomar to·*mar* take • drink
tomate ⓜ to·*ma*·te tomato
— secado al sol se·*ka*·do al sol sun-dried tomato
tono ⓜ *to*·no tone
torcedura ⓕ tor·the·*doo*·ra sprain
tormenta ⓕ tor·*men*·ta storm
toro ⓜ *to*·ro bull
torre ⓕ *to*·re tower
tos ⓕ tos cough
tostada ⓕ tos·*ta*·da toast
tostadora ⓕ tos·ta·*do*·ra toaster
trabajar tra·ba·*khar* work
trabajo ⓜ tra·*ba*·kho job • work
— administrativo ad·mee·nees·tra·*tee*·vo paperwork
— de camarero/a ⓜ/ⓕ de ka·ma·*re*·ro/a bar work
— de casa de *ka*·sa housework
— de limpieza de leem·*pye*·tha cleaning
— eventual e·ven·*twal* casual work
traducir tra·doo·*theer* translate
traer tra·*er* bring
traficante ⓜ&ⓕ **de drogas** tra·fee·*kan*·te de *dro*·gas drug dealer
tráfico ⓜ *tra*·fee·ko traffic
tramposo/a ⓜ/ⓕ tram·*po*·so/a cheat
tranquilo/a ⓜ/ⓕ tran·*kee*·lo/a quiet
tranvía ⓜ tran·*vee*·a tram
a través a tra·*ves* across
tren ⓜ tren train
— de cercanías de ther·ka·*nee*·as local train
trepar tre·*par* climb • scale
tres en raya tres en *ra*·ya noughts & crosses
triste *trees*·te sad
trozo ⓜ *tro*·tho piece
tú inf too you
tu too your
tubo ⓜ **de escape** *too*·bo de es·*ka*·pe exhaust
tubo ⓜ **de snokel** *too*·bo de *snor*·kel snorkel
tumba ⓕ *toom*·ba grave
tumbarse toom·*bar*·se lie (not stand)
turista ⓜ&ⓕ too·*rees*·ta tourist

U

uniforme ⓜ oo·nee·*for*·me uniform
universidad ⓕ oo·nee·ver·see·*dad* university
universo ⓜ oo·nee·*ver*·so universe
unos/as ⓜ/ⓕ *oo*·nos/as some
urgente oor·*khen*·te urgent
usted pol oos·*ted* you

ustedes pol pl oos·*te*·des you
útil *oo*·teel useful
uvas ⓕ pl *oo*·vas grapes
— **pasas** *pa*·sas raisins

V

vaca ⓕ *va*·ka cow
vacaciones ⓕ pl va·ka·*thyo*·nes holiday • vacation
vacante va·*kan*·te vacant
vacío/a ⓜ/ⓕ va·*thee*·o/a empty
vacuna ⓕ va·*koo*·na vaccine
vagina ⓕ va·*khee*·na vagina
validar va·lee·*dar* validate
valiente va·*lyen*·te brave
valioso/a ⓜ/ⓕ va·*lyo*·so/a valuable
valle ⓜ *va*·lye valley
valor ⓜ va·*lor* value
vaqueros ⓜ pl va·*ke*·ros jeans
varios/as ⓜ/ⓕ pl *va*·ryos/as several
vaso ⓜ *va*·so (drinking) glass
vegetariano/a ⓜ/ⓕ ve·khe·ta·*rya*·no/a vegetarian
vela ⓕ *ve*·la candle
velocidad ⓕ ve·lo·thee·*dad* speed
velocímetro ⓜ ve·lo·*thee*·me·tro speedometer
velódromo ⓜ ve·*lo*·dro·mo racetrack (bicycles)
vena ⓕ *ve*·na vein
vendaje ⓜ ven·*da*·khe bandage
vendedor(a) ⓜ/ⓕ **de flores** ven·de·*dor*/ven·de·*do*·ra de *flo*·res florist
vender ven·*der* sell
venenoso/a ⓜ/ⓕ ve·ne·*no*·so/a poisonous
venir ve·*neer* come
ventana ⓕ ven·*ta*·na window
ventilador ⓜ ven·tee·la·*dor* fan (machine)
ver ver see
verano ⓜ ve·*ra*·no summer
verde *ver*·de green
verduras ⓕ pl ver·*doo*·ras vegetables
vestíbulo ⓜ ves·*tee*·boo·lo foyer
vestido ⓜ ves·*tee*·do dress
vestuario ⓜ ves·*twa*·ryo changing room
viajar vya·*khar* travel
viaje ⓜ *vya*·khe trip
vida ⓕ *vee*·da life
videojuegos ⓜ pl vee·*de*·o·*khwe*·gos computer games • video games
vidrio ⓜ *vee*·dryo glass (material)
viejo/a ⓜ/ⓕ *vye*·kho/a old
viento ⓜ *vyen*·to wind
vinagre ⓜ vee·*na*·gre vinegar
viñedo ⓜ vee·*nye*·do vineyard
vino ⓜ *vee*·no wine
violar vyo·*lar* rape
virus ⓜ *vee*·roos virus
visado ⓜ vee·*sa*·do visa
visita ⓕ vee·*see*·ta tour
visitar vee·see·*tar* visit
vista ⓕ *vees*·ta view
vitaminas ⓕ pl vee·ta·*mee*·nas vitamins
víveres ⓜ pl *vee*·ve·res provisions • food supplies
vivir vee·*veer* live (life)
vodka ⓜ *vod*·ka vodka
volar vo·*lar* fly
volumen ⓜ vo·*loo*·men volume
volver vol·*ver* return
vosotros/as ⓜ/ⓕ pl inf vo·*so*·tros/as you
votar vo·*tar* vote
voz ⓕ voth voice
vuelo ⓜ **doméstico** *vwe*·lo do·*mes*·tee·ko domestic flight

Y

y ee and
ya ya already
yo yo I
yoga ⓜ *yo*·ga yoga
yogur ⓜ yo·*goor* yoghurt

Z

zanahoria ⓕ tha·na·o·rya carrot
zapatería ⓕ tha·pa·te·*ree*·a shoe shop
zapatos ⓜ pl tha·*pa*·tos shoes
zodíaco ⓜ tho·*dee*·a·ko zodiac
zoológico ⓜ zo·o·*lo*·khee·ko zoo
zumo ⓜ *thoo*·mo juice
— de naranja de na·*ran*·kha orange juice

INDEX

ÍNDICE

For topics that are covered in several sections of this book, we've indicated the most relevant page number in bold.

A

B

C

D

E

F

G

H

I

J

K

L

M

T

V

W

10 Ways TO START A SENTENCE

When's (the next flight)?	¿Cuándo sale (el próximo vuelo)?	*kwan*·do *sa*·le (el *prok*·see·mo *vwe*·lo)
Where's (the station)?	¿Dónde está (la estación)?	*don*·de es·*ta* (la es·ta·*thyon*)
Where can I (buy a ticket)?	¿Dónde puedo (comprar un billete)?	*don*·de *pwe*·do (kom·*prar* oon bee·*lye*·te)
How much is (a room)?	¿Cuánto cuesta (una habitación)?	*kwan*·to *kwes*·ta (*oo*·na a·bee·ta·*thyon*)
Do you have (a map)?	¿Tiene (un mapa)?	*tye*·ne (oon *ma*·pa)
Is there (a toilet)?	¿Hay (servicios)?	ai (ser·*vee*·thyos)
I'd like (a coffee).	Quería (un café).	ke·*ree*·a (oon ka·*fe*)
Can I (enter)?	¿Se puede (entrar)?	se *pwe*·de (en·*trar*)
Could you please (help me)?	¿Puede (ayudarme), por favor?	*pwe*·de (a·*yoo*·dar·me) por fa·*vor*
Do I have to (get a visa)?	¿Necesito (obtener un visado)?	ne·the·*see*·to (ob·te·*ner* oon vee·*sa*·do)